Hell in Harlan

Which side are you on, boys? Which side are you on?
Which side are you on, boys? Which side are you on?

They say in Harlan County. There are no neutrals there.
You'll either be a union man. Or a thug for J. H. Blair.

Oh, workers can you stand it? Oh, tell me how you can.
Will you be a lousy scab. Or will you be a man?

Don't scab for the bosses. Don't listen to their lies.
Us poor folks haven't got a chance. Unless we organize.

FLORENCE REECE,
HARLAN COUNTY, KENTUCKY, 1931

Hell in Harlan

GEORGE J. TITLER

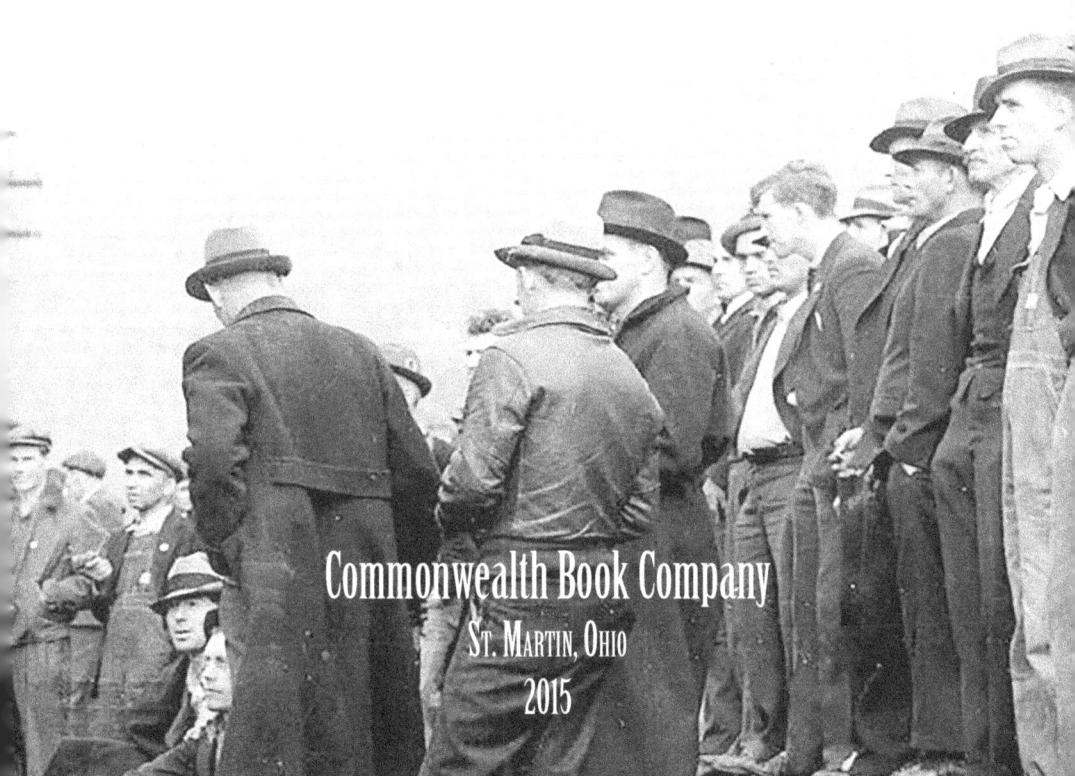

Commonwealth Book Company
St. Martin, Ohio
2015

Copyright 1972 by George J. Titler
New Foreword copyright 2015 by John Hennen
New material copyright 2015 by Commonwealth Book Company
All rights reserved. Printed in the U.S.A.

Edited by James Lynch
Commonwealth Book Company, Inc.

Illustrations & Photographs: The publisher thanks the following institutions for their generous permission to reproduce the photographs and illustrations used in this new edition: Library of Congress, National Archives and Records Administration, Historical Collections and Labor Archives, Special Collections Library, University Libraries, Pennsylvania State University, University of Kentucky Special Collections.

Cover and title page photographs: Kentucky National Guardsmen in Harlan during the 1939 strike.

Rear cover and title lyrics were written by Florence Reece in 1931, shortly after Harlan County Sheriff J. H. Blair and his men ransacked her home looking for her husband, a union organizer.

GEORGE JOY TITLER
1972

Contents

Foreword to the 2015 Edition		viii
Foreword to First Edition		xv
Preface		xvii
1	A Foothold in Harlan, 1900-1920	1
2	Big Coal Strikes Back	15
3	The Battle of Evarts	29
4	The Brief, Unhappy Life of the Communist Party in Harlan County	46
5	The La Follette Committee and Pearl Bassham	53
6	The La Follette Committee and Harlan County Justice in 1937	62
7	The Harlan County Coal Operators' Association	78
8	A Different Kind of "Lynch" Law	85

9	Blood in Harlan	97
10	The Sad Story of a Brave Man, Elmon Middleton	118
11	Happy Chandler Muddies the Waters	127
12	Even Little Boys Weren't Safe	142
13	Murder of an Innocent	149
14	The La Follette Committee Sums Up	166
15	The "Bull of Harlan" Gets to Work	172
16	A Gun for Every Man	183
17	Organizing Benham and Lynch	187
18	Elections and Harlan "Democracy"	198
19	Coal Operators Indicted	205
20	Big Coal on Trial	212
21	Strike	230
22	The Battle of Stanfill	249
22	The Final Days of Bloody Harlan	256
	Epilogue	267

Foreword to the 2015 Edition

> HELL IN HARLAN *firmly fixes Titler's legacy as a fighter for economic justice during an era of industrial warfare.*

George Titler (1895-1976) was an organizer and official for the United Mine Workers during the era of its growth and greatest strength, between 1932 and 1972. After working as a miner and UMWA staffer for many years, in 1937 Titler was dispatched by UMWA president John L. Lewis to lead the organizing campaign in Harlan County, Kentucky. As Titler's episodic memoir attests, this was a dangerous place for a union supporter.

Titler's work as the Harlan County organizing director from 1937 to 1941 placed him at the center of some of the most important labor organizing campaigns in history. Most of the rest of the country, propelled by nearly revolutionary upheavals in basic industry between 1933 and 1937, adapted to a new industrial reality in which worker militancy had forced the Roosevelt administration to respond with legislation (especially the 1935 National Labor Relations Act, or NLRA, better known as the Wagner Act) that guaranteed federal protection for workers attempting to form a union. Titler arrived to discover coal operators thoroughly organized as the Harlan County Coal Operators' Association and prepared to defend their fiefdoms, NLRA be damned. The operators, who heavily subsidized local police forces and county law enforcement officers, were almost religiously dedicated to resisting unionism in their mines.

Historically, coal operators in the Appalachian Mountains had fought unions on the basis of an economic argument. The longer distance they shipped their coal to the Great Lakes for transport placed them at a competitive disadvantage with the Central Competitive fields of the Midwest, which were thoroughly organized by the UMWA. In fact, Appalachian operators charged the UMWA with conspiring with Central Competitive operators to unionize in West Virginia and Eastern Kentucky so that Appalachian owners would be driven out of the market. By 1937, however, whatever value these economic arguments had was supplanted by a belief in the Harlan County Coal Operators' Association that the New Deal and the labor movement threatened the very meaning of American democracy and free enterprise. When the true believers of the Coal Operators Association, aided and abetted by local law enforcement, were thrown into the pit with miners who felt just as strongly that their rights as Americans guaranteed them a say about their work and a decent standard of living, industrial warfare exploded in Eastern Kentucky.

When Titler was assigned to Harlan County, miners and their families were still reeling from the deprivation of the Great Depression and failed strikes in 1931 and 1932. In those conflicts, the UMWA abandoned efforts to organize Harlan and Bell counties because the union leadership feared not only a defeat by the Coal Operators Association, but the radicalism of some of the striking miners. The organizing void in the region was briefly filled by the National Miners Union, a Communist led competitor to the UMWA. Titler, as would be expected, had little regard for the NMU and blamed it for lending credibility to the red-baiting of all strikers by the Coal Operators Association. Chapter 4, *The Brief, Unhappy Life of the Communist Party in Harlan County*, clearly articulates the contrasts between revolutionary unionism and the "bread and butter" model promoted by the UMWA.

Violence saturates Titler's memoir. His detailed accounts of gun battles, beatings, bombings, and brutalization inflicted by the Coal Operators Association's hirelings, as well as what he defines (with much, though not total, justification) as retaliatory violence against "gun thugs" by union supporters, dominate most chapters. Many labor and working class historians, again with considerable justification, are highly critical of the "business unions" that emerged from the bureaucratic machinery of post-World War II industrial relations, often identified as the "New Deal" model, given its emphasis on legalistic contracts, layered administrative procedures, and plodding mediation. It is advisable, however, that analysts not discount the psychological wounds that industrial violence left on its 1930s participants, as suggested by Titler. Many union bureaucrats of the 1940s-1960s, like Titler, haunted by constant threats of fearful violence in the 1930s, drifted toward authoritarianism in defense of their union's hard-won survival. This understandably alienated a younger rank-and-file, arguably weakening the generational solidarity needed to resist the political and legal assaults against the labor movement by the 1980s. As frustrating as the NLRA system could be, especially after a series of crippling amendments, it led to material benefits and security for millions of American workers—until the "hollowing out" of the nation's industrial base beginning in the 1970s. The collective bargaining system institutionalized by New Deal industrial relations facilitated entrenched union bureaucracy, but it must be credited with broadly realized, and unfortunately transistory, improvements in American living standards. That system of tedious but legally binding contracts, propelled in no small way by the popular memories of the brutally violent era of the 1930s, recognized that labor-management conflict could—and should be—mediated through a systematic, federally protected, collective bargaining structure. George Titler, warts and all, was a product of that system.

One of the significant contributions of Titler's memoir is that it will help educate generations of students and general readers about the definitive role played by organized workers in building American prosperity between World War II and the structural economic decline of the last forty years. For those few decades, the strength of organized labor (in the mid-1950s one in three private-sector workers had union representation) steadily elevated wages for union and non-union workers. The labor movement was the only significant countervailing influence against unrestricted corporations' economic and political authority. Unions contributed to leveling income and purchasing power among all classes and contributed significantly to the public revenues and civic life of their communities. In his brilliant memoir of growing up in a steel community, Jack Metzgar notes that for Americans to forget the accomplishments of collective struggle causes them "to underestimate what has been achieved, which leaves them demoralized about what could yet be achieved."[1] Ironically, at the end of Titler's long career, the hard-won accomplishments of the industrial union movement—the accomplishments for Appalachian communities wrought by the United Mine Workers of America—began to be overturned.

George Titler's memoir also refocuses the reader's attention on the volatile relationship between labor and state and local politics in the industrial union era. The UMWA had, against the odds, managed to organize most Harlan County mines by 1938 (the most significant exception was the operation at Benham, KY, a company town owned by International Harvester). This did not, however, indicate an enduring victory for the union, however, as companies could resist renewing contracts when they expired. Titler documents numerous local elections and police departments that he claims were corrupted by the Coal Operators Association as the operators attempted to roll back the gains made by the UMWA between 1933-1938. He harbors no generosity toward Kentucky

---

[1] Jack Metzgar, *Striking Steel: Solidarity Remembered* (Philadelphia: Temple University Press, 2000), 153.

governor A. B. "Happy" Chandler. Titler accuses Chandler of political opportunism and "union busting" when he dispatched hundreds of Kentucky National Guardsmen to crush a UMWA contract renewal strike against the Clover Fork Coal Company in 1939. Titler portrays Chandler as something of a toady for the Harlan County Coal Association and indeed, Chandler was roundly criticized by some of the regional press for overreacting to the Clover Fork strike. Eventually production resumed with a new contract.

Hell in Harlan also devotes parts of several chapters to the work of the United States Senate's La Follette Civil Liberties Committee, chaired by Senator Robert La Follette, Jr., which compiled on-site testimony on conditions in Harlan County in 1937. La Follette, a progressive Republican from Wisconsin, led a committee that was favorably inclined toward organized labor, but my most accounts not unfair toward the business interests that were called to testify. According to Patrick Manley, "the hearings exposed the heavy-handed, often brutal tactics many of the nation's leading corporations used to prevent their workers from forming unions." Eventually the committee published ninety-five volumes of testimony and is credited by labor historians with catalyzing the growth of organized labor post-1937.[2] In addition to local newspapers, Titler relied heavily on the La Follette Committee hearings for documentation of his memoir.

While Titler's time in Harlan County and the subject of this book ended in 1941, his career in the UMWA did not. In 1941 he transferred to West Virginia, and in 1942 became President of District 29. In 1966, at age 70, Titler was appointed Vice-President of the UMWA. W. A. (Tony) Boyle was the UMWA president from 1963-1972. Boyle's tenure was marked by an early form of concessionary bargaining which protected some union miners while abandoning others, and a growing perception by much of the

---

[2] Patrick Manley, *La Follette Civil Liberties Committee Hearings*, Dictionary of American History, 2003, accessed January 5, 2015 at http://www.encyclopedia.com/doc/1G2-3401802282.html, page 700.

membership that Boyle was closer to coal companies than to the miners. Over time the corruption and anti-democratic structure of the Boyle regime led to a sweeping rank-and-file reform movement within the union, coalescing as the Miners for Democracy (MFD). In 1969 former Boyle loyalist Joseph Yablonski challenged Boyle for the presidency and lost in a thoroughly corrupt election. Within weeks of Yablonski's defeat, he and his wife and daughter were murdered in their sleep in their Clarksville, Pennsylvania home. Suspicion immediately gravitated toward Boyle.

When *Hell in Harlan* was originally released in 1972, Boyle had yet to be tried for the Yablonski murders, and Titler may have believed him innocent. Titler vigorously defended Boyle against charges of embezzling union funds and making illegal campaign contributions in 1968, calling Boyle "maligned" and the victim of "persecution" by the U. S. Department of Justice. Boyle's 1969 election was overturned following a Department of Labor investigation, and in 1972 MFD insurgent Arnold Miller was elected UMWA president. Boyle eventually was convicted for ordering the Yablonski murders and died in 1985 while serving three life sentences.[3]

Although he chose to not to run in the new election, the 1972 election unceremoniously ended George Titler's distinguished 59-year UMWA career. Titler's misplaced loyalty to Boyle was arguably the result of both self-preservation and the legacy of the camaraderie wrought by the past struggles in the coalfields. It stretches belief to conclude that Titler was untouched by the culture of corruption within the UMWA hierarchy during the Boyle years, although there has been no accusation that he was involved in Boyle's descent into brutality.

---

3 The reform struggle within the UMWA has a rich historiography, including Paul Clark, *The Miner's Fight for Democracy: Arnold Miller and the Reform of the united Mine Workers* (Ithaca: Cornell University Press, 1981); Paul Nyden, *Miners for Democracy: Struggle in the Coal Fields*. PhD Dissertation: Columbia University, 1974; and Nyden, "Rank-and-File Rebellions in the Coalfields, 1964-80," *Monthly Labor Review* 58:18, March 2007, accessed on January 6, 2015 at http://monthlyreview.org/2007/03/01/rank-and-file-rebellions-in-the-coalfields-1964-80/.

Despite the difficult end to his career, *Hell in Harlan* firmly fixes Titler's legacy as a fighter for economic justice during an era of industrial warfare, and as a steward of miners' contractual protections at a time when unions played a defining role in securing the American Dream for millions of workers while checking corporate power. The fact that Titler's late career was spent defending Boyle's betrayal of those workers is tragic. But the insurgency led by the MFD, and the dismantling of the edifice of corruption that Boyle had built, is powerful testimony that the spirit of workers' rights that men like Titler fought for in Harlan County survived.

JOHN HENNEN
Morehead State University
2015

Foreword to the First Edition

It was no place for timid souls or less dedicated persons.

Here is a book by a man who put his life on the line in order to bring coal miners from abject poverty to a better way of living where today they enjoy some of the good things of life, things they richly deserve.

George J. Titler is, first of all, a fighter for justice for laboring men. I have known him for more than thirty years, known him as a two-fisted leader in the United Mine Workers of America. Almost a carbon copy of the late and great John L. Lewis.

He has never pretended to be an author. He is a truly great labor leader who has dedicated a long life to his work. His mighty footprints will linger in the coal dust and the muddy streets of coal camps long after he has passed to his reward. An able speaker and phrase-maker, it is good that in the sunset of his career he decided to set down on paper some of the almost unbelievable but nevertheless true happenings in "Bloody Harlan" county, Kentucky. This is first-hand stuff, told by a man who in his younger days, when he could have killed a man with his two powerful fists, had the raw courage to beard the Coal Barons in their den. It was no place for timid souls or less dedicated persons.

The Coal Barons in Kentucky as well as West Virginia, had long ruled with a high hand in the coal fields and they didn't want their "slaves" to be set free. Yes, the miners were slaves before the coal fields were unionized, slaves who truly "owed their souls to the company store" and worked extremely long hours for a pittance while making the coal barons rich.

George J. Titler faced bullets from ambush, sudden death, eternal harassment and certain jail terms for trying to carry freedom in the form of the United Mine Workers of America into the coal fields. This book is not fiction. It is factual all the way. At 77, ready as he says "to hang up his cap," this great lion of a man deserves high praise for setting down the facts in this book and preserving for posterity some outstanding facts which union haters would like us all to forget. If you love freedom and hate despotism this volume is your cup of tea.

Roy Lee Harmon
Poet Laureate of West Virginia
1972

Preface

> *It should be remembered, however, that this is an unvarnished but somewhat understated version of four years of hell.*

This book is the story of four of the most important years of my life, years when organized labor was tested on a blood battleground in the hills of Kentucky. Before 1937, Harlan County had been known locally as "Bloody Harlan," because of its long record of violence. During the years when I was in charge of organizing for the UMWA in Harlan County, 1937 to 1941, Bloody Harlan became nationally known. The actions of the Harlan County coal operators became a shame to the entire United States, an object of scorn to all of our citizens, including Franklin Delano Roosevelt.

Harlan County is a part of UMWA District 19 which also includes all coal miners in the state of Tennessee. Prior to being assigned to organizing in Harlan, I had worked under District President William Turnblazer in Jellico, Tennessee and also in the coal fields near Chattanooga. At my personal request, I was transferred into Harlan on New Year's Day of 1937. The main part of this book is about my experiences for the next four years.

Beginning January 1, 1937, when I left Chattanooga for Middlesboro and Harlan, Kentucky, I compiled a diary and scrap book of newspaper clippings and whatever authentic history I could salvage, and these records grew to be quite voluminous. This personal record ended in 1941 when I left Kentucky to reside in West Virginia. For more than 20 years these records have been gathering dust. My friends are insisting that before I turn in my lamp, I compile the record in the form of a brief history of the blood, sweat and sacrifice of human life expended in the coal miner's pursuit of freedom from tyranny in Kentucky.

This book is the result. Its content is based on personal recollection which I have checked wherever possible with others. Much of the material was recorded by the La Follette Civil Liberties Committee which thoroughly investigated the blood war in Harlan. For earlier history, I am indebted to an unpublished history of the County written by the staff of the La Follette Committee. Some of the material herein will shock the reader. It should be remembered, however, that this is an unvarnished but somewhat understated version of four years of hell.

It is impossible to credit here all of the men who worked hard to bring American freedom into Southeastern Kentucky. I would like, however, to single out Senators Robert F. La Follette, Jr., and Elbert D. Thomas, who exposed to the nation the atrocities committed by Harlan County coal operators. Outstanding, too, was the work of Brian McMahon and Welly K. Hopkins who were the Federal government's prosecutors during the conspiracy trial of the Harlan operators. Last but not least is John L. Lewis, the master craftsman who directed the union's successful organizing drive in Harlan County.

One of the major reasons I felt I had to write this book was the hope that it would be read by many younger workers who take the trade unions in our country for granted, those who pay their dues and think their duty of their union has ended there. Organized labor's enemies are still active in this country. Union benefits now enjoyed were won by sacrifices such as these recorded here. Unless union members remain militant and united, battles such as the four year struggle in Harlan County may again take place in our country.

Therefore, I give you four years of the history of *Hell in Harlan*.

GEORGE J. TITLER
1972

1

A Foothold in Harlan, 1900-1920

They ordered him to dress and acompany them. As he turned to get his hat, one of the gang shot him in the back of the head.

Harlan County, Kentucky, one of the major coal producing sections of the country, is located in a section of the Appalachian Mountain Range, in the extreme southeastern corner of the state. It is bounded on the east and south by Wise and Lee Counties, Virginia, and on the west and north by Bell, Leslie, Perry, and Letcher Counties, Kentucky. Its shape is that of a narrow shovel about 50 miles in length and 20 miles at its widest point. Several streams traverse the County and flow into the Cumberland River. The general appearance of the valleys through which these rivers flow is one of narrow, steep defiles. The four roads that enter the County wind along the streambeds. None of the roads is a main highway and for this reason the County is relatively isolated from the rest of the country. The only railroads in the County are spur lines for the transportation of coal.

Harlan County's neighbor to the southeast, Bell County, is the site of the Cumberland Gap which was discovered by Daniel

Harlan County, circa 1900

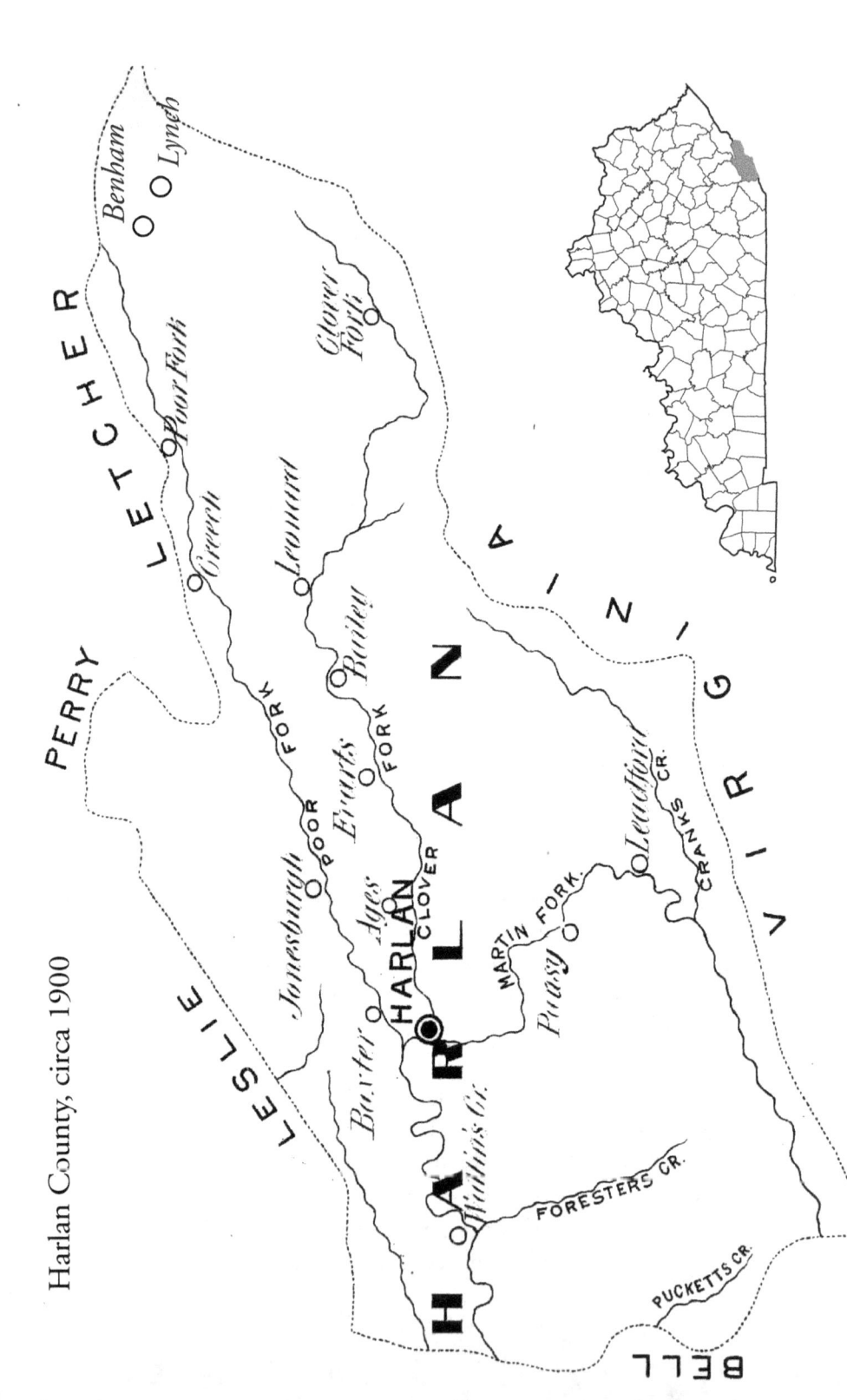

Boone in 1799 and which led to the settlement of Kentucky by a wave of pioneers that followed him west. It was through the Cumberland Gap that Abraham Lincoln's father walked on his way to settle in Kentucky where his famous son was born.

The people who settled in Bell and Harlan Counties were almost all of English origin. Because of isolation the population today is virtually all descended from those original Anglo-Saxon settlers. Much of their folklore is based on 17th and 18th Century English folklore. And their customs today are like those of a hundred years ago. When Kentucky was first settled, men carried firearms, both to protect themselves from savages and wild animals and to provide meat for the family table. A rifle, a shotgun or pistol today is as much a part of an eastern Kentuckian's customary dress as are his pants and shirt. The first possession a Harlan County boy yearns for and saves his money for is not a bike or a car but a pistol or a rifle. He is trained in their use the moment he is sensible enough to aim and pull a trigger.

It is my belief that eastern Kentuckians are no more violent than any other group of Americans except for this custom of bearing arms. In other sections of our country, a violent dispute might be settled by a fistfight or a lawsuit. In Harlan County, permanent settlement has usually been arranged only with the help of Doctor Colt.

There was bloodshed in Harlan before an ounce of coal was mined. There has been blood shed—much of it—in purely personal disputes having no connection with coal mining, unions or company thugs. The native of Harlan County is a frontiersman, proud and defensive of his freedom and his right, under Kentucky law, to bear arms if displayed openly. A man with a gun will not, when angered, bite, hit or kick another man. He will shoot. A little boy in Harlan today is still taught that he should not be carrying a gun unless he means to use it if necessity arises.

In 1910, Harlan County was sparsely inhabited by a farming population of 10,566 persons. Following the development of the coalfields, the population steadily increased until in 1930 the census recorded a total population of 64,557 persons. Nine percent of the population were Negroes and only one percent were foreign born. The larger part of the population depended for its livelihood on coal mining.

Five seams of workable coal lie on top of each other from below the riverbed to the top of the mountain, i.e., Mason, Harlan, Darby, Low Splint and High Splint. Coal from the High Splint, Low Splint and Darby seams had to be hauled down inclines off the mountain to the railroad.

Until recently there was no strip mining in Harlan County. In 1937, all of the mines were driven underground into the sides of mountains. Slopes, not elevator shafts, entered most of them. The seams varied in thickness but many of them were what we call thin, meaning that the men were not able to stand erect when they worked but crawled or stooped from one place to another.

The miners and their families for the most part lived in houses that were clustered around the entrances to the mines. In 1937, these shacks were built and owned by the coal operators and these clusters were always referred to as coal camps. Some of them had names, some of them did not. The picture of a typical coal town in Kentucky described by the United States Coal Commission in 1923 applied to the physical appearance of Harlan County in 1937:

> Each mine, or group of mines, became a social center with no privately owned property except the mine, and no public places or public highways except the bed of the creek which flowed between the mountain walls. These groups of villages dot the mountain sides down the river valleys and need only castles, drawbridges, and donjon keeps to reproduce to the physical eye a view of feudal days.

Housing in Harlan County still looks the same as it did in 1923. The only difference today is that most of the homes are privately owned and some of the owners have added electricity and indoor plumbing.

The bituminous coal fields in Harlan County are among the richest in the world. Howard N. Eavenson, of the firm of Eavenson, Alford & Hicks, consulting engineers of Pittsburgh, president of the Clover Splint Coal Co., operating in Harlan County, and formerly consulting engineer for the United States Coal & Coke Company, a subsidiary of the United States Steel Corporation, described the rapid development of the Harlan County coal fields to the high quality of the coal produced there. In testimony during the 1920's before a sub-committee of the U. S. Senate Committee on Manufacturers, he said:

> Harlan County was the last of the large coal fields opened and on account of the excellence of its product, its growth has been unusually rapid. The coal is largely used for special purposes where a low-ash and low-sulphur coal is needed. Much of it is used in by-product coke ovens and the rapid growth of the field was helped by the great demand during the war for coal yielding large quantities of bensol and tuluol, as this does, needed for explosives. Even though coal production in Harlan County did not begin until 1911, it mounted steadily from 2.5 million tons in 1916 to 15 million tons in 1928, which the total bituminous coal production for the United States in 1916 and 1928 was about 500 million net tons.

Although Harlan County did not begin to produce on a commercial scale until 1911, the coalfields of adjacent counties in eastern Kentucky and those of northeastern Tennessee rose to a position of importance during the closing decade of the nineteenth century. Actually, first commercial production in eastern Kentucky started in Laurel County immediately after the Civil War. Although this County still contains large areas of unmined coal, there is little or no coal produced there now.

Union spirit in eastern Kentucky began almost simultaneously with the beginnings of coal mining. During the 1890's, Laurel County employed about 850 miners. The average production was about two tons per man per day, the day at that time being 12 hours long. Many of these men belonged to the Knights of Labor before 1890 and were UMWA members from its founding. UMWA District 19 held its 12th annual convention in 1901, and according to James W. Ridings, now International Executive Board member from that District, the convention was attended by delegates from 53 local unions, two of which were located in Laurel County. The union spirit probably had its beginning among the miners descended from parents who had migrated from the British Isles who had been members of labor unions before coming to the United States.

During the great organizing campaign conducted by John Mitchell in 1898, just before he became president of the UMWA, union organizers entered the Southern Appalachian region in strength. By 1907 the union was strong enough to negotiate a general wage contract in the area. However, when the agreement expired in 1910, many of the operators refused to agree to a new general contract. The union, however, succeeded in negotiating and maintaining contracts with a small number of operators in the district until 1914.

After 1910, the union's position weakened throughout the Southern Appalachian area. The large companies that developed the Harlan County coalfields were traditionally anti-union. As a result, when the Harlan field was open, it operated for many years on a non-union basis. This non-union competition weakened the union throughout southeastern Kentucky and Tennessee. Membership dropped from 3551 in 1900 to only 48 members in eastern Kentucky and Tennessee in 1916.

A fresh impetus to the union movement in Kentucky and Tennessee was supplied when the United States entered World War I. The war created an enormous increase in demand for coal. This, coupled with an acute labor shortage, materially strengthened the position of the UMWA. In the late spring of 1917, the bare skeleton organization that had been maintained in District 19 was reinforced by the arrival of David Robb of Indiana and Van A. Bittner of Pittsburgh, International organizers for the UMWA. A vigorous organizing campaign was launched. The efforts of the organizers were first centered in Bell County, and on June 3 a mass meeting was held in the Straight Creek district that was attended by approximately 2,000 miners. As a result of this meeting, local unions were established at Mingo, Chenoa, Straight Creek, Elys,

Four Mile and Cumberland Road. Preparations were also made at this meeting for organizing Harlan County.

A few days later, UMWA organizers William Turnblazer and George Edmunds were added to the District 19 staff and the drive to organize the workers of Harlan County began. On June 10, a mass meeting was held at the courthouse square in Harlan Town. Approximately 2,500 miners attended this meeting and three local unions with a reported membership of about 1,500 were established. With this opening wedge, it was believed that the backbone of non-unionism in Harlan County would be broken.

First efforts, however, to deal with the Harlan County operators were fruitless. They refused to meet with representatives of the UMWA in July and a strike was authorized by the Union. Organizers in District 19 were told that they could sign separate contracts with operators who were willing to recognize the union and granting a wage increase to offset rapidly rising living costs. After several attempts to persuade the operators to sign a wage agreement, a general strike was called in Harlan County beginning August 11, 1917. The only contracts signed had been with small mines in Bell County, Kentucky, and in Tennessee.

The strike was effective. Nearly all of the coal miners in Harlan County stayed away from work on August 11. As in subsequent labor disturbances in Harlan County, there is abundant evidence that at least some of the operating companies resorted to violence in their efforts to break the 1919 strike. At the mining property of the Wisconsin Steel Company at Benham, armed guards were employed and strikebreakers were imported. A typical act of violence in 1917 was the shooting of Luther Shipman, one of the leaders of the striking miners. In the October 4 issue of the United Mine Workers Journal, this incident was reported as follows:

GUNMEN MURDER UNARMED MINER

Pineville, Ky., October 1917: On the pretense of serving a warrant on Luther Shipman, a leader among the miners on strike in this district, a posse headed by County Judge Ward of Harlan County called at the home of

Mr. Shipman. They ordered him to dress and accompany them. As he turned to get his hat, one of the gang shot him in the back of the head, instantly killing him. Then they opened a general fusillade on the other occupants of the miner's cabin and mortally wounded Frank Shipman, a relative of the other murdered man. Press dispatches, inspired by the influential men who headed this murder raid, state that there was a battle. There was no battle; the gang of gunmen had made the boast that they would shoot down the leaders and drive the other miners back to work on the company's terms. Luther Shipman was a quiet, religious man, well liked and trusted by the miners. The men are very bitter, but the leaders hope to prevent reprisals in kind.

This brutal murder was merely one of many acts of violence committed by the operators during the 1917 strike, and in many ways typifies the history of Harlan County. It should be noted that the murderers in this case included County officials. Down through the years, Harlan County's Government has more often than not been administered by coal operators and relatives, and their hirelings.

In spite of violence and coercion, the miners refused to break ranks. The records of U. S. Geological Survey, which then kept such statistics, indicate that 416,370 men days were lost in eastern Kentucky in 1917 because of work stoppages. Virtually all of this lost time was reported out of Harlan County.

The wartime economy needed all the coal that could be mined so it was not long before the Federal Government intervened in Harlan County's coal strike. Fuel Administrator Harry A. Garfield summoned the operators and representatives of the miners to Washington and insisted on a settlement. After several days of negotiations, the operators agreed to (1) general wage increase; (2) shorter workday; (3) checkweighmen on all tipples; (4) recognition of the UMWA; and (5) establishment of mine committees to handle grievances with management. Pending details regarding actual wage scale and length of working day, Harlan County miners went back to work on October 8. Final agreement was reached November 1, 1917, with the understanding that the terms of the contract were for the duration of the war.

The UMW Journal on October 11, 1917, reported that a special convention of representatives of the coal miners of eastern Kentucky and Tennessee, meeting in Knoxville, had approved the wage agreement wrung from the stubborn coal operators. The convention was addressed by UMWA Vice President Frank J. Hayes, and several International organizers including Van Bittner, William Feeney and Jack Ramsey.

Incidentally, it is interesting to note that this convention adopted by unanimous vote resolutions condemning activities of the Industrial Workers of the World. This anti-American organization, known variously as the IWW, "The Wobblies," or "I Won't Work," was a militant, radical organization, many members of which later formed the nucleus of the Communist Party in the U.S.A. All members of the UMWA are proud of the fact that the coal miners' union was the first in the nation to prohibit membership to Communist Party members. This was put in the UMWA Constitution in 1926, long before most Americans had even heard of Communism, much less recognized its dangers to our way of life.

During the following two years the UMWA was largely preoccupied with building up membership and otherwise solidifying its position in Harlan County. Organizer Thomas N. Gann was assigned to the field and by July 1918 he reported that the field was solidly organized except for the operations of the Wisconsin Steel Company (International Harvester Company) at Benham, and those of the United States Coal & Coke Company (United States Steel Corporation) at Lynch. Because of this almost complete success, the UMWA's International Executive Board decided in January 1919 that District 19 was strong enough to govern itself and the union's representatives were instructed to arrange for the restoration of district autonomy.

This decision was premature but a convention was held in March to elect district officers. Frank Keller, a six-foot, six-inch mountain preacher, who had been a member of the union six months, was called on to open the convention with prayer. He electrified the convention with his magnetic personality and they elected him

President of the District. Mr. Keller had a golden tongue but he lacked one important ingredient—experience. Due to this weakness, plus a general lack of leadership from other district officers, a $100,000 treasury was dissipated in less than one year. The district headquarters building was lost and, as a matter of fact, the district itself no longer existed in any real sense. By the end of 1920 the district was in debt and the experiment in autonomy was a complete failure.

The district's inexperienced leaders were put to the test first by the national coal strike called in the fall of 1919. John L. Lewis had just become acting president of the UMWA. The strike was a national success but in Harlan County it merely led to another outbreak of violence. When the great strike of 1919 began, the UMWA claimed a membership of 3,900 in Harlan County. With the exception of United States Steel operations at Lynch and International Harvester Company at Benham, all Harlan County mines were closed by the strike. Geographical Survey figures showed that 81 percent of the capacity of Harlan County Coal Operators' Association was out of production.

The national strike lasted from November 1 to December 12. There were two basic areas of dispute between the union and the operators. The UMWA, headed by Mr. Lewis, demanded a 60 percent wage increase and a 30-hour, 5-day week. The miners also insisted that the war had ended with the armistice and that a clause in the existing contract, which stated that the contract could not be reopened for the duration, was null and void. Mr. Lewis pointed out that the UMWA could not be held responsible for failure of the United States Senate to ratify the Versailles treaty. The operators argued that in the absence of a formal declaration by the government that the war had ended, the existing contract held until March 31, 1920. Despite injunction proceedings initiated by Attorney General A. Mitchell Palmer, the miners refused to return to work until President Woodrow Wilson agreed to appoint an arbitration commission.

JOHN L. LEWIS (1880-1969) *pictured here in 1935, was born in Iowa and there entered the mines as a teenager. He began his political career in 1906, elected as a delegate to the UMW national convention. Elected UMW president in 1920, Lewis fought for miners' rights and benefits for the next four decades. In 1964, he received the Presidential Medal of Freedom. Raised in the Reorganized Church of Jesus Christ of Latter Day Saints, Lewis maintained throughout his life strict views of sexual propriety and alcohol use. It has been reported that Lewis wanted to endorse Geroge Titler to replace him as UMWA President, but Titler's use of alcohol sunk that possibility.*

The United States Bituminous Coal Commission, which was appointed by the President to settle the question of wages and hours, handed down its decision in March 1920. The Commission's award provided for an increase of 24 cents a ton in tonnage rates; an advance of $1 a day for day and monthly workers (except trapper boys and others receiving less than a man's pay, whose pay was raised 53 cents); an increase of 20 percent in pay for yardage, dead work, room turning, and similar operations; a 48-hour week; and a contract which was to remain in effect until April 1, 1922. Compared with the rates in effect on October 31, 1919, the new scale represented an increase of approximately 27 percent.

Percentage wise this is the largest pay boost ever won by an American labor union and was the first big victory won for the nation's miners by John L. Lewis. The new contract was signed by virtually all coal operators in the United States, but antiunionism persisted in Harlan County. The operators refused to accept the award of the Bituminous Coal Commission. When the national strike was called off, Harlan County operators began another concerted effort to destroy the UMWA. District 19 Secretary E. L. Reed reported that the anti-union campaign began in the traditional manner. Several hundred miners known to be active and loyal union members were refused work. They and their families were served with eviction notices and were forced to move out of company-owned houses. The UMW Journal reported that gunmen and thugs employed by the coal companies were running wild in the Harlan coalfield. The Journal said:

> Three members of the United Mine Workers were shot down in cold blood by these ruffians and murderers on March 20 at the Banner Fork Coal Corporation Mine No. 2. The following are the names of the victims: K. S. Taylor, instantly killed. Leaves a widow and seven children without any means of support. James Burk, deputy sheriff, fatally wounded. Died the next day in a hospital at Harlan, leaving a widow and family without support. General Gibson, fatally wounded. Died on an operating table in a hospital at Harlan, leaving a family without support. One of the gunmen, Jim Hall, was severely wounded and sent to a hospital at Harlan.

According to the UMW Journal, Jim Hall was one of six thugs paid $10 a day by the coal operators to intimidate union members. He was reported to have boasted that he killed a miner a month. During a fight where he killed three men, he himself was wounded in spite of the fact that he wore a steel breastplate for protection against bullets.

On May 1, 1920, the UMW Journal printed a letter to the editor that detailed other instances of violence committed by employees of the Harlan County coal operators. The correspondent said that at Wilson-berger a coal operator tried to evict union member J. B. Bryant from a company house. He refused so the house was dynamited while Mr. Bryant, his wife and six children were asleep. Through a miracle they survived. This letter also said truthfully that two men—Rockingham Smith and Boyd Kelly—who had been tried, convicted and sentenced to 20 years in prison for killing the two Shipmans in 1917 had not only not served a minute of their sentences, but that one of them, Smith, was in 1920 chief constable of the County Court of Harlan County. This letter also reported that there were about 75 gun thugs working for the operators in Harlan County and that, among others, they had murdered Lee Clark, a UMWA local union secretary and a city policeman in Harlan.

With miners clinging tenaciously to the UMWA, however, the operators finally capitulated and the operators signed a new wage agreement on August 12, 1920. In accordance with the Coal Commission award, tonnage rates were increased 24 cents a ton and yardage. But in the agreement the operators inserted a clause providing "that men shall not be discriminated against on account of membership or nonmembership in any organization nor shall any member of any organization interfere with or discriminate against those who are not members, nor shall men who are not members interfere or discriminate against those who are." This made the contract essentially an open-shop agreement and permitted a more orderly liquidation of the union by the operators later on. It should be remembered that this agreement was signed by the district officers who did not have the experience to realize what this clause in the contract signified.

Almost at once, according to reports of the miners, the checkweigh men disappeared from the mine tipples, notwithstanding the fact that the Kentucky law provided:

> That when a majority of the miners engaged in digging or mining coal in any coal mine in this state, request the owner or owners, or operator of said mines to allow said miners to employ, at their own expense, a person to inspect the weights at said mine, and see that all the coal digged and mined by said miner is properly weighed and accounted for, and do and perform only such other duties as will insure that said coal is properly weighed and correctly accounted for, said owner or owners or operator or

operators shall permit such person to be employed by said miners making the request. Provided, the person so employed by said miners has the reputation of being an honest, trustworthy, discreet, sober and upright man. Said checkweightman shall be duly elected by a majority of the employees engaged in mining and loading coal and said election shall be properly conducted by secret ballot at the principal entrance to the mine.

Local strikes in protest against contract violations of this kind were discouraged by the union's national leaders because they recognized the fact that the post-war depression made strikes of any kind virtually impossible of success. As a matter of fact, although the Harlan County operators said that they had reached an agreement with the union, no union-management relationship existed in Harlan County after World War I. By 1921 even the wage provisions of the contract were openly ignored by the operators.

It was reported in one of the leading coal trade journals that operators in the southeastern Kentucky districts, including Harlan County, had cut wages from 27 to 30 percent. The article went on to indicate that while many operators paid the union scale during the latter part of 1920 and the early months of 1921, the union was never officially recognized and operators disregarded the dues check-off entirely. It was further reported that the miners in the district were so desperate for employment that they readily accepted the pay cuts.

A vivid indication of the inroads made in the union ranks in Harlan County during the depression of 1921 was reported by the government publication, "Mineral Resources of the United States," which showed the maximum extent to which the important coal producing districts were shut down by the great strikes of 1919 and 1922. As against 60 percent of the productive capacity of Harlan County rendered idle by the strike of 1919, only 21 percent was affected by the strike and on this account over-emphasized the shutdown in the district. In the official summary of the coal industry for the strike years, it was stated that strike losses in the Harlan field "were insignificant in 1922."

2

Big Coal Strikes Back

> *Harlan County coal operators were making money hand over fist and it was a golden era of full employment for gun thugs.*

Breach of contract soon degenerated into a rough, tough union-busting drive by the Harlan County coal operators. Its complete success is a matter of record. It was many a long year, nearly twenty in fact, before Harlan County was again organized by the UMWA.

Typical of the strong-arm methods used by the operators are those outlined by Chester C. Watson, a miner who was working at Black Mountain at that time and who is now a retired representative of UMWA District 29 in West Virginia. He recently wrote:

> In January 1922 I went to work for the Black Mountain Coal Corporation at Black Mountain, Kentucky, (Post Office Kenvir, Kentucky), which mine was owned by the Peabody Coal Company, Chicago, Illinois.
>
> The Local Union at Black Mountain, No. 4492, United Mine Workers of America, had a membership of approximately 900 members and was working under a one-year, closed-shop contract, with complete check off of union dues, etc.

There were two mines at Black Mountain, north and south. Coal from these mines was carried by conveyor belts from the top tipple down the mountain to the railroad tipple.

In 1923 when the Local Union sent a contract committee to Chicago to get a new contract signed by the Peabody Coal Company, they were told that the coal company had to compete in the coal market with the non-union mines in Harlan County and the Black Mountain Local Union would have to organize these nonunion mines and bring them up to their standard and if this was not done, the Peabody Coal Company would not sign another one-year contract with the UMWA. The Black Mountain Local Union sent committees to the other mines in Harlan County but was unable to organize them.

This contract expired on March 31, 1924, and having no contract, the Local Union went on strike April 1, 1924. On September 1, 1924, the Company brought in fifteen guards, deputized as deputy sheriffs, to Black Mountain with high-powered rifles and machine guns. Machine guns were placed on each top tipple and the mine was declared open for operation. A few outside men were brought in and started to work.

Forty-two house eviction cases were tried before County Judge Willie Bob Howard and the men involved in the house cases which included all the Local Union officers, mine committees and men active in the Local Union, were ordered by Judge Howard to vacate the company houses.

On September 23, 1924, the Local Union met and disbanded. All members were given transfer cards. Employees at the Black Mountain Mine were required to go into Superintendent J. T. Smith's office to be given a clearance slip for re-employment and had to vacate the company houses and leave Harlan County to get employment.

The Union had been broken at all other Harlan County mines for more than one year and they were operating non-union. When this strike was broken in 1924, none of the non-union mines in Harlan County, all of which were members of the Harlan County Coal Operators' Association, would employ a man from Black Mountain.

Many of the men who worked at Black Mountain transferred to Local Union No. 5355 after Local Union 4495 at Black Mountain folded up. No. 5355, at Evarts, was a recruiting local with members from Kildav Woods and Black Mountain. It had jurisdiction at no mine.

The men at Black Mountain had remained loyal to the UMWA much longer than other miners in Harlan County. Some of them went to work at Black Mountain on a non-union basis. Mr. Watson was typical of others who left Harlan County and worked elsewhere. He went to Twin Branch, West Virginia, in 1928 and worked for the Fordson Coal Company. In 1928, Harlan County was no place for a union man to live.

Harlan County in the 1920's was an area where coal miners starved to death while most of the rest of the citizens prospered. The prosperity of the rest of the County was based on the poverty of the miners. Harlan County coal operators were making money hand over fist and it was a golden era of full employment for gun thugs. This prosperity for the coal operators and their hirelings was strictly local as far as the national coal industry was concerned. For the coal industry as a whole, the post-war era of national prosperity was a grotesque illusion. During the lush period from 1923 to 1929 when virtually all other industries, except agriculture, were being swept forward by an apparently endless economic boom, production of bituminous coal fell off sharply. Mine sales realizations were cut 36 percent, more than 3,000 commercial mines went out of business, and nearly 202,000 soft coal miners lost their jobs. The enormous profits of the years immediately following World War I were transformed into a new loss for the industry of more than $1 million in 1929.

Exactly the reverse took place in Harlan County. Production rose from 8,581,000 tons in 1923 to 14,093,000 tons in 1929, a gain of more than 80 percent. At the same time, the number of men employed advanced from 9,280 to 10,831, an increase of 17 percent. It is true that prices paid to Harlan County coal operators dropped in about the same proportion as elsewhere but this loss was partly offset by an increase in productivity per-man-per-day. Explanation for the conspicuous prosperity of coal operators in Harlan County is the fact that they were the first operators group in the country to go non-union and, therefore, the first to cut wages. They began the wage-cutting, price-cutting competition that very nearly destroyed the coal industry in this country. Because they were first, they were able to keep one step ahead of operators, most of whom had not gone non-union until 1927. But in 1929 the price-cutting squeeze caught up with the Harlan operators. Although production remained high and wages went to almost unbelievably low levels, the Harlan County coal operators joined the rest of the industry in the industry-wide depression.

The operators' anti-union arsenal was full of weapons. One, as described by Mr. Watson, was violence and the fear that went with it. There are others, among them a device the operators called the "individual contract" and which the UMWA has always referred to as "yellow dog contracts." Under terms of these so-called agreements, the miner in writing signed an individual contract that stated that he would not belong to the UMWA or any other labor organization as long as he remained in the employ of the company with which he signed the contract.

According to a contemporary report of the U.S. Government's Bituminous Coal Commission, the yellow dog contract suppressed civil liberty and "has been used as a basis for securing injunctions against the attempts to organize the field by any means whatsoever." These contracts were also used as a basis for claiming damages from the UMWA. Miners appealed to the Coal Commission against these contracts. Their appeals were apparently read and filed. Typical was one addressed to the Commission in May 1923, by a group of miners in Perry County, Kentucky. It said:

> Honorable Gentlemen: We, the undersigned, coal miners and mine workers of Auxier, Lothair, Heiner, Hardburly, Domino, Cornettsville, Christopher, Chavies and Hazard, Kentucky, humbly pray that the United States Coal Commission will restore to us American wage workers the right to belong to or join the United Mine Workers of America, which the coal operators of this section of Kentucky have taken away from us. The coal operators forced us by coercion through their personal agents to sign a contract that we will not join the United States Mine Workers of America. If we do not sign the coal company's contract then we are forced out of our jobs and forced out of the coal company's houses. We are free American wage workers, and we ask the right to belong to any American organization we see or think is to our interest as Americans. The coal operators have and belong to their own organizations.
>
> They are most tyrannical and unscrupulous to us coal miners. They employ gunmen and private spies to report us miners if we join any labor organization and discharge us. They make statements in the newspapers

that the miners of northeastern and eastern Kentucky are well pleased with the conditions imposed upon us by coal operators and their gunmen and private spies. The statements made by coal operators and their private hireling emissaries are absolutely untrue. We are far from satisfied. In fact, we are as slaves under the conditions imposed upon us by the coal operators. Again we ask the United State Coal Commission to help us to be free American wage workers. We humbly pray you to help us to restore democracy for all American producers in the mountain counties of northeastern and eastern Kentucky. This is our prayer. Please help us.

The Commission did nothing.

Some observers of union activities in Harlan County implied that the UMWA, in the face of bitter anti-union attitude of the operators, made no real effort to organize the miners in the field between 1920 and 1930. This is considerably less than accurate. Throughout the twenties repeated efforts were made by the union to re-enter the field. A concerted drive, for example, began in the latter part of 1923 just after the work of the U. S. Coal Commission had been completed. Union organizers were quickly driven from Harlan by the operators' gun thugs.

For the next two years the union was virtually extinct in Harlan County. Communication with the outside world was nil. Most of the men had watched the union pushed out without a whimper. They were eager to work under any conditions and at first the wage cuts had been small and changes in working conditions had been slight. Little by little, however, a true era of poverty and degradation for the coal miners of Harlan County began and continued. The men wanted the union back but for the time being it was too late. Two letters to the editor of the Journal tell much of conditions in Harlan County in 1925-1926, and also express the desire for a return of the union, coupled with the realization that this could not take place.

The first letter appeared in the February 15, 1925, issue of the Journal:

> I am writing so that brothers in other parts of the country may know of conditions in District 19. The larger mines in the Bell and Harlan County fields are working pretty steady, but the conditions under which the men are forced to work are deplorable. I am told by several men in this district that they are working hard loading coal but cannot make half enough to support their families. Wages have been reduced to less than one-half what they were a year-and-a-half ago. There has never been such a slaughter in wages since the operators have been successful in putting the union out of business in this particular field. The miners let the operators take the union away from them and are now asking when will the union come to their rescue.
>
> The miners certainly have good leadership since the International Union has taken over the district. The fault has been that the majority of miners have lost sight of their own welfare and allowed the operators and gunmen to get the upper hand. Our president, William Turnblazer, has never sanctioned a reduction in wages. On the other hand, the men in this district have not backed him up in his stand against a reduction. Sanford Snyder, an international organizer, has been in this field for nearly three years and is one of the best field workers ever sent here. He is outspoken against a reduction.
>
> I know the spirit of the union is stronger in the field at this time than it was in 1917, but in my opinion there is no use now bothering with the matter. Of course, such action is hard on the good men of the district, but I think that when the union comes in here again it will come to stay, for it is coming by the stomach route this time—the men feel the need of it.
>
> For example, look at the condition of the miners in the coal camps of the Liberty Coal & Coke Company since the union has been driven out. I am told by traveling men that the condition of the men is awful in this camp with the exception of the salaried men and contractors. There have been more men maimed and crippled and killed in the few months that the union has been out of there than there were during the entire twelve or fifteen years under union conditions. I hope that the union may prosper and some day come back to our relief.

The second letter to appear in the Journal:

> I am located at Verda, Harlan County, Kentucky, District 19, and have been for four years. I think the men of Harlan field have seen their mistake now. The coal that we were receiving 50 cents a ton for loading when

the United Mine Workers left this field, with 60 cents rib yardage and 7 cents for slate, now is 40 cents a ton in rooms and 42 cents in entry without any rib or yardage and no checkweighman at all. I have seen a whole trip go over the scales without being weighed. I believe the men working here see where they missed it when they let the union go. The men posted notices about a checkweighman election and some of them were fired. I have always been a union man and it makes the red blood boil when I see such things. I long to see the men get enough of it.

Conditions became progressively worse during the months that followed. According to one observer, wages of day men in 1926 ranged from $2.00 to $3.50 for a 12 to 16 hour day, while the wages of miners and loaders were reported to be as low as 20 cents a ton.

Another Verda miner wrote the Journal: "There are women and children in Harlan County that go to bed hungry because the husband and father cannot make enough to feed them. Day men are paid from $2.00 to $3.50 for twelve to sixteen hours a day. They run coal from 5:30 in the morning until 8 or 9 o'clock at night. Diggers are promised 40 cents a ton, but when it is weighed the weight they get only shows 20 cents a ton, because the same cars on which they formerly got paid for 4,000 pounds now weigh only 2,000 pounds."

Toward the end of 1926, due to a windfall of unexpected business for the American coal industry resulting from the British coal strike, there was a brief revival of union activity in Harlan County. But in spite of the favorable circumstances, not much headway was made. To defeat this new campaign there is evidence that many of the companies discharged workers and evicted them from the company-owned houses when it was discovered that they had joined the union.

The operators were literally getting away with murder and the fact that the 1926 organizing drive failed was almost entirely due to the fact that Sheriff Ward of Harlan County was a creature controlled and paid by the operators. His duties were actually to coerce, maim and murder any man with the audacity to speak up for the union. William Turnblazer reported to District 19's membership that he and other UMWA officers were attempting to have Sheriff Ward removed from office by Gov. W. J. Fields. He said: "We do not intend to allow Sheriff Ward or his paid gunmen to chase any organizer out of Harlan County."

But Ward was not removed. And if he did not chase any organizers out of Harlan, he and his thugs prevented them from recruiting very many new members. After this, the union spirit in Harlan County was dormant but refused to die. On May 1, 1927, the UMWA called a mass meeting in Harlan Town and for the first time in several years an International officer came to Harlan. He was the union's new Secretary-Treasurer, Thomas Kennedy, an anthracite miner from Hazleton, Pa., who had succeeded William Green in 1925 when the latter became president of the American Federation of Labor.

The meeting was a complete success in spite of the fact that local officials did everything they could to destroy its effectiveness. The city water supply was cut off during the day at the behest of the operators. Obtaining a drink of water was more difficult than getting a "shot of corn." But Tom Kennedy, Bill Turnblazer, Peggy Dwyer and other speakers of the day were able to revive the spirit of unionism and 1,058 miners were reinstated in the UMWA and taken into full membership. Local unions were re-established in virtually all coal camps in the Harlan territory.

This new spirit did not last long. The unqualified opposition of the operators coupled with the fact that Harlan coal miners had become accustomed to defeat proved too much for the union and by the end of 1927 efforts to organize the workers had again been abandoned. Organizing activities were at a virtual standstill in 1928, but in 1929 interest was revived by reports that acute distress prevailed in the mining communities throughout southeastern Kentucky. As a result, a first hand investigation was made by the editor of the UMW Journal.

The Journal article described poverty and starvation in the non-union coalfields of southeastern Kentucky. The editor said he "discovered that wages of miners ranged from $1.50 to $2.80 a day and that they got only two to three days work a week." In addition, he reported "all of the principle coal companies are running company stores, and the men who earn these pitifully small wages must trade at these stores. Very few men draw even a cent on payday."

He said that the coal operators themselves were as economically distressed as were their employees. He concluded: "All of this is definite proof of the correctness of the position of the UMWA for years past that wage reductions will not help the coal industry."

As a result of these conditions, the UMWA tried a new approach. In May, a petition was circulated among the business and professional men in the field requesting Mr. Turnblazer to call a public mass meeting for the purpose of discussing the problems of the coal industry. The meeting was held in Pineville on May 26 and was attended, according to reports, by "a large crowd of miners, operators, business and professional men, bankers, and the general public." This group adopted a series of resolutions calling on the Federal Congress to pass legislation regulating the bituminous coal industry because of the state of economic anarchy and depression existing in America's most basic industry. Officials of the International Union, led by John L. Lewis, had been pressing for passage of such legislation for several months.

The resolutions were taken to Washington and presented to President Herbert Hoover by Mr. Turnblazer and J. B. Helton, Sheriff of Bell County, the latter a good friend of the union. The government took no action, however, and whatever interest there had been in the sorry plight of Harlan miners once more languished.

The stock market crash of October 1929 and the desperate depression that followed merely accentuated an economic crisis that Harlan coal miners and operators had been enduring for several years. The following excerpt affords a glimpse of conditions existing at the outset of the depression from a letter to the editor of the UMW Journal by a miner living in Benham:

The mines are operating every day with few exceptions. Yet, it is a sad sight to see the little children clad in dirty clothes and nearly barefooted and their fathers wearing overalls on Sunday. The surroundings are decidedly deplorable with the exception of a few places. Other coal companies of this district have reduced wages from time to time until today it is just meat and bread proposition, and not enough of that. The small merchants have been thrown into bankruptcy, and here of late they have begun to talk in favor of unionism as the only hope for the miner and the restoration of business. It will be remembered that a few years ago they were lined up with the coal operators.

As the depression deepened there was a further succession of wage cuts and by the fall of 1930 the UMWA had once more entered the field in force. On Labor Day a mass meeting was held at Wallins Creek. Here again, the ostensible purpose of the meeting was the consideration of "ways and means of stabilizing the coal industry."

The meeting was addressed by Kentucky's Gov. Flem D. Sampson, Mr. Turnblazer and District 5 President, P. T. (Pat) Pagan. It was decided that a letter should be written to President Hoover asking him to call a conference of industry, government and labor union officials to try to arrive at a solution to the increasingly dangerous problem of unemployment. Although this appeal was likewise ignored in Washington, the miners were ripe for organization and the UMWA made gradual progress in the field during the remainder

Early UMWA organizing drives in District 19 were met with fierce resistance from coal operators. Miners could be fired for attending meetings, and "outside" organizers, such as Carl Williams pictured here, suffered violent treatment.

of 1930. A final fillip was furnished to the union movement by the announcement of a ten percent wage reduction in February 1931. The miners' bitterness at this move enabled the union to start a vigorous organizing campaign. It began with distribution of a circular describing the conditions that prevailed throughout the coalfields of southeastern Kentucky. Copies of the circular were sent to President Hoover, Secretary of Labor William Doak, and several members of Congress. The circular was printed in the Congressional Record at the request of Congressman J. Will Taylor of Tennessee. On the last page of the circular was the following appeal addressed to the miners:

> WANTED - 20,000 coal miners of District 19 to affiliate with the United Mine Workers of America; to assist in stopping wage reductions, long hours of labor, miserable working and living conditions.
>
> We have a plan whereby you may now join the organization by mail or otherwise, and prevent any discrimination against you. For further information in connection therewith, we advise you to get in touch with Lawrence Dwyer, P. O. Box 462, Pineville, Kentucky, and William Turnblazer, P. O. Box 96, Jellico, Tennessee.
>
> Join the union of your craft. Do not delay! Organize immediately! This is your opportunity. It is your only salvation, and in the words of the immortal Lincoln, "We cannot live half free and half slave." Let us hear from you.

This was followed by a mass meeting in Pineville early in March. According to the UMW Journal, approximately 2,000 miners attended the meeting and all who had a dollar joined the union. Alarmed at the revival of the union movement the operators began discharging union members, plus some of the miners who had simply attended the Pineville mass meeting. As a result of this action, Mr. Turnblazer addressed a telegram to President Hoover on April 1, 1931, asking for aid.

The telegram pointed out that Harlan coal operators were discharging employees merely because they had attended a public meeting. Not only were the employees fired but were evicted from their homes. They had no place to live and nothing to eat. Mr. Turnblazer stated: "They have appealed to that great American mother, that wonderful angel of mercy, the American Red Cross, and they have asked for bread and were given a stone."

He also informed the President that Governor Sampson, of Kentucky, had been appealed to "to no avail." The telegram also said: "These miners are hungry. They are anxious for work. The coal companies refuse them. The American Red Cross refuses them relief or assistance." The Turnblazer telegram concluded by quoting Daniel Willard, president of the Baltimore and Ohio Railroad, who had stated publicly: "In such circumstances, I would steal before I would starve."

President Hoover replied that "Judge Payne, Chairman of the American Red Cross, informs me that he is sending one of their agents into the locality you mention to investigate the situation." M. R. Reddy, the Red Cross representative, however, reported that the problem of relief was entirely in the hands of the local chapters and that national headquarters could not intervene. The local chapter of the Red Cross did lend its aid to the starving miners. In effect, it merely subsidized their starvation diet with handouts of flour. This action was almost meaningless and, in fact, merely made the process of starvation a little slower.

During the next few months, incipient rebellion smoldered menacingly in Harlan County. Unemployed miners began to march. One day, according to Mr. Turnblazer, "2,800 men marched into Harlan and demanded food. Merchants and others collected $350 and gave it to them." Late in April a drift mine at Shields was bombed and a tipple of the Harlan Collieries Company was burned. Later, sixteen vacant homes owned by the Three Point Coal Company were burned. Further violence was inevitable.

The top finally exploded on May 5 when the famed "Battle of Evarts" took place. Many people who have heard of this incident believe that scores of men died in the so-called battle. Actually, only four men were killed. Tension had begun to build up a few days earlier when the Black Mountain Coal Company discharged a large number of men and began evicting their families from company-owned houses. The dismissed miners met at Evarts, an independent (non-company) town about nine miles from Harlan. Word reached the miners that Jim Daniels, a deputy sheriff who was known throughout Harlan County as "the Kaiser" was on his way to Evarts with three carloads of deputies to clean out the town. Just outside of Evarts, the deputies and miners met. There was a fusillade of rifle shots and when the smoke had cleared away three deputies and one miner were dead.

The next day, according to an Associated Press dispatch, Governor Sampson ordered several companies of State Troops to Harlan County. This was after an all-day conference between the governor's representatives and labor leaders. After the conference, the following statement was signed and issued to the press:

> In the best interests of citizens of Harlan and Bell counties, we hereby request that Governor Sampson send sufficient soldiers to these counties to preserve order.
>
> We also desire and insist that no transportation of outside or foreign labor be sent into Harlan and Bell Counties while the troops are in the field and for the duration of martial law.
>
> The miners have the right of free assemblage and the right to join and solicit members for their organization and we agree that all meetings should be held in the daytime. We agree that all mine guards be disarmed and their commissions revoked. We, the undersigned, agree to cooperate to the fullest extent to bring about a settlement of these conditions at the earliest possible time.

The Battle of Evarts became a national sensation. It marked the beginning of the end of UMWA inertia in Harlan County. It marked the start of a new organizing drive that continued fitfully until 1941 when the operators finally signed a contract with the union based on the national wage agreement. It also projected the Communist Party into Harlan County which meant that the UMWA had it to fight as well as the coal operators and state and county officials bought and paid for by the mine owners. In the next few chapters, I will describe the battle of Evarts and the conflicting stories told about it, and a few of the colorful characters that were involved. I will also briefly recount the activities of the Communists in Harlan County. The latter accomplished little but made a lot of noise.

3

The Battle of Evarts

> *Virtually every man in Kentucky straps his guns on in the morning when he dresses and feels naked if he goes to the breakfast table unarmed.*

The Battle of Evarts took place on May 5, 1931. It was in reality more of a skirmish than a battle. It lasted only fifteen minutes. No more than fifty men were involved. Three company gun thugs (or deputy sheriffs, whichever you prefer) and one picketing miner was killed. Several others were wounded but recovered. But in spite of the small casualty list, Evarts was soon a household name in the United States. The murder and conspiracy trials that followed were reported on the front pages of all national newspapers. The Communists tried to seize control of the union spirit in Harlan and the famous novelist, Theodore Dreiser, then a Communist tool, wrote nationally syndicated newspaper stories about Harlan County coal miners.

The story of the battle has since become shrouded in myth. There are many who believe that hundreds of men died. The account I have gathered together should set the record straight. It is based on official court records and conversations with scores of those involved. One version of the battle is based on testimony given by witnesses for the Commonwealth who were attempting to convict the miners of murder or conspiracy. The testimony of these witnesses for the operators acquits the miners. The second version of the Battle of Evarts is based on what the defense—the miners themselves—had to say. It also acquits the miners. The record is clear.

Commonwealth Version

Before going into the details of testimony presented by anti-union witnesses, it might be well to place the battlefield in geographical perspective. It should be remembered that the men were picketing the Black Mountain Mine but were unable to enter the town of Black Mountain because it was company owned. A company mining camp, Verda, is located about four to five miles from Black Mountain. The town of Evarts, a non-company community, is located half way between the two company camps.

Events leading up to the gun battle began early on the morning of May 5, 1931, when a Black Mountain Coal Corporation truck drove past a group of UMWA pickets in Evarts. A strikebreaker named John Hickey who was accompanied by his son, Roscoe, and another scab named Roy Hughes drove the truck. As the truck passed by, one of the miners, Oscar Dykes, according to testimony at the conspiracy trial, shouted: "There they go. We'll lay for them when they come back."

Shortly afterward a number of striking miners gathered at the Louisville and Nashville Railroad depot in Evarts and another group went to the Verda end of Evarts where they stationed themselves. The L & N agent, O. M. Howard, testified that he telephoned E. B. Childers, superintendent of the Black Mountain Mine, and Harlan County Sheriff John Henry Blair notifying them that the strikers had gathered to stop the truck. Sheriff Blair admitted on the witness stand that he had talked by phone to Howard, Childers, and Jim Daniels, chief of the Black Mountain group of thugs. The sheriff further stated that he had ordered Daniels to "bring a bunch of mine guards from Black Mountain to Evarts" and instructed him to wait at the L & N depot to meet fifteen deputy sheriffs Blair was sending from Harlan. The mine guards and deputies would then, according to Blair, have escorted the truck past the pickets at Evarts. Five of the mine guards who survived the battle presented consistent testimony at the various trials of union men for murder or conspiracy. According to their stories, Daniels was in charge of a group of ten mine guards who traveled in three cars. They were armed with rifles, which were kept out of sight. All of them said that as they passed through Evarts no one said anything to them nor did anything to them. They passed various miners at the railroad station and more along the road. None of these molested the guards.

Still driving slowly, (some swore their greatest speed all the way from Black Mountain was fifteen miles per hour, others eight to ten), they neared the battle scene, an open spot on the edge of Evarts with a clear road to Verda and Harlan. Here they said they saw two Negroes and a white man standing beside a small water birch tree. When the last car had passed one of the Negroes raised his hand and a shot was fired. Daniels ordered the cars to stop. He got out on the righthand side, passed around the front of the car to the left side, and with his Browning rapid-fire rifle in a position to shoot, leaned upon a five-foot bank and looked over. According to the thugs, a shotgun immediately roared and Daniels, shot in the head, dropped to the ground dead.

Shooting became general. A battle raged for fifteen minutes. Some witnesses testified that more than a thousand shots were fired. Two more mine guards, Otto Lee and Howard Jones, were killed; two other guards, E. M. Cox and Sherman Percifal, were badly wounded.

That is the condensed testimony of the Commonwealth witnesses based on court records. It set forth all alleged facts in their stories of that morning's tragedy.

The Real Story

The defense conceded the truck had passed through Evarts to Verda and that some men had gathered to picket and persuade Hughes not to scab at Black Mountain. The defense proved, through Mrs. G. I. Michael, a Commonwealth witness, that Daniels and his mine fellow-guards, instead of driving to the scene at fifteen miles an hour or less, had sped there at forty miles or more per hour. She testified she left Black Mountain ahead of the deputies and although she drove twenty-five to thirty-five miles per hour, two cars of deputies passed her before she had traveled the mile and a half between Black Mountain and Evarts and the third passed her in Evarts. Instead of moving leisurely, Daniels and his crew sped eagerly to the fray.

Defense witnesses testified Daniels and his men began shooting at the pickets before stopping their cars that the pickets scattered and hid behind rocks and in small depressions for protection from the gunmen's withering fire. To gain a more advantageous position for achievement of their deadly purpose, Daniels and his men got out of the cars and with their rifles blazing advanced toward the trapped pickets. Daniels was intent on killing some pickets who had jumped over the side of the road behind a low cut bank to escape the guards' bullets. Stalking his prey, he leaned over the bank, emptied his Browning gun many times, crouched back to reload, and fired again and again. Daniels tried too long and too often. Reinforcements arrived to protect the ambushed pickets. There was testimony that as soon as the fight started half of the people of Evarts entered the battle on the side of the pickets from across the creek. The next time Daniels aimed over the bank he was killed.

Although all the mine guards swore Daniels was killed right after he reached the cut bank, the testimony of H. B. Turner, a merchant who appeared for the Commonwealth, gave full support to the evidence of the defense witnesses. Turner was coming in a taxi from Harlan to Evarts and was three hundred yards away when the shooting begun. He got out of the car and walked to within 250 feet of the fight, where he had a clear view of the battle. His testimony proves Daniels was not killed until at least five minutes after the shooting started.

"He was lying on the lower side of the bank," Turner swore. "He had gone up the bank and it looked like he was trying to shoot every once in a while he would raise his head up and somebody would shoot from somewhere else and he would dodge back down, and I watched him there until it looked like somebody shot his head off and he fell right there."

On cross-examination, Turner testified he saw Daniels rise up and look over the bank "something like four or five times." The defense demonstrated throughout that Daniels and his men were the aggressors, that instead of the mine guards being ambushed it was the mine guards who ambushed the pickets.

Three mine guards and one union coal miner were killed. Forty-three mineworkers were indicted for the killings of the gunmen. William Turnblazer, who was not in Harlan County but 100 miles away in Jellico, was indicted. The first eight men were charged with murder and tried in the Harlan courts. The operators were unable to get convictions before a mountain jury.

Three men, William Hightower, Ezra Phillips and William Hudson, were convicted of conspiracy by a Bluegrass jury and were pardoned by Governor Lafoon in December 1935. Four others, Jim Reynolds, W. B. Jones, Chester Poore and Al Benson were also convicted but were not freed until 1941.

W. B. Jones' trial for conspiracy to commit murder ended on December 1, 1931. Other conspiracy trials concluded as follows: Chester Poore on July 28, 1932; Jim Reynolds on September 22, 1932; and Al Benson on January 8, 1933. The conspiracy change was a smoke screen. Since it had been made so clear that it was the pickets, not the deputies, who were bushwhacked, since manifestly the killing of the three mine guards was done in self defense, the prosecution, a willing tool of the coal interests, found it necessary to resort to the conspiracy charge to secure convictions.

The prosecution proceeded against the accused on four theories: 1. That there was a conspiracy to kill Daniels, Childers and Sheriff Blair in order to replace them with officials who would be more friendly to the miners. 2. That there was a conspiracy to kill Daniels because he was to testify in May in Harlan at the examining trial of Bill Burnett, a union miner charged with (and later acquitted of) the killing of Jesse Pace. 3. That there was a conspiracy to kill deputies who, according to a letter alleged to have been read by defendant W. B. Jones at a union meeting May 4, were coming from Harlan with warrants for the arrest of five hundred miners and who planned, after the arrests, to ravish the miners' wives and daughters. 4. That there was a conspiracy to prevent a scab, named Roy Hughes, from moving his furniture next day from Verda to Black Mountain.

Attempting to prove these allegations, Fred Lester, Commonwealth witness in the Jones trial, testified: "Then he, (Jones) went ahead and said to them. 'All that has not got high-power rifles,' he said, take shotguns, and them that has not got shotguns, take pistols, and anybody that has not got a pistol, get a red handkerchief, and anybody that hain't got any gun at all, get some rocks,' and said, 'if there is any of you not able to throw rocks, get a red handkerchief, you can wave it.'"

Hugh Lester's testimony was a shameless echo of his brother Fred's story. Hugh said " and he (Jones) said, 'Every man get him a gun, and them that has not got a gun can get a pistol and if they hain't got a pistol, get a load of cracked rocks; and he says, them that has not got rocks, get a red flag or a red handkerchief and wave it.'" All of this was purported to have been said by Jones in a meeting of the Local Union the night before the battle.

Other Commonwealth perjurers also changed the "red handkerchief" into "red flag." But the enthusiastic prosecutors failed to school their witnesses sufficiently. There was no testimony showing that on May 5 anyone carried red handkerchiefs or red flags, or threw rocks.

Many of the state's witnesses who testified about the May 4 meeting were persons who themselves had been charged with the murders and were testifying to save their own lives. Examples: Fred, John and Hugh Lester had been indicted on a charge of poisoning a nephew to obtain $20,000 insurance. They also were indicted as participants in the May 5 battle. Both the May 5 murder charges and the poison murder charges were dismissed after they had testified for the Commonwealth, but Fred, chief beneficiary, was unable to collect the insurance.

What does the evidence actually show on the four conspiracy theories?

> 1. That union miners had petitions bearing thirty thousand signatures asking Governor Laffoon to remove Sheriff Blair and other county officials because of terrorist acts. Much testimony proved the union members had gone out of their way to secure removal of those officials peacefully and legally.

> 2. There was no conspiracy to kill Daniels to keep him from testifying against Burnett. Frank White and George Lee, deputies who took part in the fight when Burnett killed Jesse Pace, and who were far more important witnesses than Daniels, were permitted to pass through Evarts enroute from Black Mountain to Harlan an hour or more before the battle, and they were not molested. Dolly Hudson Daniels, widow of Jim Daniels, later told Governor Chandler that on the morning of May 5 Superintendent Childers came to her house and ordered her husband to the scene of the picketing and "wouldn't let him wait long enough to get breakfast or shave." She urged the governor to pardon the prisoners. Her statement further proves that Daniels was not preparing to go to Harlan that morning as the Commonwealth alleged. His May 5 journey to death had one purpose—to shoot it out with the pickets at Evarts. The Commonwealth produced no evidence to show that any preparations were made by the union miners to defend Burnett; no lawyer had been retained; no witnesses subpoenaed. After the Jones trial this part of the "conspiracy" was barely mentioned.

> 3. The majority of the Commonwealth's witnesses testified that from twelve to fourteen pickets were at the battle scene, obviously an insufficient number to stop an invading army of deputies coming from Harlan to arrest five hundred miners and then ravish their wives.

4. No denial was made of the effort to picket the truck containing the furniture of the scab, Roy Hughes. Picketing is part and parcel of every strike. The testimony of both Hughes and the driver Hickey that they did not know until the morning of May 5 that they were going to bring the truck through Evarts, making it impossible for a conspiracy to have been hatched at the May 4 meeting to stop the truck with guns.

What actually happened to bring on the battle? Let us sum up the evidence again to make the picture clearer. The Commonwealth's case: The L & N depot agent telephoned Childers and Sheriff Blair, advising them of the picket line. Blair and Daniels talked several times over the telephone. Blair ordered Daniels to bring his men and meet the squad of deputies coming from Harlan "at the L & N depot," then escort the truck to Black Mountain. Daniels and his men drove peacefully down the road and were suddenly fired upon from ambush.

The defense proved by Commonwealth witnesses: That Daniels and his men drove swiftly, at least forty miles per hour with their rifles hidden. Daniels rode in the front car and kept his own car in the middle to avoid recognition. Daniels didn't stop at the L & N depot where he had been supposedly ordered to wait for the Harlan deputies, but drove no more than 1,600 feet to the battle site; that pickets were looking toward Harlan for the truck while Daniels and his crew sped up behind them; that Daniels was not killed until five minutes after the battle started and only after he had made several attempts to shoot a man who was crouched down behind the cut bank; that Daniels was twenty feet away from the car when he was killed.

Without quoting defense witnesses for corroboration, this conclusion is the most probable: Blair and Daniels plotted over the telephone to wipe out the pickets by a surprise attack. While the pickets were looking toward Harlan for the truck to come from Verda, the Black Mountain mine guards were to sweep down and shoot them in the back. The other fifteen deputies coming from Harlan would attack from the opposite direction. Thus the pickets would be caught between two fires. The plan miscarried because Daniels attacked too soon while the fifteen Harlan deputies were still at Verda. (Note: The battle occurred at a place where the road makes a right angle turn).

If Jones had been tried purely for murder, any jury—either from the Blue Grass or the mountains—would have acquitted him. He was nowhere near the scene of the shootings. But the Commonwealth filed "conspiracy" charges and used maudlin stories of "red flags" and "black oaths," plus other gibberish as evidence to bolster up this fantastic charge. Much of the Commonwealth's case depended on the jury putting credence in the belief that the Battle of Evarts had been precipitated by a group of blood-thirsty miners who wanted only to wipe out the deputies.

Five of the surviving mine guards, according to their own testimony, were permitted to get into one of the cars and leave the battle scene. A sixth, Sherman Perciful, testified that although badly wounded he walked away. The seventh, E. M. Cox, testified that one of the miners "hollered at me to throw down my gun and run and I would not be hurt."

When the taking of testimony in the Jones trial ended, most observers expected a prompt acquittal. But they had not anticipated the next move of the prosecution. Commonwealth's attorney, W. C. Hamilton of Mount Sterling, was selected to play the final trump card in his summation to the jury. His notorious "bonfires of rejoicing in Moscow if you acquit this man" speech is one of the most brutal violations of court procedure in history. The Knoxville News-Sentinel, a Scripps-Howard daily newspaper, which has never been noted for its friendliness to organized labor, followed the Jones trial carefully. On December 11, 1931, it said in a lead editorial:

> William B. Jones, secretary of the United Mine Workers in Harlan County, Kentucky, has been convicted of murder in the first degree and sentenced to life imprisonment . . . The climax of this trial came as attorneys argued it before the jury. It was not featured by a review of the

facts of the battle. Instead, denunciations of unionism and of "Reds" rang through the courtroom.

Read these excerpts from the arguments:

With an admonition by the Commonwealth's attorney, W. C. Hamilton, not to let the American flag surrender to the Red flag, the fate of W. B. Jones, miner and union organizer, was placed in the hands of the jury.

Hamilton devoted more than a third of his four-and-a-half hour speech to a denunciation of the I.W.W. and Communism. There was no proof in the trial that Jones belonged to either organization.

Hamilton pointed out that the United Mine Workers' oath fails to say 'in the name of Almighty God' but says instead 'in the name of each other.'

Emphasizing the importance of the verdict, the Commonwealth attorney said 'in Russia they will read the fate of this man' and 'if you turn him loose there will be celebrations in thousands of places, and in Moscow the Red Flag will be raised higher.'

The Commonwealth attorney condemned Jones for using an American flag in the parade of miners: 'He carried an American flag in his hand but the Red flag was in his heart. Before Saturday night you will know what I am saying will materialize. In Pineville or Harlan there will be a celebration of Reds, and property will have no more value than human life is regarded there now.'

The organization to which Jones belonged is affiliated with the American Federation of Labor . . . but whether or not Jones had radical inclinations is beside the point. This fact is important:

There is no fair-minded man who has followed the Jones trial who can help from wondering in his own mind whether the Harlan County labor leader was convicted and sentenced to life imprisonment for murder or for being a labor leader.

The miners were ably defended by Capt. Ben Golden, former prosecuting attorney of Bell County, father of James Golden who ably represented the miners of southeastern Kentucky for many years, and J. M. Robeson, former congressman from Kentucky for many years, assisted by W. Bridges White of Mt. Sterling. When the Court of Appeals upheld the verdict against W. B. Jones, it said in the ruling: "It is earnestly insisted that the verdict of the jury should be set aside under the evidence but the well-settled rule is that the credibility of the witnesses is for the jury."

In November 1935, the twelve Bluegrass jurors petitioned Governor Chandler to set Jones free but he refused. On December 24, 1936, a delegation of thirty-five persons called on Governor Chandler, including William Turnblazer, myself, and Dolly Daniels, widow of the chief mine guard, Jim Daniels, who was killed in the Evarts battle. She told the governor she believed that all the prisoners were innocent.

A true picture of what took place at Evarts on that fateful morning was later given to me personally by Martin Kurd who was a picket during the battle and later went to work for me as an organizer when I came to Harlan County. Kurd recalled that the Battle of Evarts took place just across the Clover Fork River, about 100 yards from the main street of the town. He was close to Ezra (Big Segar) Phillips when he shot Jim Daniels in self-defense. He recalled that a few minutes after the shooting started by the Black Mountain mine guards and the twelve or fifteen pickets that the brick building just across the river became a fortress. Half the town was soon involved. Guns blazed from the roofs and windows. It is little wonder that people were aroused. They had been angered by the story that five hundred thugs were going to swoop down on the town, kill union miners and rape their wives. This had added fuel to anger caused by an incident a few days before the battle when deputies had thrown a white waitress in jail with a drunken Negro miner and left her all night in the same cell with him. I would tend to doubt this story as hearsay except for the fact that the miner himself verified the story to me.

These facts were made known to Governor Chandler in 1935 along with a statement by Sherman Percival, one of the Black Mountain guards who was the recipient of sixteen bullets during the Battle of Evarts. After testifying that he was unable to identify anyone as having taken part in the battle, Perciful told the governor that George Dawn, a principal Commonwealth witness, had said: "Damn it, say you saw them whether you did or not." Perciful urged that the prisoners be freed, but in spite of his pleas and the pleas of Jim Daniels' widow and members of the juries who convicted Jones and Perciful, the governor refused to release the prisoners.

One of the rewards of a lifetime of service to a labor union lies in friendships I have made with various colorful and dedicated men down through the 35 years. Three of the principals on the union side at the Battle of Evarts later worked with me and I came to know them well. I have already mentioned Martin Hurd who worked with me from 1937 to 1941 helping to organize the miners in Harlan County. At the time of the Evarts' trials, Hurd was threatened and intimidated by the state but he stood his ground and testified to the truth. I first met Martin Hurd in May 1937 when he came to me and asked for a job. I told him I had a full crew. He said, "O.K., I will help organize for nothing." He worked for a week and convinced me he had a great deal of ability so I put him on the payroll.

Hurd was not only a good organizer but also a colorful, carefree character. He was a 6' 2" tall, light skinned Negro with a build like an Adonis and an eye for the ladies. He dressed well and owned several tailor-made suits. His wife worked for Dr. P. O. Lewis. She knew he was fickle and after several years became fed up with his activities as a philanderer. During a heated argument she took a razor and slashed his beloved suits to ribbons. She accused him of having made love to every quadroon, octoroon and sepia in Kentucky. She then got on the train and left town. Martin was a lost ball in high weeds. No one to cook for him; no one to press his clothes, and no one to love him when he was broke. He then got a bright idea. He sent his wife a telegram that he was dead and asked her what to do with the body, signing the name of a local undertaker. Mrs. Hurd hurried back to Harlan to claim Martin's remains and there stood Martin smiling at her when she got off the train. She fainted. They were a normal couple. They kissed, made up, and lived happily ever after (I think).

When he was working with me he got into a different kind of trouble, which typified the manner in which Harlan County authorities persecuted representatives of the union. He was charged with carrying his pistol concealed. This was a ruse used by local officials to harass union men. Perhaps to understand the nature of the judge, a brief explanation of Kentucky's unique weapons law is in order. The state has always emphasized in its custom and legislation the fact that a man has a right to bear arms openly. You could (and still can) carry a dozen pistols if you left the end of the barrel in sight. Usually it hung below your coattail. If the coattail hung lower than the end of the barrel, you were in violation of the law for carrying concealed weapons.

Virtually every man in Kentucky straps his guns on in the morning when he dresses and feels naked if he goes to the breakfast table unarmed. It was common practice for two or more deputy sheriffs to swear out a warrant or an affidavit that they saw John Doe of the UMWA in public carrying a concealed weapon. Usually they said they saw the gun in the union man's hip pocket when his coattail blew back. Such cases were tried in the County Court. If a man demanded a jury trial under the illusion that this would render him a fair shake, a deputy would go out in the Harlan courthouse yard and summon the first six men he saw. Usually they were bums who sat around and waited for jury duty. They were paid $2.00 each per case and the $12.00 was added onto the cost of those convicted. If a man was found not guilty, no costs were paid and the jury worked for nothing, which, I do not think I need to point out, led to 100 percent convictions. So the "wino" jury convicted and received the $2.00 which just about covered the cost of a bottle or two of wine. This was Harlan County juries.

In addition to being charged with carrying the concealed gun, Hurd was also formally charged with hiring an assassin to kill all the Harlan County officials. This charge was ridiculous but it was a regular method of harassment used against every union organizer in Harlan County. The Harlan Enterprise told the story as follows:

HARLAN, MARCH 26, 1938. The story of a plot to murder a group of county officials, former officials and peace officers of Harlan County was told by a witness in the Harlan Circuit Court today in a sudden move to place Martin Hurd under a peace bond. Hurd, a 36-year-old United Mine Workers organizer, was charged by David Crockett, Negro coal miner of Gary, West Virginia, who Sheriff Herbert Cawood said appeared voluntarily and swore that Martin Hurd offered him a new car and $500 for each death, $150 a month and expenses, to kill Daniel Boone Smith, Theodore Middleton, Lee Fleenor, Captain Russell of the Lynch police force, Bill Hollins, and two men by the name of Young and Little. The peace bond warrant against Hurd was signed by Charles Elliott, deputy sheriff for Sheriff Herbert Cawood.

Hurd said he went to Gary to visit his uncle and Crockett asked for a lift to Lynch. The girl who drove Hurd's car from Gary to Harlan said Crockett and Hurd slept all the way and discussed nothing. The old perjury mill was still grinding. The case was finally thrown out of court.

Martin Hurd was one of three men who were involved in the Battle of Evarts who later worked with me in Harlan County and whom I came to know and respect. The second man was actually in charge of organizing in Harlan County for several years before I moved in from Tennessee. He was Lawrence "Peggy" Dwyer who had been an international representative of the UMWA since 1911. His nickname came from the fact that he had one leg cut off at the knee when he was working in the coal mines. He was an Irishman and the father of eleven children. Peggy was an aggressive organizer who would fight anything that walked or crawled if he felt the cause was just. All of his life he had been a good union man And during his early years in West Virginia he suffered for it. Well known because of his union tendencies, Peggy once moved into a company house at a West Virginia mine, which promptly instituted action to evict him. It usually took three weeks to get service for a legal eviction. As soon as one notice was served on him, Peggy would move into another empty company house and wait out the three weeks for another eviction notice. Finally, Peggy himself got tired of moving every three weeks so he went to the mine, carrying his pistol, and told the superintendent he was annoyed at moving all the time, that he had a family to keep and was willing to work. He added briefly that if the superintendent did not give him a job he would kill him. The superintendent believed Peggy meant what he said so gave him a job and the two got along for a number of years without any more trouble.

This did not stop Peggy's organizing activities. The superintendent had to put up with them during these years, whether he liked it or not, because one of the things you could not stop him from doing was talking about the United Mine Workers of America.

Peggy was a great storyteller. One of his favorites concerned a time when he was fiscal agent for strike relief during the Cabin Creek-Paint Creek strike in West Virginia in 1912 and 1913. He went to the union's international headquarters in Indiana and got $3,000 relief money in cash, which he carried back to West Virginia in his hollow wooden leg. Another story involving his wooden leg concerned an automobile accident. Peggy always drove a Model A Ford when I knew him and had trouble controlling it because of the fact he only had one leg. One time, I remember with a great deal of delight, he lost control of the car and it ran over a bank. The car was demolished but Peggy escaped unhurt except for the fact that his wooden leg was broken in two in the middle. When he came crawling up the bank with what appeared to be one leg broken off below the knee, a woman, part of a large crowd of tourists who had gathered to see the blood, fainted because she thought he had really lost his leg.

Dwyer was not only an Irishman, he was a lucky Irishman. During his years in Harlan several attempts were made to kill him but he never was hurt. His car was fired into on several occasions from ambush and his living quarters in Pineville were blown up on two different occasions.

Another of Peggy's favorite stories involves one of the times his house was dynamited. On this occasion the dynamite was put close enough to his bed so that instead of hurting the intended victim when it blew the house up, it merely blew Peggy, bed, mattress and all against the ceiling and he came down without a scratch. However, a bottle of ink had been dislodged from the dresser by the explosion and the cork came out, throwing ink all over Peggy's face. In the darkness after he had come back to earth, Peggy felt this ink on his face and thought it was blood. When he was able to get a look at himself in the light, he found that it was ink and with his usual display of humor in telling the story, he said, "I have heard of people with red blood, yellow blood, but that was the first time I ever thought I was a blue blood."

In addition to his other attributes, he was a man of great kindness. He would give you the shirt off his back, or ninety cents of his last dollar if you needed it. He was a great American. He retired at the age of seventy-four to his farm in Shoals, Indiana, and died a year later. I always suspected he was bored to death by inactivity.

The third man involved in the Battle of Evarts, whom I later came to know well and still respect as a friend, was Bill Gibbs. After the battle, he was indicted and held in jail for sixty-seven days because he couldn't raise $30,000 bond. He was finally released by a Circuit Judge, D. C. (Baby) Jones without a trial. Jones had good reason to release Bill Gibbs. He knew that he was held in jail without reason and that Gibbs was not a man who forgave easily. Baby Jones probably learned this from his bodyguard, a tough character named Two-gun Marion Allen who had worked with Gibbs in Harlan County coalmines. I am sure the reason that Judge Jones felt he needed a bodyguard was fear that some decent citizen of Harlan County would kill him. Gibbs had a reputation as a gunman but was also well known for the fact that he had never picked a fight in his life. In his early days he had killed a man by the name of Anderson after Anderson had killed Bill Gibbs' brother. Undoubtedly Two-gun Allen convinced Baby Jones that it was jeopardizing both of their lives to keep Bill Gibbs in jail unless they could prove he was guilty of some crime. Gibbs was released after the judge attempted to get him to agree that he would not retaliate for the false imprisonment.

Bill Gibbs then went quietly back to work as a coal miner at the Black Mountain Mine. During the 1930s he could usually be found there on a picket line or at a union meeting. In 1941 Gibbs was successfully framed by the Harlan County Coal Operators and went to the penitentiary for killing a mine foreman of the Berger Coal Company. Gibbs spent several years in the penitentiary on a one-to-ten-year sentence, after which he was paroled. Soon after he had been freed, a man named Bernard Long confessed on his death bed that he, Long, had killed the mine foreman and that Bill Gibbs was innocent of that crime. Gibbs resided at Grays, Kentucky, on a hillside farm until his death in 1963. The state has done nothing to rectify this injustice. I believe that the legislature should, in spite of the many years that have passed, pass legislation enabling the state to pay Gibbs' widow for the time he was falsely imprisoned. This will probably never be done and is merely another installment of sacrifice that union miners pay for freedom.

This is the story of the famous Battle of Evarts. It was a symbol of the UMWA's fight for freedom but at the time was merely another abortive attempt to unionize Harlan County.

4

The Brief, Unhappy Life of the Communist Party in Harlan County

> *At this point in the history of Bloody Harlan, both the Communists and the UMWA had been driven out.*

The Evarts battle marked the beginning of an epidemic of local strikes. The first was at the operations of the Harlan Gas Coal Company where two hundred miners—virtually the entire working force—laid down their tools. A few days later, after the arrival of the troops ordered into Harlan by Governor Sampson, three more mines were closed by strikes and Secretary George Ward of the Harlan County Coal Operators' Association estimated that four-hundred and fifty miners were on strike. This rash of work stoppage was partly due to the operators' failure to carry out the provisions of the agreement which called for disarming of mine guards. The spread of strikes in Harlan County is borne out by data based on official records of the U. S. Bureau of Mines. The figures show that at one time or another during the year, 1,574 miners were involved in strikes and that a total of 37,034 man days were lost because of strikes. This is in striking contrast with the record from 1923 to 1930 when in four of the eight years no strikes were reported by the operators and in the other four years less than three operators reported strikes.

UMWA officials were convinced that strikes in Harlan County at that time would be futile. The union refused to sanction them or to render any substantial assistance to the miners. Apparently the UMWA was greatly concerned over anti-union publicity after the Battle of Evarts. In any event, after the collapse of a strike at the mine of the Creech Coal Company on June 17, the UMWA withdrew completely from the field.

This left Harlan County open to organizing efforts by dual unions, efforts that were destined to fail but which strengthened the hands of the Harlan County operators because it enabled them to accuse anyone working to better the lot of the miners of being a Communist. These accusations had some element of truth in them simply because the dual union was Communist-dominated. Known as the National Miners Union, it was formed in Pittsburgh about 1925 when it was a part of the Industrial Workers of the World (IWW). The National Miners Union believed in direct political revolution as the only means to better the lot of coal miners and other workers, and attacked the UMWA for its more conservative line of action. They succeeded for a time in persuading some misguided Harlan County miners to join their union. These men were made desperate by starvation and persecution and, grasping at straws, signed up with the so-called "Save the Union Movement" when the UMWA withdrew from the field. The union's leaders believed that for a time it would not be practical to fight the Harlan County coal operators and the Communist Party on the same battlefield at the same time.

In spite of the complications caused by entry of Communism into Harlan County, there was little violence. Colonel Carrel, who was in charge of the Kentucky troops in Harlan County, reported that the only incident of violence took place on June 11 when a coal miner named John Casteen was killed by a gun thug, Bill

Randolph, at Cawood. Randolph was quite a character. He was a big, handsome six-foot motorman at Three Point who succumbed to the lure of money and joined the thug gang. He was known to have killed five men and to be without fear. He once went into Harlan when Theodore Middleton was chief of police and kicked his buttocks in an attempt to force the police chief to draw a pistol on him, but for once Theodore Middleton ate crow. Randolph was killed by Clarence Middleton, shot behind the ear when he was not looking. In any event, his murder of Casteen was the only violence in the early summer of 1931, and by the middle of July most of the mines had resumed operation. As a consequence, the National Guard troops were withdrawn from Harlan on July 23, 1931.

The withdrawal of troops from Harlan County was the signal for the resumption of warfare. By this time the operators had apparently decided to drive all forms of unionism out of the county. Charles Rumford Walker's summary of developments that took place after the troops had left, which is largely substantiated by testimony before a Senate Subcommittee of the Committee on Manufacturers is given below:

> The union (NMU) formed women's auxiliaries to aid in organizing relief; soup kitchens were set up, and new NMU locals formed. The UMWA warned the miners of the danger of the Communist-controlled NMU. The operators opened their attack shortly after the Pittsburgh convention of the NMU. On July 20, there was a raid on the home of Bill Duncan, Pittsburgh delegate. On July 23, Jesse Wakefield's car was dynamited during the night. On July 25, twenty-eight additional thugs were imported, increasing the force to sixty-five. The operators were thoroughly aroused and ready to fight with every weapon at hand. A report went about that orders had been given to the new thug army to "shoot, kill and slay four Red leaders" in Harlan County, and that they were to do this within two weeks or it would be too late to stamp out the NMU.
>
> On July 26, 1931, the union held a picnic attended by 2,000 miners, their wives and children, at which open speeches were made. Eleven heavily armed deputies came to the picnic but left. The miners had armed themselves.

It is interesting to note that on July 30 Judge Willie Bob Howard in a labor case found occasion in court to condemn roundly the NMU and to offer words of praise and defense for the United Mine Workers of America. Only a few months before this in the spring of the year he had condemned the UMWA and warned the miners against it. This about-face we found characteristic of operators and officials of Harlan. Now that the UMWA was dead in Harlan, the corpse came to be spoken of with touching respect by its old enemies.

From July 30 to August 3, there were strong efforts on the part of the operators to prevent the holding of a state convention of the NMU at Wallins Creek. Wholesale raids on miners' homes were accompanied by a great deal of illegal searching of automobiles. The convention was held however, on August 2 in spite of the terror which had led up to it. Miners guarded the entrance to Wallins Creek and five hundred Negro and white elected delegates were present including women. Late at night after the convention two car-loads of NMU men were arrested and personal property taken from them. The arrest was without warrant or provocation.

On August 10, the Evarts soup kitchen was dynamited. This was one of seven maintained by the NMU. Shortly after the dynamiting, Finley and Caleb Powers who were guards at one of the other soup kitchens were arrested on charges of 'banding and confederating.' They were unarmed and at the time of their arrest and were fixing the fires for the next day's cooking. Other acts of terrorism committed against the union are to be found elsewhere in the committee's record. Their repetition here is unnecessary; they did not succeed in halting the spread of the union. Two miners were shot and killed by thugs in the Harlan soup line in cold blood.

As a result of the reports of suffering and violence, nation-wide attention was centered on Harlan County. Large numbers of newspapermen, individual investigators, and delegations visited the region to verify the reports. One of the first of the investigators to visit the field was Louis Stark of the New York Times, and the results of his investigations were published in that paper in the latter part of September. The first of the delegations was the so-called Dreiser Committee, sponsored by the National Committee for the Defense of Political Prisoners. This was followed by a committee headed by Waldo Frank. Then, early in 1932, a rapid succession of delegations visited Southeastern Kentucky, but not all of these forays were able to get into the region to complete their investigations. A group of Columbia University students got as far as Middlesboro (Bell County) and then were escorted to the state border by a group of public-spirited citizens under the leadership of County Attorney Walter B. Smith of Bell County. Another student group from Commonwealth College were badly beaten before being escorted out of the state.

The dramatization of the conditions prevailing in the region brought about a brief investigation by a Senate Subcommittee of the Committee on Manufactures. Early in 1932, the following resolution was introduced in the United States Senate:

> Resolved, That the Committee on the Judiciary, or any duly authorized subcommittee thereof, is authorized and directed to investigate the conditions existing in the coal fields in Harlan and Bell Counties, in the Commonwealth of Kentucky, with a view of determining particularly (1) whether any system of peonage has been or is being maintained in such coal fields; (2) whether the postal service and facilities have been or are being obstructed or interfered with therein, and if so, by whom; (3) whether citizens of the United States have been arrested, tried or convicted in violation of the Constitution or laws of the United States; (4) whether firearms, ammunition, or explosives have been shipped into such coal fields from states other than Kentucky, and if so, by whom shipped and by whom paid for; (5) whether any unlawful conditions exist or have existed in such coal fields which interfere or have interfered with the production for interstate shipment, or otherwise with the interstate shipment, of coal from such coal fields; and (6) the causes leading up to the conditions reported to exist in such coal fields. The committee shall report to the Senate as soon as practicable the results of its investigations, together with its recommendations, if any, for necessary remedial legislation.
>
> For the purpose of this resolution the committee, or any duly authorized subcommittee thereof, is authorized to hold such hearings, to sit and act at such times and places during the sessions and recesses of the Senate in the 72nd Congress until the final report is submitted, to employ such clerical and other assistants, to require by subpoena or otherwise the attendance of such witnesses and the production of such books, papers, and documents, as it deems advisable. The cost of stenographic services to

report such hearings shall not be in excess of 25 cents per hundred words. The expenses of the committee shall be paid from the contingent fund of the Senate upon vouchers as approved by the chairman.

The subcommittee was composed of Senator Bronson Cutting, Senator Edward P. Costigan and Senator D. H. Hatfield of West Virginia. Senator Hatfield did not agree with the majority report and filed a minority report. Because of the limitations imposed on the subcommittee by the restrictions to voluntary appearance of witnesses in Washington, the Senate investigation was necessarily incomplete. Nevertheless, enough evidence was obtained in three days of hearings to warrant the following conclusions:

> As suggested at the outset of this report the subcommittee has reached the conclusion that a prima facie showing has been made of autocratic and other antisocial conditions and of violated legal and constitutional rights. The charges are too grave to be ignored and in fairness require additional testimony more searchingly and effectively made available in and out of the affected coal mining area. The subcommittee's experience in the preliminary inquiries has persuasively indicated that authority to visit Kentucky and to subpoena witnesses, conferred in a formally authorized investigation, are vital to the complete disclosure of underlying and relevant facts, without which serious efforts to consider or formulate remedial legislation will be definitely hampered. The Committee therefore recommends the prompt adoption of Senate Resolution 178, with the one amendment above specified.

Senate Hatfield disagreed with the majority report in a letter dated July 11, 1932 to Senator Costigan. He set forth reasons for his disagreement. Hatfield based his objections to what he called the disrupting influence of a U. S. Senate investigation of the Cabin Creek-Paint Creek strike while he was governor of West Virginia. He said: "It delayed an adjustment of the strike after a contest of a year and a half." He said that the UMWA was opposed to the investigation and said that the agitators for a probe emanated from radical agitators. Hatfield also said he believed that "it is quite possible that it (the investigation) would incite new antagonisms that are dormant at the present time."

In spite of the recommendation of the subcommittee, the investigation was not conducted and any national interest in Harlan County was diverted by the gloom of the nation-wide economic depression.

It was at this point that the NMU died in Harlan County, if indeed it had ever lived there. This is perhaps most vividly illustrated by the fact that a strike was called by the Communists in Harlan County in 1932 but not one single man-day lost was reported during the year on account of work stoppages. At this point in the history of Bloody Harlan, both the Communists and the UMWA had been driven out. A sharp change occurred in 1933 when it would have appeared that success for the union was not at all possible.

5

The La Follette Committee and Pearl Bassham

> *The hillbilly syndicate that operated this vicious system could and would liquidate anybody who dealt with the union.*

One of the most famous investigations ever conducted by the United States Senate took place in the late 1930s. It was conducted by a special committee headed by Senator Robert La Follette, Jr., the progressive Republican from Wisconsin. Its purpose was to ferret out and expose brutal methods used by large corporations in fighting labor unions. Senator La Follette, his associates and staff studied company spies in the Chrysler Corporation; a strike-breaking agency run by a gentleman widely known as "Chowderhead" Cohen; and inevitably interference with civil liberties in Harlan County, Kentucky, by the coal operators. The report of the La Follette Committee has long been a matter of public record. Testimony filled ten books, two of which were devoted to Harlan County. What was testified to seems unbelievable today. Nevertheless, it is true. What the La Follette Committee ascertained in 1937 was true in the years prior to the investigation and, by and large, conditions remained the same until 1941.

A typical witness before the committee was Pearl Bassham, vice president and general manager of the Harlan Wallins Coal Corporation which then operated four mines in Harlan County that produced over one million tons of coal a year, employing over 1,200 men.

By 1937, when the La Follette Committee conducted its investigation, I was assigned to Harlan County and knew Pearl Bassham well. He was a small, middleaged man about five foot six inches tall, with a bald head and a set of beautiful big teeth like a horse. He showed them all when he smiled. As far as union men were concerned, his smiles meant nothing except, perhaps, that he wanted to show his big beautiful teeth. He always gave me the impression—then and later—that he was a man in love with only one thing, money. He rose from the job as motorman in one of the Harlan Wallins mines to vice president of the company almost over night.

In this chapter I will detail what Bassham told the committee simply because he was typical and fairly honest in his answers. In the first place, he admitted that his company opposed union mem-

SENATOR ROBERT LA FOLLETTE, JR. (1895-1953) *was the son of the famous Wisconsin Progressive governor "Fighting Bob" La Follette. Following his father's death in 1925, "Young Bob" won his father's senate seat, which he lost, ironically, to Joseph McCarthy in 1946. A fierce advocate for organized labor, La Follette's Civil Liberties Committee exposed nationally the astonishing methods corporate giants employed to suppress unionization, including industrial espionage.*

bership for its employees. He bluntly stated to the committee on May 4: "It has been our attitude up until two or three weeks ago to discharge men who became members of the union." Because of the La Follette investigation, Bassham explained that in April he had "issued instructions that no one is to be fired on account of joining the union."

He also averred that every miner employed by the Harlan Wallins Coal Corporation was forced to sign a "yellow dog" contract binding him not to join any "mine labor organization." The contract read in part:

> Harlan Wallins Coal Corporation, Incorporated, employer, and (blank) employee, agree as follows: That so long as the relation of employer and employee exists, between them, the employer will not knowingly employ, or keep in its employment, any member of the United Mine Workers of America, the I.W.W., or any other mine labor organization, and will not aid, encourage or approve the organization thereof, it being understood that the policy of said company is to operate a non-union mine, and that it would not enter into any contract of employment under any other conditions.

Bassham conceded that the "yellow dog" contract violated provisions of the National Labor Relations Act. Nationally known as the Wagner Act, this law had been passed in 1935 to protect further the rights of employees to organize and bargain collectively through labor unions. As a weak excuse, Bassham stated that the yellow dog "was a contract that has been in use ever since I came with the company and we just continued it." He further testified that he had "not had an opportunity to acquaint himself" with the National Labor Relations Act." It is not surprising that the UMWA had never been able to organize a local union at any of the mines of the Harlan Wallins Coal Corporation. Bassham's "explanation" was that "our people have never seemed to want the union."

Every miner who lived in the Harlan Wallins Coal Corporation camps was forced to rent a company-owned house and sign a company house lease. The lease required the occupant to vacate the premises immediately upon leaving the employ of the company. Miners discharged for violating the "yellow dog" contract by joining the union were immediately required to pack up their possessions and move on. Each man who worked at Verda (The Harlin Wallins company town) had to rent a house whether he used it or not. Single men living in the homes of their parents also paid house rent. There was one house in Verda which was rented to eight single men at one time and yet it was unoccupied.

When coal miners are paid on the basis of quantity of production, accuracy and honesty in weighing the coal is important to the miners. Coal companies usually hired a person to weigh the coal as it was unloaded at the tipple. One of the objectives of the United Mine Workers of America has always been recognition of the right of employees also to employ a checkweighman to see that miners paid by the ton are given honest weight at the mine scales. It has been proved on a national scale that men were cheated of approximately forty to fifty percent of their pay at mines where checkweighmen were not employed.

When the first contract was signed at Verda in 1937 between the union and the Harlin Wallins Coal Corporation, a state mine inspector by the name of Guthrie was called in to inspect the scales and a checkweighman was put on the tipple. When Guthrie attempted to balance the scales he had to drill pounds of lead out of the scale weights. He reported to me that the false weights were costing the miners tonnage pay on seventeen gondolas (850 tons) of coal a day. The company had also been losing money because it was alleged that this non-weighed coal was sold separately. This money did not revert to the company but was a gravy train for some high company officials.

In Kentucky since 1886, the State law has required the employer to accede to the demand of a majority of his employees when they demand that they be permitted to employ a checkweighman to protect their interests, and provided for an election to determine as to whether or not a checkweighman is to be employed by the miners.

There were no checkweighmen at most of the mines in Harlan County in 1937. A union organizer testified that there were checkweighmen at only two mines in the entire county. Both were Black Mountain mines. Robert E. (Uncle Bob) Lawson, general manager of the Cornett-Lewis Coal Company located at Louellen, in Harlan County, testified that he knew of five checkweighmen in the county. He claimed that the reason more were not employed was due to the reluctance of the miners to pay for them. There was, however, no checkweighman at his own mine. His lame explanation was: "I have tried my best on four different occasions in public meetings to get my men to elect one, and they won't do it. They don't want to pay one." On the other hand, a union representative, Marshall Musick, who had worked at Lawson's mine testified that the miners had checkweighmen at the mine until their union was broken in 1934. He said that after the union was busted, both checkweighmen were run out of the company camp and were not replaced. Nor were there checkweighmen at the mines of the Harlan Wallins Coal Corporation. Mr. Bassham stated that the men had not demanded any. His employees claimed that they were denied the right to have checkweighmen. Any miner who "demanded" would have been chased off company property. He probably would have been beaten up for his audacity.

The denial of the right to have checkweighmen was not the only grievance Harlan County miners had against the operators. Even more important was the fact that wages, hours and working conditions were pitiful when compared with standards achieved in unionized coal mines.

To illustrate this, let me say that no Harlan County miner was paid for what we call "dead work." This coal miners' term means work that is non-productive, such as installing timbers to support the shaft or mine roof, loading out slate and cleaning up other refuse. In unionized mines, this work was paid for at an hourly rate. Not in Harlan County, though. The man was paid for the actual tonnage he loaded and he did this other heavy labor gratis. And he was required to work until his place was cleaned up before he could leave for the day—what old-timers call the "clean-up" system. Of course, he had an option. He could be fired.

The Harlan County miner was paid less than his organized brothers and worked more hours for his pittance. The only pay raise given by the Harlan County coal operators was fifty cents a day in 1937 and was granted because it was thought that this huge wage boost would take the steam out of the UMWA's organizing drive.

What little money paid to the men at the Harlan Wallins mines was quickly taken away from them, many times without the man having seen or touched it. In those days, Harlan County miners were paid semimonthly at an average wage of $75 a month. It was customary for the employees, who were naturally always hard-pressed for money, to draw advances on their pay. And the kindly Harlin Wallins Coal Corporation permitted this. But there was a catch. The company deducted 15 percent from all advances in cash or company scrip. The latter did not have anywhere near the value of cash because the company did not redeem the scrip at its "face value" but at an additional discount of 15 percent.

The miners had little opportunity to make their purchases except at the company store of the Harlan Wallins Coal Corporation, which was operated by the Verda Supply Company, a separate company created by Pearl Bassham. The men lived in a town built on company property. Independent merchants were not permitted to open shops in the camp which would compete with the company store. The miners even faced the threat of being discharged if they failed to patronize the company store and went outside the camp to do their marketing. This placed the company store in a position to exact its own prices from the miners. The miners testified that they were forced to pay exorbitant prices.

The truth of these charges is shown by the swollen profits made by the Verda Supply Company in spite of the fact that it was obliged to accept a ten percent discount on company scrip (five percent less than other merchants who accepted company scrip). Pearl Bassham permitted three other persons to share the

Verda Supply Company gravy with him at an investment of $1500 each. For the first year of its operations (1935) the Verda Supply Company paid dividends of $2400 to each of the four persons, a 170 percent return on their investment in one year, a profit which Bassham described as "pretty good."

Even the medical services which the company arranged for its employees, at their own expense, was turned to a source of profit for the company. The miners were forced to agree to a monthly check-off from their wages for medical services, two dollars a month for single persons, and $2.50 for married persons. The company employed two doctors at a monthly retainer to provide its employees with what it called necessary medical treatment, but did not pay them all the money it collected from the miners for medical service. Mr. Bassham himself admitted: "We pay the doctors $1250 per month. We collect from $1800 to $2400. The remainder goes to the company."

Underpaying the doctors increased the company's profits but the quality of medical treatment available to the miners suffered correspondingly. Furthermore, the doctors had to pay for drugs and supplies out of their curtailed remuneration. They had an incentive, therefore, to run their offices as economically as possible.

One of the miners employed by the Harlan Wallins Coal Corporation told the La Follette Committee that due to an accident in the mine, his jaw bone was shattered. He went to the company doctor, who merely gave him some pills. He later went to the company hospital for treatment, but proper care was not provided. After infection had set in because of improper treatment, he was compelled to go to a private physician at his own expense to effect a cure. Here, again, the miner had an option. He could pay for proper medical care or he could allow himself to die because of the abuses inherent in the company doctor system, or he could quit and allow his family to starve.

Another ingenious method of exploiting his employees, devised by Bassham, was a semi-monthly second-hand car lottery, which should be called a rattletrap raffle. Every two weeks the foreman in the Harlan Wallins mines "were given chances" which they carried through the mines on company time and "sold" to the employees. One of the foremen testified that the men were compelled to buy chances on pain of dismissal and that he never failed to dispose of all tickets he was forced to sell. The lottery tickets were prepared by the company, and the money for them was collected from the miners by means of a check-off on their wages. Company officials handled the drawing of the lots on a wheel belonging to the company. As much as $800 was collected in this way from the employees for each car that was raffled off. The car was not exhibited to the employees before the raffle and they complained that they were forced to take dilapidated cars, worth practically nothing. Bassham readily admitted that "all the men together are paying more than the car is worth."

The company compelled its employees to kick in on this rattletrap raffle for more than ten years. During that period, Bassham admitted that he had disposed of "eight or ten" of his own private used cars in this way. I am sure that the number he foisted on his employees was nearer to one hundred than ten. He had a Ford agency in Harlan and had plenty of used cars to raffle off. Several of the company's supervisory officials had also taken advantage of this method of disposing of their own cars at a profit. W. W. Lewis, president of the Bank of Harlan, secretary-treasurer of the Cornett-Lewis Coal Company and treasurer of Harlan County, was permitted, as a special favor, to dispose of his used cars at the expense of the employees at the Harlan Wallins mines. A similar courtesy was extended to Daniel Boone Smith, commonwealth attorney for Harlan County and Bell County. From time to time, the company too raffled off its own used cars. The raffle transactions were so profitable that Mr. Bassham estimated that the company approximated an $1800 or $1900 profit on them in 1936 alone.

Bassham explained that the raffling of used cars was a regular part of the company operations. By this he meant that it was another little racket the company had going for it. Bassham conceded that he "might" be taking advantage of his employees in forcing them to participate in the car raffle. He said that the raffle was very profitable to the company and that the cars were "very easily sold." He admitted to the La Follette Committee that his ability to exploit the miners through the raffle was based upon the fact that they depended on him for their employment. A member of the Committee, Sen. Elbert Thomas of Utah, asked him: "Why don't you quit the mining business and go into this raffling business?" Bassham replied: "I would not be able to sell the chances, sir, if I did not have the mines."

Conditions in Harlan County varied in the different mining camps—from bad to miserable. Certain operators denied their employees were exploited as harshly as the employees of the Harlan Wallins Coal Corporation. However, in 1935, the secretary of the Harlan County Coal Operators' Association went to the State capital at Frankfort to lobby on behalf of the coal operators of Harlan County against legislation which was solely intended to correct abuses on wages paid employees, but they were also in a position to capture markets from operators in other districts who abided by the union standard of hours, wages, and working conditions.

Of all the operators and companies in Harlan County in 1937, there were only four whom I regarded as decent human beings. These men were victims of a Frankenstein monster, a system, over which they had no control and which, I believe, they hated and feared. The hillbilly syndicate that operated this vicious system could and would liquidate anybody who dealt with the union. This was proved by the attempt to dynamite the house of the superintendent of the Black Mountain Coal Company. The decent men to whom I refer are Armstrong Matthews at Closplint, A. J. Asbury at Black Mountain, R. W. Creech, owner of the Creech Coal Company at Twila, and Elmer Hall at Three Point.

6

The La Follette Committee and Harlan County Justice in 1937

> *Among the deputies Sheriff Middleton appointed from January 1, 1934, to March 1, 1937...4 had been sentenced for murder, 14 had been sentenced for manslaughter, 3 had been sentenced for malicious shooting with intent to kill.*

There were only five incorporated towns in Harlan County—Harlan, the county seat, Cumberland, Wallins Creek, Loyall, and Evarts. The largest of these did not have a population exceeding five thousand. There were about thirty company towns, including the following: Verda and Molus, the company towns owned by the Harlan Wallins Coal Corporation; Louellen, the company town of the Cornett-Lewis Coal Company; and Closplint, the company town owned by the Clover Splint Coal Company. At the eastern end of the county were the company towns of Benham and Lynch, which were occupied by miners who worked at the captive mines of the Wisconsin Steel Company and the United States Coal & Coke Company, the latter a subsidiary of United States Steel Corporation. Over forty-five thousand citizens of Harlan County lived in company towns.

In an incorporated town, the local government was in theory controlled by officials duly elected by the residents. In a company town, local government was administered by the employer as a part of his business. Social life and community activities, normally regarded by Americans as a matter of individual choice, were permitted in company towns only at the whim of the employer. The right to have guests, to come and go without asking leave—even the use of Federal mails—were all concessions which were granted or denied in company towns according to policies adopted by the company management. Typical was Verda, the company town of the Harlan Wallins Coal Corporation, directed by Pearl Bassham, who maintained close control over all community activities. The road which led from the public highway to Verda was owned by the company and had on it a sign which read "Private Property—Keep Out." Even the post office at Verda was located in a building owned by the company and on company property. Bassham admitted to the La Follette Committee that it would be possible not only to prevent any person from entering the company town, but also from entering the company building where the United States Post Office was located.

Across the highway from the private town of Verda, a large tree towered over the road. Fifty feet high in its branches was a tree-house. This was no children's playground, however. It was a pillbox where the Harlan Wallins gun thugs stationed themselves, like guards on a penitentiary wall, to watch the camp. From their vantage point, they could see anyone who entered or left the town. Stranger, beware!

The road leading to the company town of Louellen was barred by a locked gate. The key was available only at the company office. In explaining this barrier, "Uncle Bob" Lawson, general manager of the Cornett-Lewis Coal Company, which owned Louellen, told the Committee: "Now, if anybody comes in there and wants to go inside, they just ask—not a regular person that lives there—but they come over to the office and get the key and go where they want to and come back."

There was even a private jail in Louellen. It was in a section of the theatre building and, according to a former employe of the company, was used to "lock up United Mine Workers" and "men who became intoxicated."

I personally examined this jail which was not used by the company after May 1, 1937. It was in a large basement room with two small barred windows. There were no toilet facilities because the town of Louellen had no sewer system. Miners were confined in this hell-hole for two or three days at a time with little or nothing to eat and had to use the corner of the room as a privy. A miner caught associating with a union organizer would be thrown in this so-called jail, usually under a false charge of intoxication. He served whatever time the mine manager thought sufficient. The company-paid deputy sheriff would take him before a company-elected Justice of the Peace. The helpless man would then be fined and the money to pay it was arbitrarily taken out of his pay.

In 1937 in Harlan County an employee with a grievance against his employer did not have any impartial authority within his community to hear his case. His only recourse was to appeal to county officials. The character of the few elected county officials was consequently of vital importance to the miners.

Five officials in Harlan County were primarily charged with enforcement of the law: the High Sheriff, the County Attorney, the County Judge, the Commonwealth Attorney, and the Circuit Court Judge. The Circuit Court of the Twenty-sixth Judicial District of the Commonwealth of Kentucky had jurisdiction over major cases, both criminal and civil, arising in Harlan and Bell Counties. The Court was attended by the Commonwealth Attorney, who directed the conduct of all criminal cases within the district. The Court Judge had a lesser jurisdiction than the Circuit Court Judge, attending only to local matters affecting the county government, or minor civil suits, or petty offenses. The position was open to non-attorneys. For instance, the incumbent from

1934 to 1938, Morris Sayler, was a merchant. He had absolutely no legal training. The County Attorney was ordinarily assigned to the duty of preparing cases for presentation to the grand jury under the direction of the Commonwealth Attorney.

The chief executive official of Harlan County was the High Sheriff. His duties were described to the Committee by Sheriff Theodore R. Middleton, who took office on January 1, 1934. According to Middleton, duties of the Sheriff of Harlan County included enforcement of law and order, protection of life and property, and to wait on the courts and serve the proccesses of the courts.

The Sheriff also collected state and county taxes, and was required to file bonds covering faithful performance of his duties and the funds which came into his possession through the collection of taxes. Prior to the adoption of the deputy-sheriff law on May 31, 1938, the Sheriff was authorized at his discretion to appoint deputies in such numbers and with such qualifications as he thought best, subject only to confirmation of the County Judge. For his services, the Sheriff was compensated through fees and commissions which he received in performing the functions of his office; a limit of five thousand dollars per year, plus expenses, was fixed by the State Constitution as the maximum amount which the Sheriff was permitted to retain, and it was his duty to turn back to the state all fees and commissions in excess of that amount.

From 1930 to 1934, the High Sheriff of Harlan County was John Henry Blair. Blair conducted himself in office in such a way as to convince the miners that he was acting in collusion with or employed by the coal operators. During his term, Harlan County was in the grip of deep depression, and thousands of miners were unemployed. Those who had jobs received a series of severe pay cuts. Privation and unemployment among the miners had inevitably created a tense atmosphere. The Committee found that Sheriff Blair and his deputies "preserved order" through extra-legal and autocratic means.

Sheriff Theodore R. Middleton, who succeeded John Henry Blair on January 1, 1934, conducted his campaign for election on a platform which promised to put an end to collusion between county officials and coal operators, and to extend equal protection of the law to miners as well as to their employers. In his campaign, he rallied behind him all the citizens of Harlan County who were opposed to lawless acts perpetrated by law enforcement officers while John Henry Blair was sheriff. The Rev. Carl E. Vogel, pastor of the Cornett Memorial Methodist Church in the City of Harlan from September 1930 to September 1935, stated the issues of the campaign of 1933 as follows: "The issues were very clean cut. The issue was the cleaning up of the situation in Harlan County relative to the collusion between the Harlan County Coal Operators' Association and the officials." He further stated that Sheriff Middleton, in his campaign had stressed that issue above all others.

The La Follette Committee discovered that the background of Sheriff Theodore R. Middleton before he took office was not one calculated to inspire confidence. In 1920, after Army service from 1913 to 1919, and attainment of the temporary rank of Second Lieutenant of the Infantry, he applied for appointment as an officer in the Regular Army. His application was rejected by the examining board on the grounds that he had appeared as a witness in a trial of a soldier in France and as the report stated: "... contradictory statements made in two letters written by applicant and his testimony at trial of soldier, thoroughly discredit applicant's reliability as a witness. Lacks veracity. Recommend he not be commissioned in the Regular Army. Very poor material."

After he left the Army, Middleton operated a poolroom in Harlan County. In 1926 he served a five-month sentence in a Federal penitentiary after a conviction for selling liquor (moonshine) in violation of the National Prohibition Act. After he left prison, he operated a restaurant in the City of Harlan until he was appointed to the police force of the city by his uncle who was then chief of police. His first-hand knowledge of the criminal mind was undoubtedly his main qualification for his new job. He succeeded his uncle in this position which he held until his election to the office of High Sheriff in 1934.

Middleton waged a good campaign for election. As a politician, he was a pro. He solicited the support of the miners in Harlan County who were members of the United Mine Workers of America. International Representative Lawrence "Peggy" Dwyer told the La Follette Committee that Middleton had made the following pledge to the miners: "He swore to his God Almighty, in my presence and in the presence of others, if we would endorse and support him and he would be elected, he would give us, the miners, the same protection as the other citizens of Harlan County."

Middleton further promised that if he were elected Sheriff, he would not renew the appointments as deputy sheriffs of what he called "the gunmen" who had served under Sheriff John Henry Blair. Middleton was opposed by W. J. R. "Willie Bob" Howard, former County Judge, who was publicly supported by the coal operators. The election was bitterly contested, and in an effort to prevent stuffing of the ballot boxes, Middleton and some of his supporters engaged in a series of gun battles with members of the opposing faction which resulted in the death of at least one man and the wounding of several others. These battles were stopped only by the calling out of the National Guard. The election ended with a victory for Middleton and the so-called reform ticket.

As soon as he took office, Sheriff Middleton ignored the pledges he had made. After his election, he was obliged to file bonds for one hundred and sixty thousand dollars covering the performance of his official duties. Middleton turned to the coal operators who had signed the bonds for Sheriff John Henry Blair to obtain them as his own personal sureties.

Middleton's testimony to the Committee with respect to the underwriting of his administration by the coal operators is illuminating:

> Senator LaFollette: Now, Mr. Middleton, when you compare the sureties of your bond with these on Sheriff Blair's bond, you will find that six of the large coal operators of Harlan County who signed sheriff Blair's bond also signed this, and three of these men were members of the executive committee of the Harlan County Coal Operators' Association. How

could you make good on your campaign promises if you immediately put yourself under obligations to the same operators who were responsible for Sheriff Blair's administration?

Mr. Middleton: Well, I don't know. I guess there have been a lot of campaign promises that have not been fulfilled.

Sheriff Middleton was a man of small means when he took office. According to his own estimate, his possessions on January 1, 1934, did not exceed ten thousand dollars in total value, and his annual income was less than three thousand dollars. Between January 1, 1934, and April 12, 1937, when he appeared as a witness before the LaFollette Committee, Sheriff Middleton's personal fortunes took a sharp turn for the better. In the three-year period, his net worth had increased to at least $102,728. This increase in his assets was not due to his salary as sheriff, which was limited by the Kentucky Constitution to a maximum of $5,000 a year. His average annual income from other sources amounted to $6,500 a year. When pressed by the Committee for an explanation of his sudden acquisition of wealth, Sheriff Middleton merely replied, "I am just as puzzled about it as the Senator is." He then took refuge in claiming his constitutional privilege against self-incrimination, what has now become widely known as "taking the Fifth."

> Senator, I believe at this point I will claim my constitutional right and respectfully decline to testify any further on my financial transactions, for fear they may involve me in a law suit with the Federal Government on my income tax. I am afraid my answers here to your questions might tend to incriminate me.

One of the factors which contributed to Mr. Middleton's sudden affluence was his use of State funds in private business transactions. The Sheriff maintained separate bank accounts in the Harlan National Bank for his personal account, the State tax account, the delinquent tax account, and the general account for the income and expenses of the sheriff's office. Although the sheriff was supposed to maintain these special accounts separately, he testified that he intermingled the State funds with his personal funds. To facilitate this practice, he prepared a rubber stamp which carried four endorsements, all of which were placed on the back of checks which came to the sheriff's office, authorizing the deposit of the checks in any of the four accounts maintained by the Sheriff in the bank. The Sheriff admitted to the Committee that the funds were interchangeable.

A cursory examination of the sheriffs bank account disclosed that he used at least $10,700 of tax money in connection with speculations on the stock market which were conducted through the firm of Westheimer & Co., Cincinnati, Ohio. The Sheriff did not attempt to deny that this was true.

While the Sheriff was happily counting his money, the miners who had supported him in his election continued on short rations. The principal source of complaint against the administration of Sheriff Middleton lay in the caliber of the men whom he appointed

SHERIFF THEODORE MIDDLETON *attempting to explain how his net worth grew from $10,000 to over $100,000 in three years while earning a $5000 salary.*

to serve as deputy sheriffs. The Sheriff was authorized to deputize mine guards who were appointed by the coal companies to act as peace officers within company towns. These deputies were armed, were authorized to make arrests and to exercise the police authority of the State generally throughout the county. Except for the Sheriff himself, located in Harlan town, the county seat, far removed from many of the mining camps, the citizens of Harlan County had no police protection except that afforded by the deputy sheriffs who were paid by their employers, the coal operators. Although wielding Public authority, the deputy sheriffs reflected the interests of their employers and not the public interest. They were company thugs—no more, no less. Therefore, it was of utmost importance to the miners in Harlan County that the High Sheriff exercise restraint and judgment in granting deputy sheriff commissions to guards employed by coal companies. The record of Theodore Middleton showed a reckless abuse of this power.

The Sheriff himself needed only three deputies to operate his office. These were a chief clerk who kept the books of his office, a chief deputy who attended to the service of papers and to the removal of prisoners from the County Court to the jail or the State penitentiary, and a tax collector who supervised the collection of taxes. According to the testimony of his chief deputy, other deputy sheriffs "hung around" the office of the Sheriff and occasionally performed special services, but they were not regarded as regular employees of the Sheriff. For his own purposes, however, it appears that the Sheriff charged the County with the salaries of some deputies he had appointed but were not regularly engaged in public duties. The State law permitted the Sheriff to deduct expenses of his office, in addition to $5,000 for his own remuneration, from the fees and commissions which he collected in behalf of the State. Each year the Sheriff filed with the Harlan Fiscal Court a statement showing the expenses of his office including payments to some deputies whom he listed as having been paid from public funds. The amounts so listed were deductible as expenses from the public funds in his control. The lists filed by Sheriff Middleton showed

18 deputies on his pay roll in 1934, 8 in 1935, and 9 in 1936. Testimony to the Committee showed that these lists were grossly in error, if not entirely fictitious. How the deputy sheriffs were paid is not clear. The Sheriff disclaimed any responsibility in the matter.

A limited survey conducted by the committee disclosed that 181 of the 369 deputies appointed by the Sheriff between January 1, 1934 and March 1, 1937, had been employed as police officers by certain coal companies, and these records were corroborated by the Sheriff. In the case of two deputies, who were guarding the property of several coal companies in February, 1937, the Sheriff paid their salaries and was reimbursed by the coal companies on a pro rata basis. At least one deputy, Ben Unthank, was on the pay roll of the Harlan County Coal Operators' Association. The data made available to the committee was too fragmentary to permit any disclosure as to the actual number of the deputies who were on the pay rolls of the coal companies. With reference to the caliber of the men who were deputized by Sheriff Middleton, the record leaves no room for doubt. Men convicted or indicted for homicide and other crimes were commissioned, armed with guns, and sent out in the county "to preserve the peace." Sheriff Middleton testified that no effort was made to set any standards which applicants for the position of deputy sheriff were required to meet. Commenting on the character of his deputies, he said, "I think it is fairly good, some of them. Some of them may not be so good."

What became of the "salaries" which were paid out is illustrated by the sad experience of Henry M. Lewis, chief deputy sheriff under Sheriff Middleton. According to Mr. Lewis, he and his two colleagues were paid at the rate of $110 each month in 1934. In 1935, all three appeared as being paid at the rate of $200 per month. The same rate continued for 1936, except that Mr. Lewis' name did not appear on the list submitted to the court by the Sheriff. The Sheriff explained that this omission was an "oversight," which had passed unnoticed because he did not keep "a very elaborate system of bookkeeping." Mr. Lewis, however, did not keep the $200, but was required to "kick-back" $90 of it to the sheriff, leaving only $110 as his salary. Later he was "raised" to $125 per month.

> Mr. Lewis: He said he needed some little money so as to make the check $200 and I gave him back $90 and after awhile I gave him back $75.
>
> Senator Thomas: How did you come to an agreement as to the difference between $90 and $75?
>
> Mr. Lewis. He gave me a raise of $15; he told me he would raise me $15 a month.
>
> Senator Thomas: And he would take it out of the kick-back?
>
> Mr. Lewis: Yes.

Mr. Lewis testified further that it was his understanding that the other two salaried employees also turned in their "kick-backs" to Sheriff Middleton. It is possible that the "salaries" of the other deputies, who performed no regular services, followed the same course to Sheriff Middleton's pocket. The Sheriff refused to testify on this subject because he said it would "involve me in a law suit with the Federal Government on my income tax."

In addition to the three deputies who were regularly employed in the sheriff's office and who were paid out of county funds, the Committee found that Sheriff Middleton freely granted other deputy sheriff commissions.

Between January 1, 1934 and March 1, 1937, the Committee found 369 deputy sheriffs received commissions from Sheriff Middleton. This unusual figure was accepted by the Sheriff, who testified that "I imagine that is something near the number." It was not possible to establish the exact number of deputies because of the haphazard method with which the Sheriff kept his records. Some of the deputies appointed by the Sheriff were not even entered on the books of the county court as having been approved by the County Judge. Sheriff Middleton testified that he did not "make any distinction" with respect to their powers and duties between such deputies and those who had been duly confirmed.

At the time the Sheriff testified before the Committee on April 15, 1937, according to the records examined by the Committee, there were 163 deputies holding active commissions. This figure appeared to surprise the Sheriff, who said: "I have relieved a bunch of deputy sheriffs and I don't think I ought to have over a hundred." He admitted, however, "I am not positive of the exact number I have got."

A number of the Sheriff's own relatives were commissioned as deputy sheriffs. Of these, several were of such notoriously violent character that the circuit court judge on several occasions publicly castigated them. Slemp Middleton, brother of the Sheriff, served as a deputy sheriff in 1934 and in 1936. He was indicted six times by the grand jury on different charges. On September 17, 1934, in ordering one of the cases removed to a different county for trial, the Circuit Court Judge declared:

> The Defendant, Slemp Middleton, has been in a great deal of trouble in Harlan County, and stands indicted in the Harlan Circuit Court in several different cases, and because of his violence and lawless habits is now in the Harlan County jail on default in filing a peace bond. He is regarded as one of the most dangerous men in Harlan County, and the Court feels, in view of the great amount of criminal conduct that he has been connected with, that the motion of the Commonwealth's Attorney ought to be, and the same is hereby sustained, and this case is removed to the Boyle Co. Circuit Court, and assigned for trial in said Court.

HENRY M. LEWIS *explaining to the La Follette Committee how the "kick-back" system worked in Harlan County between the coal operators, the Sheriff's office, and deputies.*

The Sheriff also appointed as deputy sheriffs other members of his family who had been involved in criminal conduct, including, among others, his cousins John Merle, Charles and Milt Middleton. So violent were the members of the Middleton family that on September 17, 1934, the circuit court judge, in ordering the removal of the trial of John Middleton on an indictment for willful murder, gave the following grounds for his ruling:

> Because it is personally known to the Judge of this Judicial District that for several years last past, there has been more crime in Harlan County than any county in the State of Kentucky, that there has been almost a total disregard of the law, and of the life and liberty of the people, and there now exist more than 800 Commonwealth cases on the dockets of the Harlan Circuit Court, many of the charges being against the Middleton family, which is one of the largest families in Harlan County, and a great deal of intimidation of witnesses, and even killing of witnesses have taken place in this county, local jurymen are afraid to do their duty.

The criminal conduct on the part of the deputies appointed by Sheriff Middleton was not committed merely by those who were members of his own family. The grand jury of Harlan County on May 5, 1934, in its final report, urged that the Sheriff take steps to remove from office such deputy sheriffs as were charged with violating the laws which they were supposed to enforce. The report stated, in part:

> We recommend to this court and to the Sheriff of Harlan County, Mr. T. R. Middleton, that the following persons be discharged from their positions as Deputy Sheriffs of Harlan County: Henry C. Stepp, Milt Middleton, Charlie Middleton, Logan Middleton, Merle Middleton, Bill Lewis, Tom Trent, and Palmer Cox.
>
> Your Grand Jury reports that each of these men are under one or more indictments for felonies, and in the opinion of the Grand Jury are no longer suitable to serve as officers charged with the enforcement of the very laws they stand indicted for violating.

It is apparent that in practically every homicide which has occurred in Harlan County since the first of the year, officers figure prominently. A good officer should have the respect and support of all the citizens, but when he violates the law, he should be given no more consideration than any other individual. We beg to state that until such time as these men have been cleared of the charges against them, they should not be allowed to serve as officers.

Sheriff Middleton testified that he had no recollection of the orders or the circuit court, nor did he recall that recommendations of the grand jury were officially brought to his attention. It is certain, at least, that he took no action to remedy the situation which had justifiably aroused the indignation of the citizens of Harlan County. Among the deputies whom Sheriff Middleton appointed from January 1, 1934, to March 1, 1937, 37 had served sentences in the State reformatory at Frankfort for one or more violations of State law; 4 had been sentenced for murder; 14 had been sentenced for manslaughter; 3 had been sentenced for malicious shooting with intent to kill, and the others had served sentences for robbery, burglary, and grand larceny. Three deputies had been convicted for felonies and served time in the Federal penitentiary for violations of Federal law. In addition to these convictions, 64 deputies had been indicted one or more times by the grand jury of Harlan County mostly for crimes of violence. The Sheriff, after hearing the list of convictions and crimes charged against the deputies whom he had appointed to serve as peace officers, made no comment on the character of his appointments.

The oldest and largest families in Harlan County were the Howards and Middletons. In 1934 Theodore Middleton appointed as deputies 18 Howards, 18 Middletons, 9 Saylors, 8 Balls, 6 Joneses, 5 Turners, 5 Sargents, or 69 deputies from seven families.

The coal companies shared the responsibility with the Sheriff for employing men with criminal records to act as guardians of their property. Tom Trent, indicted by the Harlan grand Jury in 1934 for mayhem, malicious shooting and wounding, operating an automobile while drunk, and for being drunk in office, was employed as a peace officer in the company town of Benham by the Wisconsin Steel Company, a subsidiary of the International Harvester Company. Lee Fleenor was employed as a deputy from August 26, 1933 to April 1, 1934, by the Clover Splint Coal Company. Newell G. Alford, secretary-treasurer and general manager, testified that Fleenor "left the employ of the company very suddenly when he was placed under arrest following a charge of murder in the courthouse." It seemed that Fleenor had settled a personal grudge against Bige Howard, another professional "peace officer," by shooting him down like a dog on the steps of the County Courthouse. Fleenor was sentenced to fifteen years in the State penitentiary on November 30, 1934, for this offense. Prior to his employment by the Clover Splint Coal Company, he had been indicted for murder in two cases and for malicious shooting in a third case in 1932. Mr. Alford said that the company had no knowledge of these indictments by the Harlan County grand jury, although he said it made a practice of investigating the records of its deputy sheriffs.

Pearl Bassham testified that the Harlan Wallins Coal Corporation made little effort to investigate the records of the deputies whom it employed. His company employed two deputies at its Verda mine from 1933 through the first half of 1936. These men were both Middletons, Merle and Charles, and both had long criminal records. In 1936, two more deputy sheriffs were added, Wash Irwin and Frank White. Wash Irwin also had a long criminal record. At another mine owned by the corporation in Harlan County, two other deputies were employed, Robert Eldridge and Jess Johnson, both of whom had criminal records. Mr. Bassham testified that the selection of the deputies whom he employed was the responsibility of the Sheriff. He said, "I did not have any purpose because they had had a criminal record in hiring them. Part of them were recommended to me by some sheriff or they were already deputy sheriffs when I hired them." But it seems to me that the only sure way to secure employment as a deputy sheriff in those days was to be a well-known jailbird.

This record appalled the La Follette group, and in its report, the Committee wrote:

> It is apparent from the above discussion that during the period under investigation by the committee, there were a large number of deputy sheriffs in Harlan County, many of them desperate criminals, selected in a haphazard manner, and appointed with little formality. None of the deputies, except the three working in the office of the sheriff, were regularly employed on a public pay roll. The majority worked as company policemen in the different coal camps. Some worked as company police at large under the direction of Ben Unthank, a deputy on the pay roll of the Harlan County Coal Operators' Association. A large group, without any apparent regular source of income, were available to exercise the public authority delegated to them by the Sheriff on behalf of such persons as were willing to pay them. Such was the state of law enforcement in Harlan County.

7

The Harlan County Coal Operators' Association

> *Miners were slaves. If they demanded the rights to which free men were entitled, they were bullet bait.*

In its investigation into civil liberties violations in Harlan County, Kentucky, the La Follette Committee eventually discovered that the County was under the iron thumb of an organization called the Harlan County Coal Operators' Association. The Committee said that the Association "has been an integral, though unofficial part of the government of Harlan County."

That is an understatement. The Association owned, operated and ruled the County as a private fief, which its members felt had been granted them by the Almighty in perpetuity with coal miners to slave in the pits for them just like the "vassals and stout varlets" who slaved in the mines of Medieval England.

The Association was formed in October 1916. The Committee stated: "One of its principal functions is to provide a means for taking collective action against labor organizations in Harlan County." Although phrased in ambiguous terms, the testimony of George S. Ward, secretary of the Association, revealed that the position of the Association was one of unqualified opposition to any attempt on the part of the miners in the County to organize.

Between 1927 and 1936, inclusive, there were thirty-eight local companies that were members of the Association at one time or another. These companies contributed a total of $438,795.42 to the Association during the ten-year period. In the years 1933 to 1937, twenty-six or twenty-seven companies were active members of the Association. The captive mines of the United States Steel Corporation and of the International Harvester Company, however, were not affiliated.

In 1935 the Harlan County Coal Operators' Association had twenty-six paying members who contributed a total of $41,729.99. These individual contributions were assessed on the basis of the amount of coal produced by each member company. Of these twenty-six members, one, the Black Mountain Corporation, operator of a captive mine, was owned by the Peabody Coal Company and contributed $4,531.37 in 1935 or 10.8 percent of the income of the Harlan County Coal Operators' Association. There were sixteen other member companies of the Association under the control of non-resident interests. The Harlan Wallins Coal Company, which was controlled by certain financial interests in Nashville, Tennessee, contributed $6,552.68 to the Association in 1935, or 15.7 percent of its total income. These two companies, therefore, contributed 26.5 percent of the total income of the Association. The contributions of the seventeen absentee-owned mining companies in Harlan County in 1935 totaled $27,305.78 or 65.4 percent of the total income of the Association for the year. The locally-owned coal mining companies contributed a total of $14,424.21, or 34.6 percent of the total income. Obviously, the principal support of the Harlan County Coal Operators' Association came from absentee-owned mining companies, whose executives cared nothing about "a few" local shootings.

The Association was governed by an executive board composed of the president, vice president and eleven non-office holding members. Between 1933 and 1934, membership on the executive board remained fairly constant. According to the testimony of Pearl Bassham, representatives of the largest contributors to the Association were elected to serve on the board. The membership of the board was as follows from 1933-37:

> President, S. J. Dickerson, Mary Helen Coal Corp.
> Vice President, B. W. Whitfield, Harlan Collieries
> Secretary, George S. Ward, Association Secretary
> Elmer D. Hall, Three Point Coal Co.
> D. B. Cornett, Cornett-Lewis Coal Co.
> R. C. Tway, R. C. Tway Coal Co.
> Pearl Bassham, Harlan Wallins Coal Corp.
> E. J. Asbury, Black Mountain Corp.
> R. W. Creech, Creech Coal Co.
> L. P. Johnson, Crummies Creek Coal Co.
> J. C. Stras, Kentucky Cardinal Coal Corp.
> Elzo Guthrie, Harlan Fuel Co.
> W. A. Ellison, Mahan-Ellison Coal Corp.
> C. B. Burchfield, Black Star Coal Co.

To state it mildly, the Association maintained a close interest in Harlan County politics. Secretary George Ward denied this to the La Follette Committee, but this pointless statement was undoubtedly made merely for the record. As a matter of fact, he had, while acting as secretary of the Association, held the office of High Sheriff, having been appointed to an interim term for one year (1926-7) by the County Judge, Willie Bob Howard, who was his brother-in-law. In April, 1937, Mr. Ward served as chairman of the Republican Committee in Harlan County. The County Democratic chairman was the Association President, S. J. Dickenson. The Association had both parties sewed up tight. In addition to this, Lee Ward, George's brother, served as Chief Clerk, and after Henry M. Lewis resigned, as chief deputy under Sheriff Middleton.

Apart from its direct participation in public affairs in Harlan County, the Association was able to assert the authority which it held by virtue of the combined power and wealth which its membership controlled in the county.

The influence which the Harlan County Coal Operators' Association exerted on the county officials was enhanced by business connections between county officials and members of the Association. For example, Daniel Boone Smith, after he was elected Commonwealth Attorney in 1934, accepted monthly retainers amounting to $175 a month from the Harlan Wallins Coal Corporation, the R. C. Tway Coal Company and the Mary Helen Coal Corporation, all three companies being represented on the executive board of the Harlan County Coal Operators' Association. Prior to his election, Smith had on "one or two occasions" been consulted by or had done work for two of the companies, but he described this business as "in the nature of isolated instances . . . and not of any major significance."

Pearl Bassham not only paid a monthly retainer to Smith, but he also permitted him to raffle his used-up used cars to the miners at the Harlan Wallins mine. Incidentally, this rattletrap raffle racket was in direct violation of a Kentucky law that Smith was supposed to enforce.

Another staunch member of the Association's political team was the Sheriff. Prominent Association members had "gone his bond" when he came into office, among them the busy Pearl Bassham. The latter also cut Sheriff Middleton in on the exorbitant profits realized at the Verda company store. The Sheriff was one of the lucky four who made a twenty-four hundred dollar killing in one year on a fifteen hundred dollar investment.

In March 1936, the Sheriff entered into another lucrative business transaction with his bosom buddy, Bassham. The latter arranged for the purchase of some coal lands in Harlan County for fifty-five thousand dollars, taking a one-third interest himself, with the other two-thirds split evenly between Middleton and County Judge Morris Saylor. He then arranged for the Harlan Wallins Coal Corporation to lease the land, paying royalties of 6-1/2 or 6-3/4 cents per ton for coal extracted therefrom, with a minimum annual royalty of five thousand dollars each to Sheriff Middleton and Judge Saylor. Bassham transferred his own third interest over to the Harlan Wallins Coal Corporation. The Sheriff did not pay cash for his third interest of $18,333.33. He borrowed $8,333.33. from the Bank of Harlan on a note secured by the Harlan Wallins Coal Corporation. Apparently the Sheriff paid the balance of ten thousand dollars out of his own funds. The transaction, therefore, netted the Sheriff at least a return of five thousand dollars in one year on a ten thousand dollar investment, less about $416 interest on his loan.

Another profitable business enterprise owned by the Sheriff was a dairy farm. His main customers were the commissaries of coal companies affiliated with the Harlan County Coal Operators' Association, including the Harlan Wallins Coal Corporation.

The County Judge, Morris Saylor, after he took office, likewise had profitable business opportunities, thanks to Bassham. He, like Sheriff Middleton, "owned" one-fourth of the Verda Supply Company, which paid 170 percent dividends a year. He also was in on the coal royalty deal.

The Harlan County Coal Operators' Association undeniably was the most potent factor in the political life of Harlan County. It had the Sheriff in its pocket —the most powerful elected officer in the County. It also owned the County Judge, whose duty it was to confirm the appointments of deputy sheriffs. In addition the Commonwealth Attorney, Daniel Boone Smith, whose duty it was to prosecute violations of the criminal statutes, including crimes committed by deputy sheriffs, was on the payroll of three coal companies who were represented on the executive board of the Association. The political situation was thus taken care of, rather cheaply, too, when judged by today's standards. There remained only the task of selecting a person to ride herd on the army of desperadoes whom the sheriff had appointed as deputy sheriffs. The man chosen for this assignment was Ben Unthank, "field man" of the Harlan County Coal Operators' Association.

Unthank was a deputy sheriff, on the payroll of the Association. The Association maintained for his use a large war chest upon which he drew to pay for the espionage and terrorist activities which he initiated and directed. The details of the relationship between Unthank and the Association were obscured because the Association successfully blocked the Committee's investigation on this item. Secretary Ward admitted that all the records relating to the activities of the Association with regard to labor matters had been destroyed. He said: "Well, just to be frank, I have anticipated an investigation for the last three or four years, and while I was not ashamed of the record, I just did not feel like keeping a record that could be revealed to anybody that wanted to see it."

Senator La Follette said: "But, Mr. Ward, the only implication that can be drawn from the destruction of the records is, in any situation such as you have described, that the person responsible for their destruction has something that he wants to conceal, otherwise they would not be destroyed."

Mr. Ward merely shrugged and said: "Well, that is the situation, and the implication will just have to be drawn." Mr. Ward disclaimed any knowledge of Ben Unthank's activities, or of the persons whom he hired with the funds of the Association. The Committee obtained from the Association two cancelled checks for February, 1937, one drawn to cash for $1,252.69 and one to George Ward for $1,075.00. Mr. Ward testified that he turned the total amount of $2,327.69 over to Ben Unthank in cash for his "payroll." He said this was his usual practice.

Unthank never testified before the Committee. In spite of diligent efforts made to locate him, he remained in hiding until the inquiry into Harlan County had closed. Ward not only failed to assist the Committee in locating his top gunman, he testified that when Unthank reappeared, he would be paid the salary he had "earned" in the period he was dodging service by the Committee.

Mr. Ward did admit that Ben Unthank was employed by the Association to handle the "organization situation" created by efforts of the United Mine Workers to organize Harlan County coal miners. Mr. Ward also revealed that during periods when the union was conducting a more vigorous campaign than usual, it was the practice of the Association to double its dues. The extra money was needed to hire more gunmen and to "pacify" the restive miners.

The La Follette Committee knew before the hearings that geography made union organization difficult. Isolated by mountains, in 1937 Harlan County was also isolated politically from the rest of the United States. Freedom existed only for the cynical gang that ran the County and bought its politicians. Miners were slaves. If they demanded the rights to which free men were entitled, they were bullet bait.

8

A Different Kind of "Lynch" Law

> *U.S. Steel wielded absolute power over its employees who lived in Lynch and could deprive them and their families of job, home, and purchasing power.*

The La Follette Committee learned a lot about the facts of life in Eastern Kentucky while investigating civil liberties violations in Harlan County. One of the first items of knowledge its members acquired was that Harlan County coal operators not only owned politicians, law officers and coal miners, but that they also owned and governed entire towns. Although they are locally known as coal camps, some of the company towns in Harlan were as large as small cities. Biggest of these was Lynch, which is located at the Eastern end of Harlan County.

In 1937, Lynch—streets, houses, and all public buildings—was owned by U. S. Steel Corporation through its subsidiary, the United States Coal and Coke Co. Its only public thoroughfare was a highway through the town. Today, Lynch is much like any other small town in the United States. But in 1937 its unhappy inhabitants were isolated from the rest of the world by a system of company surveillance that can only be compared with Russian prison-work camps in Siberia.

All employees of the company who lived in Lynch had to live in company owned houses. If a miner was laid off or discharged by the Company, he was immediately required to vacate his house. The only stores in Lynch were those owned by the United Supply Company, another U. S. Steel puppet. There were no independent stores within a radius of five or six miles. The company issued scrip to pay wages in advance of payday. This scrip was redeemed by the company from employees and individuals only, but not independent merchants. U. S. Steel wielded absolute power over its employees who lived in Lynch and could deprive them and their families of job, home and purchasing power.

The population of Lynch was between eleven and twelve thousand. It was an unincorporated town, and officials or employees of the company, as ordered by the general superintendent of the mines, administered all affairs of the town. When questioned concerning the reason for Lynch's remaining unincorporated, Harry M. Moses, the general superintendent, stated that the principal reason was economy. He also stated that the company thought it necessary to have control over all the streets and other sections of the community, aside from the State road, because Lynch was essentially a town for the employees of the United States Coal & Coke Company, and there was no means of making a living in Lynch except to work for this company.

The police department of the United States Coal & Coke Company was organized along military lines, consisting in normal times of a captain, a lieutenant, a sergeant, and a number of patrolmen—usually a total of thirteen men. In order that these men might have the power to make arrests or otherwise take action to maintain the peace, three of the men were commissioned as deputy sheriffs and eight as county patrolmen.

The Lynch police force was originally organized by H. A. Chambers, superintendent of police of the H. C. Frick Coke Company, another of the coal mining subsidiaries of U. S. Steel. The president of H. C. Frick, with headquarters in Pittsburgh, Pennsylvania, was executive head of all the coal-mining subsidiaries of the United States Steel Corporation. Until April 1936, expense accounts of the Lynch police force had to be sent to Mr. Chambers. Reports by J. R. Menefee, captain of police of U. S. Coal & Coke Company, continued to go to Mr. Chambers until November or December 1936. These expense accounts which were sent to Superintendent Chambers, were approved by C. F. Ruch, assistant to the president of the H. C. Frick Coke Co. Six of the men on the Lynch force came from the H. C. Frick Coke Co. in Pennsylvania and had prior industrial police experience, probably with the infamous "coal and iron police." In addition, the United States Coal & Coke Co. sent its supervisory officers to a police school conducted by the H. C. Frick Coke Co. at its Washington Run mine at Star Junction, Pennsylvania.

The U. S. Steel police in Lynch performed most of the duties that are normally assigned to the office of a public police force in any city. It was the duty of company police to apprehend criminals, and to be constantly on the lookout for certain individuals "billed entirely over the country as criminals." They also made regular sanitary inspections of the town, enforced quarantines and otherwise aided in compelling compliance with health regulations.

Lynch, like all towns in Harlan County, was an isolated community and could be entered by few routes because of the mountainous nature of the terrain surrounding it. It was a comparatively simple task for the company police to check on activities of union organizers when they attempted to operate in Lynch. The United Mine Workers of America began an organizing drive soon after the passage of the National Industrial Recovery Act of 1933. In this first try, the United Mine Workers did not send outside organizers into Lynch.

Despite spying and threats by Lynch's company police, a local of the UMWA was organized in July 1933. Because of the fear of its members that they would be discharged if it became known to the company that they were attending union meetings, the local held its first meetings at night in a field outside the city of Cumberland. When the union felt strong enough, it held an open meeting in a hall in Cumberland, which was attended by about five hundred miners. Two members of the Lynch police force and two members of the Benham police force stood outside the hall and noted the men who attended the meeting. Soon thereafter, the company began to summon union members to the office of the mine inspector, a Mr. Henry, where they were told that they would be fired if they joined the union. Preparations were made in July and August of 1933 to bust this drive, when the police department at Lynch bought $657.68 worth of tear gas and tear gas equipment from Federal Laboratories, Inc. In addition, Lynch police bought five hundred 30-30 rifle cartridges. They had forty-one rifles, twenty-one revolvers, and four shotguns already on hand.

Another move by the company to thwart the UMWA was formation of a company union. W. V. Whiteman, then general superintendent of Lynch, called a meeting of all employees. He summarily announced who would run for office and who would conduct the election. Nor were the miners given an opportunity to vote on the question of whether they desired to have a company union. Formation of the company union was followed by a systematic campaign of discriminatory discharges of UMWA members, following which they were immediately evicted from their homes. When the union took two of its cases of discrimination before the Bituminous Coal Labor Board, the company refused to recognize the jurisdiction of the board and ignored the board's order to reinstate the discharged men. The refusal of U. S. Coal & Coke Company to comply with decisions of the Bituminous Coal Labor Board was followed by the discharge of seventy-five more UMWA members, and the local at Lynch had to be dissolved. U. S. Steel in 1933 successfully told the Government to go to hell.

The United Mine Workers inaugurated a second organizational drive in Lynch in December, 1934. A crew of twelve organizers, under the direction of International Representative Dale P. Stapleton, began an intensified drive in January 1935. The police force at Lynch was increased from its normal roster of thirteen to twenty men. The police again purchased from Federal Laboratories $1,000.20 worth of tear gas and related equipment. In April 1935, after the drive of the United Mine Workers was frustrated, the force was gradually reduced.

The first job for the company police was exclusion of union organizers from Lynch. In December 1934, William Milton Hall, organizer for the United Mine Workers, together with two of his co-workers, William Miller and John Stines, drove into Lynch. When Hall visited a miner in his home, he was followed by a company policeman and warned: "Hall, we have told you our last time, this is the fourth time that you have been in this town and you are going to stay out of here." Hall said, "I am very sorry if I am undesirable around here." He said, "You are. We know what you are doing here."

The police also subjected all strangers to strict surveillance; especially those who dared to visit known or suspected union men. Even relatives were not exempted. James Westmoreland, president of the Lynch local, related that police would not allow his sister-in-law, a student at Berea College, to stay at his house while on vacation from school. She was planning to stay a week, but after staying one night, John William Vinson, a deputy, came into the house. He did not give any reason, just told her to be gone by twelve o'clock. She did not believe he meant it, but at twelve o'clock he came back and told her to "get gone" and if she did not, he would put her out. She got in her car and left. Mr. Westmoreland's rent was paid, checked out of his wages, and he was not discharged but was still working for the company.

The fact that union organizers were excluded from the streets on which the men lived made it difficult for them to communicate with the miners. In an effort to overcome this obstacle, the organizers utilized a sound truck from which they made speeches from the State Highway. They were not long permitted to use so simple a device. Despite the presence of an officer, an unidentified man walked up to the sound car, while Dale Stapleton was speaking, and broke the wires that ran from the microphone to the loud speaker.

After this took place, Officer Greenlee of the Lynch company police arrested the driver of Mr. Stapleton's car for not having a chauffeur's license, despite the fact that he had an operator's license and a driver's license.

The police even censored reading matter. Mr. Stapleton told the Committee: "The men who were distributing the literature, some of it handbills, some United Mine Workers Journals, were followed to the homes of the miners, and as this literature was given to the people in their homes, the officers followed them directly to the door and would take the literature from the hands of the party who had received it, and destroy it."

But the organizers wouldn't quit. Unsuccessful in their other efforts to approach the miners, the union used an airplane to drop circulars on Harlan County communities. This was not very successful, for anyone who touched these circulars laid himself open to a sound beating. An affidavit by a miner, Simon Williams, in the Committee's report, stated:

> One day in March, 1937, an airplane flew over Harlan County dropping circulars. A Lynch policeman drove up in a car to where we were standing at Frog Level between Benham and Cumberland and asked if there was anyone who would dare pick up the circulars. A colored boy picked up one and the policeman slapped him down and whipped him and run him out and told him to get away and not fool with him. He mistreated the boy something awful.

The activities of Lynch police were not confined to their own town. Mr. Stapleton testified that a meeting had been arranged in the hotel at Appalachia, Virginia, on February 20, 1935, between a group of UMWA organizers and E. H. Hollingsworth, president of the company union of United States Coal & Coke Company, to talk over the possibility of a transfer into the United Mine Workers of America of the company union membership. Theodore Roosevelt Clarke, UWMA organizer, testified concerning this meeting:

I was present in the hotel at Appalachia at that time. I was in the next room to Chief Menefee of Lynch. The weather was cold. The room that we were in, the room was No. 204, I believe it was. He was in the next room to us, and there was a connecting door between the two rooms, and we heard somebody talking rather loud in there and it was concerning us organizers in Lynch. So the radiator was right by the door and we were trying to get some heat in the radiator, so after I found out he was talking about us, I made it a point to see who was doing the talking through the keyhole in the door, and straight in front of the keyhole was Chief Menefee, and he was talking to some fellow—I could not see who he was. I could just see his legs and feet. The fellow who was talking to Captain Menefee made this remark, leaving out the cuss words, he said 'Why do you not kill him?' and Chief Menefee said 'We cannot afford to do that.' He said, 'If we do, it will start a Senate investigation here, and we cannot stand that.' So we were sandwiched in there. They had a gang of gunmen between all of our rooms. So the go-between man, Hollingsworth, he came up the fire escape. He said 'For God's sake, get out of here; you are framed.' I asked him how he knew and he said, 'I have seen about twenty-five thugs in town, and some of them are in the hotel now.' I saw a few of them but I did not know any of their names at that time. We immediately got out of the hotel because we thought it was the best policy.

When Mr. Menefee was questioned on this matter by the committee, he denied categorically that he had a room at the hotel in Appalachia the night of this meeting. However, he retracted this denial when a copy of his expense account for February 20, 1935, was offered for the record showing that he claimed $1.50 for room rent at Appalachia on this day, and $1.80 for three meals at Appalachia.

In their efforts to combat the United Mine Workers' 1935 organizing drive, the Lynch company police force was helped by Sheriff Middleton and a crew of deputy sheriffs from the western portion of the county. The organizers sought to enter Lynch to conduct a mass meeting on January 6, 1935. They were met by Sheriff Middleton and a group of about 25 deputy sheriffs who prevented them from entering the town. One of the organizers, William Milton Hall, who did get through, managed to give a brief speech before he was seized by the deputies. Mr. Hall identified among the deputy sheriffs present, Ben Unthank, Frank White, and George Lee. A deputy sheriff of Letcher County, Robert Hart, entered Lynch at the time of this union meeting to serve a murder warrant on a person who was said to be at this meeting. As soon as Mr. Hart entered Lynch, Sheriff Middleton's deputies arrested and disarmed him. Several hours later he was released, but only after the deputy sheriffs smashed his gun with a sledgehammer. This assault was probably inspired by the fact that Hart was a member of the United Mine Workers of America.

On February 9, 1935, Sheriff Middleton and his deputies again interfered with the organizing drive in Lynch. The United Mine Workers had rented a building in the incorporated town of Cumberland, which is about a mile and a half from Lynch and Benham, as headquarters for locals in those two towns. On the afternoon of February 9, Sheriff Middleton and a group of ten deputies raided these local union offices and arrested the organizers present. They stayed and continued to arrest organizers as they appeared. In the course of two hours they had arrested a total of 23. These organizers were all searched as they were arrested. They were shown no arrest warrants, and were allowed no bond.

William Milton Hall, one of those arrested, testified: "I was one of those arrested on February 9. I don't know the rest of them. I was not shown a warrant when I was arrested. I asked the Sheriff if we would be allowed to file a bond and he said no, we could not. He did not explain why, just said he would not take a bond, that is all."

The organizers were taken to the jail in Cumberland where they were packed into a cell so tightly—eleven persons in a space two feet by six—that all were compelled to remain standing. Counsel for the Mine Workers characterized the situation as being similar to that of the Black Hole of Calcutta. Later they were all taken to the county jail in Harlan under the escort of a group of deputy sheriffs. They were kept in jail until February 11, 1935. On the afternoon of the following day, all the men were brought before County Judge Saylor and arraigned on charges of "public nuisance." On the motion of County Attorney Elmon Middleton, all of the charges were dismissed.

However, two of the organizers, William Milton Hall and Tom White were served with warrants in the courtroom, charging them with the use of boisterous language and provoking an assault on another. Hall was given a jury trial at which a colored driver for the United States Coal & Coke Company testified that Hall had sworn at him. On the basis of this testimony, Hall was fined ten dollars and costs. The case against Tom White was dropped on condition that he would stay out of the county. The United Mine Workers protested vigorously to Governor Ruby Lafoon against these malicious arrests on trumped-up charges for vagrancy. The Governor issued a special order to the Kentucky National Guard setting up a special commission to investigate the state of unrest that existed in Harlan County. Brigadier General Henry H. Denhardt headed the Commission and it was on the basis of the findings of this Commission that Governor Laffoon issued his charges against Sheriff Middleton.

At that time, Tom White was International Board member from UMWA District 13 in Iowa. I was a District Board member in Iowa. When Tom came back and told the story of his experiences to the boys in Iowa, he did not tell us he was scared. He had us believing that he was enjoying his duty in Bloody Harlan. But when I later talked with the boys who were with him in 1935, I found out that they were all frightened and that Tom was reluctant to leave the jail. He said it was the only safe place in Harlan County.

In the language of a detective, "rough shadowing" means to keep a man under open surveillance in such a manner that not only he knows he is being followed, but anyone he meets becomes aware of it, too. James Westmoreland testified that as soon as he was elected president of the UMW local in Lynch in 1933, he was treated as follows: "After we organized this union and got a substantial number of members, and I was elected president of the local, I was not able to carry on my duties and activities and responsibilities as president of the local. Whenever I would come up out of the mines, a policeman would meet me at the mouth and follow me to the bathhouse and stand over me in the bathhouse. He would not allow me to speak to anybody; followed me to the store or home, or wherever I went, and those policemen would be right with me. This prevented me from speaking to the other members of the union. I knew it would be futile and place those in an embarrassing position, on the part of those that I would speak to; therefore, I never did say anything. The deputies that followed me around were Victor Creech, Captain Russell, John Yelenovsky, Frank Smith and William Vincent. They followed me from the mouth of the mine into the bathhouse and stood there while I was taking a bath, and they followed me when I went to the store or anyplace else. These police just walked up and down in front of my house—two of them—taking a turn about; one in the night and one in the day. My friends could not visit me or they would be placed where they would be liable for a discharge.

Evidence of the existence of a spy system in Lynch, Kentucky was found by the Committee through examination of the expense accounts of Captain Joseph R. Menefee, of the Lynch police force. These expense accounts showed that shortly before the 1935 organizing drive in Lynch, Mr. Menefee had rented post office boxes at Norton, Virginia, headquarters of the UMW organizers carrying on the drive, and at Appalachia, Virginia, just across the line from Harlan County, another base from which the organizers operated. When the Committee asked why he had rented these boxes, Mr. Menefee was unable to explain, but finally admitted

JAMES WESTMORELAND *testifying about his treatment at the hands of the Lynch company police force.*

that his men were doing espionage work, and received their orders by mail.

In view of all these activities of the company police in the company town of Lynch, it is easy to understand the complete failure of the attempts of the United Mine Workers to organize the miners of Lynch, in spite of many years of effort, until the company changed its labor policy.

These conditions lasted as long as the United States Steel Corporation and its subsidiary, The United States Coal and Coke Company, were opposed to the recognition of bona fide unions and attempted to eradicate them from the communities in which they operated. The restrictions on organizational efforts continued at least until March 1937. John Young Brown, Attorney for District 30 of the United Mine Workers, related a conversation with the superintendent and the captain of police on March 6, 1937, as follows:

> I got to Gary, West Virginia, at about five o'clock Saturday afternoon, March 6 of this year, and had a conference with Mr. Henry Moses and Captain Menefee. Mr. Michael Carrell (U. S. Steel labor relations man) had come over to Gary, and he was there when I got there and Mr. John Hanratty, who was in charge of the Pikeville office of the United Mine Workers, went over with me and also a young organizer by the name of Tom Raney from Pikeville, Kentucky, who drove us over there while we had the conference. I told Mr. Moses that my purpose there was to see if we could not get permission for the organizers to walk along the side street, and to ring doorbells and to peacefully talk to members of the organization about coming into the United Mine Workers. He told me that the policy of the company had not changed any. I had previously told him that it was our information that since the signing of the steel contract with the C I O that we would not be met with the same resistance that we had previously met in Lynch, Kentucky. He told me that he had no notice of any change in the policy of the company, and he stated that their policy would be the same as it had always been. I said 'Do you mean by that, that if our organizers are on your company property on any of these side streets, that they will be arrested for trespassing?' He said, 'for trespassing, or such other offenses as they may commit.'

The trouble at Lynch was soon over. With the signing of a contract with the Steel Workers Organizing Committee in 1937, covering the plants of United State Steel Corporation, the mining subsidiaries were subject to pressure from the parent companies to fall in line. The H. C. Frick Coke Company, a subsidiary of the United States Steel Corporation, signed a contract with the United Mine Workers of America in April 1937. The United States Coal & Coke Company in Lynch also signed a contract covering the union's own membership with the United Mine Workers of America in the summer of 1938. Thus one motive behind the suppression of civil liberties no longer existed, and the police department of the United States Coal & Coke Company could confine its activities to the simple and essential object of guarding property and life, against encroachments by lawbreakers. Evidence indicated that the worst aspects of Lynch had been alleviated for the time being, as a result of the recognition of the right of the organization.

9

Blood in Harlan

"Thugging" is hunting organizers and union men the same as you hunt deer.

The La Follette Committee on Civil Liberties had read the newspapers and was aware that Harlan County was no place for a timid soul. But the fighting little Progressive from Wisconsin had fought for this investigation in the Harlan coalfields and would not back down. Much of the testimony sickened him, but he and the Committee members and staff worked diligently until the job was done. Their lengthy report was a nation-wide sensation, and public indignation eventually made the Harlan coal operators realize that mass murders might be going out of style, even in Harlan.

In this chapter I will briefly relate some of the activities of gunmen in Harlan. All of this information can be verified by reading the report of the La Follette Committee. The gun thugs told of in these chapters were, of course, mere hirelings of the rich operators. But do not pity them.

They deserve nothing but contempt, for they were as sorry a group of characters as ever strutted briefly in the public eye.

The stage was set for a blood bath in Harlan when President Roosevelt in 1933 signed the National Industrial Recovery Act, which guaranteed workers the right to organize into unions and bargain collectively. District 19 of the UMWA, which included Harlan County, immediately, started an organizing drive. Lawrence "Peggy" Dwyer was assigned in June 1933 to act as organizer in charge in Harlan County to secure new members. Proceeding cautiously at first, for fear of suffering violence at the hands of deputies employed by the coal operators, "Peggy" and his aides soon picked up steam. At the end of four months, the union was strong enough to compel the coal operators affiliated with the Harlan County Coal Operators' Association to sign an agreement with the UMWA, effective October 2, 1933, and extending to March 31, 1934. The agreement was binding only upon members of the Harlan County Operators Association who employed members of the United Mine Workers of America. At that time, there were approximately two thousand miners in Harlan County who had joined the union. The union met with bitter resistance from the Association. It raised emergency funds for use in "resisting the efforts to organize the county." Ben Unthank, who at that time was a deputy sheriff under John Henry Blair, handled this money for the High Sheriff of Harlan County. Unthank, who was an expert thug, proceeded to carry on a campaign of terror against the organizers. In this he was ably assisted by Deputy Sheriffs Frank White and George Lee.

In the summer of 1933, Unthank approached Larkin Baker, assistant organizer under Dwyer, and bribed him to act as a spy for the Harlan County Coal Operators' Association. Baker reported to Unthank on activities of the union, based on information which he obtained in his work as organizer, and later in his position as labor vice president of the Kentucky State Federation of Miners. He received $75 a month plus expenses from Unthank, the payment being handled through John Surgener, a merchant in Harlan town, whose son was married to Unthank's daughter. At the same time, Unthank also hired Chris Patterson, an unemployed miner who had been crippled in a mine accident to spy for him. Patterson had lost a leg and had his back broken, but had drawn very little workmen's compensation. He had also been an organizer for the Communist-led National Miners Union. A third man employed by Unthank at the same time was Richard C. Tackett, a former Baldwin-Felts professional strike breaker, who had been commissioned as a deputy sheriff under John Henry Blair. These three men, under the leadership of Unthank, assisted in a determined course of action to stop the organization of mine workers. The first step in their conspiracy was to eliminate the chief organizer, "Peggy" Dwyer, by threatening his life.

The initial attack against Mr. Dwyer came three weeks after the beginning of the union drive in June 1933. Mr. Dwyer went into Harlan County for the purpose of visiting the local union at the mining camp at Liggett. Larkin Baker notified George S. Ward, secretary of the Harlan County Coal Operators' Association, of Dwyer's intended trip. On his return from Liggett, Dwyer, accompanied by Jim Bates and Bob Childers of the United Mine Workers, was driving along a winding road four miles from the city of Harlan. While passing beneath a cliff covered by a clump of bushes, a volley of shots hailed from the top of the cliff and sprayed bullets over the car. A local gun thug, the same Marion "Two-Gun" Allen who was bodyguard for Judge D. C. "Baby" Jones, was standing by his car along the highway and gave the signal to Unthank's bushwhackers by firing a shot in the ground.

In describing the ambush to the Committee, Dwyer recalled:

> The first shot struck the glass four inches from my face, throwing the glass all over me, and then shots just ripped into the car, the side of the car, and all around. The young man I had driving the car, Mr. Reed, kind of lost control of the car and it started off the road, and I grabbed the wheel and straightened it, and I patted him on the back and said, 'Gloster, don't get excited' and just as I said that, one of the men in the back seat, Bob Childers, shouted out to me, 'Peggy, I am shot in the back.' I said, 'Oh, no.' In just the next breath Jim Bates, the other man said, 'I am shot in the hip.'

> After about a space of two hundred feet, I guess, I got the car straightened, the wheels straightened, and I looked back, and as I looked back I saw the man coming from that cliff and bushes onto the highway. They had a car parked there. I recognized one of the men positively; that one that I recognized was Ben Unthank, and I would not be positive—but I think the other was Frank White.

This time the organizers escaped with only two casualties. Dwyer was still unharmed. But a month later the attack on him was resumed. His home at that time was located in Pineville, about eighteen miles from Harlan County. He told the Committee that in September 1933 "I was stopping in the Parrott's apartment in Pineville. At about 2:40 in the morning we had a dynamite explosion that tore up the house I was stopping in, broke all of the windows in all of the houses in that community, but I was not injured."

Chris Patterson testified that Larkin Baker and his wife had told him that Baker had set off the dynamite near the house, acting under Unthank's instructions. The dynamite was furnished by Unthank who paid Baker a hundred dollars for doing the job. Baker denied any connection with the dynamiting; however, he testified that after it took place, he "took alarm" at his job and attempted to break away from Unthank. He said:

> After the explosion went off in Pineville, why, I quit the job, and Unthank, he never stopped from time to time until he got me out away from home, and at Pineville over there where he could talk with me again, and I dodged him as much as possible, and then when he did get hold of me and when we did get away from town at the end of the woods where we could talk, I told him that I had quit, and he had my pay day, a couple of my pay days in his pocket, and he insisted on me taking it and continuing on. I tried to get loose and I couldn't; he would not allow it. He told me that he would expose me, lay the dynamiting on to me if he seen fit to. That was the first time. And I could not get away from him.

Unthank was undaunted by failure in his first two attempts to eliminate Dwyer. In November, Larkin Baker was sent to Pineville to make a sketch of the apartment in which Mr. Dwyer was living. Then, on November 24, 1933, Baker, Patterson, Tackett, and Unthank went to Pineville. They "floated around the beer rooms and messed around there until it got about 12 o'clock." And then, under cover of night, they went to Dwyer's house and again dynamited it. "Peggy" Dwyer was thrown out of bed, but his good luck held. He received only minor injuries. Chris Patterson testified that he obtained the dynamite from Unthank and gave it to R. C. Tackett to set off. Tackett claimed that the others had set off the dynamite because he had pretended to be too drunk to do the job. Baker admitted receiving fifty dollars for his part in the dynamiting, and Patterson testified that he had received a hundred dollars from Unthank, fifty dollars of which he turned over to Tackett.

While Unthank and his fellow conspirators were plotting to murder Dwyer in Pineville, the union was encountering similar hazards in Harlan County itself. In the summer of 1933, a preacher, B. H. Moses, who lived in a church at Black Bottom, near the mines of the Cornett-Lewis Coal Company and the Clover Splint Coal Company, had permitted union members to meet in his church. Moses told the Committee what happened to him in retaliation:

> There were four sticks of dynamite placed in the building. My wife and four children were there sleeping. I was away from home at the time and the next day I returned home, and my little daughter went into the church building. You see, there were rooms that I lived in beside the part that we used for a church, and the little girl went in the building and found the dynamite in there, and she came running out and told me there was something in the church house, and I went in there and I found four sticks of dynamite with fifty foot of fuse, burned within about eighteen inches of the cap, and it went out. There had been a mass meeting supposed to be on a vacant lot the day before we found. This dynamite, and at the time of the mass meeting it was raining and they asked me to turn them in the building, and I did so, and that night the dynamite was placed in the building.

He appealed to the Sheriff for protection. Several days later, Allen Bowlin, a deputy sheriff, warned him that his life was in danger from the two companies." Mr. Moses described the atmosphere of terror surrounding the church: "I went in home one morning and a few minutes after I walked into the house, a lady came crying and said that her husband told her to come and see me as quick as I can that they were aiming to kill me. The men that were my friends, men that were laying in the weeds around my house at night to protect me, they told me it was getting so hot, they thought it was best for me to get away for awhile." Mr. Moses left his church and moved into the Black Mountain camp. A few days after he left, the church building was dynamited and completely destroyed.

High Sheriff John Henry Blair and his deputies also took an active part in the continual harassing of miners attending organization meetings. The first union meeting for the miners of Harlan County took place June 1933, at Pineville, in Bell County. The meeting could not be held in Harlan because of fear of the gun thugs. According to the testimony of Mr. Dwyer, deputy sheriffs from Bell County had to be posted on the road to keep Harlan County deputy sheriffs away from Pineville. They stopped "two or three cars on the outside of the city, and the cars had gunmen, deputy sheriffs in them, loaded with rifles, shotguns and pistols." "They didn't enter Pineville," Dwyer said.

RICHARD C. TACKETT *(right) in the custody of U.S. Marshall Robert Bonham at the La Follette Committee hearings, where he testified about his involvement in the bombings of Lawrence "Peggy" Dwyer. Tackett was a deputy sheriff under J. H. Blair.*

In July 1933, Theodore R. Middleton was chief of police of the town of Harlan and was a candidate for the office of High Sheriff. To obtain the miners' support, he promised protection to them if they held their meetings within the corporate limits of Harlan Town. When a meeting of the miners was arranged, he roped off the streets and five thousand people assembled undisturbed under his protection. Middleton also attended another meeting held by the miners at the town of Evarts on October 1, 1933, and stood guard next to the speaker. In spite of his presence however, a volley of high-powered rifle shots fired from a nearby hillside broke up the meeting. The persons who fired the shots were not apprehended.

As previously recounted, these and other acts of violence and terrorism throughout the county aroused the citizens against the administration to the point where they elected Theodore Middleton as Sheriff.

When the new administration took office, it gave promise of living up to its pro-union campaign pledges. One of the first acts of the new High Sheriff was to arrest Ben Unthank, Larkin Baker, Chris Patterson, R. C. Tackett and John Surgener on January 1, 1934. They were charged with conspiring to dynamite "Peggy" Dwyer's home at Pineville in November 1933. The Harlan County Coal Operators' Association came to their defense. An attorney named Harvey Fuson appeared as their counsel. In part payment for his services, Baker gave Fuson two hundred and fifty dollars, which had been given to him by Unthank. Baker, Patterson and Tackett continued to receive their regular stipends from the Harlan County Coal Operators' Association while they were in jail. All five defendants were indicted and Patterson came up for the first trial on March 2, 1934. He was found guilty and sentenced to ten years in the penitentiary. Following the conviction of Patterson, the prosecution failed to press the other cases, and they were filed away.

This brief interlude of reform came to an abrupt end. Rumor drifted to the miners that the Sheriff was intending to reappoint Unthank and the other "road-killers" as deputy sheriffs. Dwyer went to see the Sheriff and discovered to his dismay that the rumor was true. Sheriff Middleton hung his head and told him: "Well, Peggy, I was forced to do it on obligations I entered into during the primary." Unthank, still under indictment, and his cohorts were reappointed by Sheriff Middleton and confirmed by the County Judge, Morris Saylor, who had also swept into office on the "reform" ticket.

The October, 1933 contract of the United Mine Workers with members of the Harlan County Coal Operators' Association expired March 31, 1934, and was extended for one month. When the operators refused further extensions of the contract, members of the United Mine Workers ceased work. In Louellen, company town of the Cornett-Lewis mines, eviction notices were served on strike leaders, and on May 19, 1934, the president of the local, Marshall A. Musick, was arrested by five deputy sheriffs, including Unthank, Frank White and George Lee, and was arraigned on a charge of criminal syndicalism. After being confined for nine and a half hours, he was finally released on a $5,000 bond. On May 21, Mr. Musick was brought to trial. At the trial Judge Saylor informed Mr. Musick that Superintendent Lawson of the Cornett-Lewis Co. was willing to dismiss the case against him as well as all the pending eviction cases if the men went back to work. The necessity for a decision on this offer was obviated, however, by the news from District President Turnblazer that the Harlan County Coal Operators' Association contract with the UMWA had been renewed until March 31, 1935, and the men could go back to work. Mr. Musick was promptly released.

When Marshall Musick was arrested, he was entering the church to preach a funeral sermon of a brother coal miner. He explained to Unthank that the deceased had requested that he preach his funeral sermon. He invited the deputies to attend the funeral with him and said he would be willing to go with them after the services. Unthank said, "To hell with you. Tell it to the Judge." The miner was buried without ceremony.

Although the United Mine Workers of America succeeded in renewing its contract with the Harlan County Coal Operators'

Association, the union made no gains in membership in Harlan County. Coal operators continued to interfere with the right of union organizers to talk to the miners. Pearl Bassham admitted that he did not permit union organizers to enter his company town.

Drastic measures were taken by Mr. Bassham to discourage union activity in his camp. He hired his own group of strong-arm men, who were assigned the task of harassing and beating union organizers and union members. Their activities under Mr. Bassham's bidding were supplementary to the efforts of other deputies under the leadership of Ben Unthank. Bassham recruited his "thugs" on the basis of their reputation for violence. A lengthy criminal record was all the recommendation needed for a job. In June 1933, he brought Bill C. "Thug" Johnson from West Virginia. Johnson had worked as a strike guard for the Baldwin-Felts Detective Agency and had, on two occasions, been indicted for murder. Johnson's reputation as a tough had preceded him to Harlan County. He was made a "cut boss" (section foreman) and was instructed to "fire all union men" at the Harlan Wallins mine. In addition, while in the pay of the company, Johnson gave much time to "thugging" under the direction of Merle Middleton, a deputy sheriff paid by Mr. Bassham and a cousin of Sheriff Theodore R. Middleton. Johnson explained his duties to the La Follette Committee:

> Thugging is hunting organizers and union men the same as you hunt deer, except I never did kill nobody—in Harlan County. When I went to work with Jim Matt Johnson, we were hunting union men. I was told that we would catch them and take them out and bump them off. There was a whole crowd of us. We could call a crowd of from fifteen to twenty-five, pretty quick.

The Jim Matt Johnson referred to was no relation to "Thug" Johnson, but he was also a professional Baldwin-Felts strikebreaker from West Virginia. Both Johnsons were big men, ugly in looks and disposition. They were big enough to beat up most men and mean enough to shoot anyone in the back if the pay was right.

By the summer of 1934, Harlan County miners were again at the mercy of armed gangs of tough hirelings of the coal operators.

Unthank and his assistant goons, Frank White and George Lee, led one band of men chiefly composed of deputy sheriffs. Merle Middleton headed Pearl Bassham's thug gang and he was known as "chief thug." At first the camps where union members lived were not interfered with, but the miners were not permitted to hold public meetings. Organizers were ambushed on the highways as they attempted to drive through the county on union business.

From 1934 to 1937, Bassham's deputies, particularly White, were assigned to duties as "shack rousters." The "shack rouster" invaded the homes of the miners every Monday morning, without a warrant, with a bullwhip. If a man was found in bed, he was presumed to be drunk or hung over, and was whipped out of bed and marched to work. I personally have talked to men who were forced to go to work suffering from pneumonia, appendicitis or rheumatism.

In June 1934, the union called a mass meeting to be held near Verda, Pearl Bassham's company town, to encourage miners to join the union. Union members in other coal towns started toward Verda to attend the meeting. Immediately the gangs went into action. Lee and White, and a band of deputies appeared at Verda, on orders from Sheriff Middleton. The Harlan-Wallins gang led by Merle Middleton, supplemented their forces. "Thug" Johnson said: "We had orders to keep organizers and union men and all automobiles out of Verda and patrol the road and turn them back from each way. This road comes two ways, you understand—coming down and coming up—and I was down the road sometimes and up the road sometimes."

This "Thug" Johnson character may not have had much command of the English language, but he sure had that road figured out. It ran two ways—up and down—and I'm sure that after "Thug" puzzled over that, he had to let his brain rest for a week or two from overstrain.

One group of union men walked down the right-of-way of the railroad leading from the Black Mountain camp toward Verda. B. H. Moses, the preacher, told the Committee that when they reached the Kildav camp near Verda, they were met by deputies: "There was somewhere I suppose in the neighborhood of 75 or 80 men in the crowd of so-called peace officers that were armed with pistols, shot guns and rifles." From the road above the embankment, the deputies poured out of cars brandishing pistols and guns, turned the miners back and herded them to the Draper camp.

One of the deputies, Ted Creech, who was also superintendent of the Creech Coal Company of which his father was president, was carrying a submachine gun. He testified that he could "not recall back that far," but he claimed his memory served him well enough to deny under oath that he ever had a submachine gun or machine gun in his hands in Harlan County. However, Mr. Creech's machine gun attracted the attention of some of the other members of the gang. Deputy Sheriff Hugh Taylor recalled the machine gun very vividly and "Thug" Johnson had the following recollection concerning Mr. Creech's weapons: "He took me to a car—I don't know whether it was his car or not, but a car—and showed me over some guns. One was a machine gun."

Shortly thereafter, in June 1934, the miners attempted to hold another union meeting in Harlan County. W. P. Merrell, former Governor of Kentucky, was invited to address the gathering. Once more the deputy sheriffs, led by George Lee, and the "thug gang" of Merle Middleton prevented the miners from passing along the public highways to reach the meeting. Marshall A. Musick, a minister of the gospel, who had lived in Harlan County for 14 years, and was then employed by the Cornett-Lewis Coal Company at Louellen, was proceeding to the meeting with a group of approximately 50 miners when they encountered a band of 17 deputy sheriffs and "thugs" at a railroad crossing near High Splint. As in the attack at Verda, carloads of deputies drove up to the miners, and unloaded and proceeded with drawn weapons to drive the miners back. The miners scattered and ran up the railroad tracks that were beside the highway; but many were overtaken by the deputies and were severely kicked and beaten. Lee came upon Mr. Musick and jabbed him with his automatic rifle, fracturing a hipbone, which rendered him helpless. Merle Middleton then rushed in and proceeded to kick him, repeatedly, across the entire railroad right-of-way, which were three tracks wide at that point.

"Thug" Johnson testified that Merle Middleton had brought his thug gang with him, first arming them with shotguns and rifles taken from the office of the Harlan-Wallins Coal Corporation. "Thug" said he got the following instructions: "My orders are not to let nobody stop. I was to keep them from going on the road and tear all the signs down that were posted. I pulled some signs down myself."

Johnson said he watched as Merle Middleton was kicking one man, and testified that Middleton cried: "Whoop 'em up, Johnson!" meaning, according to Johnson, "he wanted it done in a bigger hurry." The incident was witnessed by Rev. Carl E. Vogel, at that time minister of the Cornett Memorial Methodist Church, in Harlan town, who described it as follows:

> And while on my way, just as I approached the railroad crossing on the highway at Benito, Kentucky, the road was blocked, with the exception of perhaps enough room for one car to pass on my left; and I pulled up behind the cars that were parked there and observed that there was something of more or less a riot or disturbance taking place on the highway, and I watched for possibly four or five minutes, and when another car of deputy sheriffs passed by and happened to see me, knowing of my presence there, they went up to the head of the line of cars, and upon arriving at the head of the line of cars, they immediately got out and flagged me by, and I drove by in low and observed what was taking place as best I could. The deputy sheriffs were driving back on that public highway a group of miners in their shirtsleeves who were coming down toward Benito. They were driving them back up the valley toward Clover Splint and High Splint and Louellen. The deputy sheriffs were armed with rifles and pistols. The miners were not armed. No physical resistance had been offered by any miner under my observation, but I did see the deputy sheriffs use their weapons at least in one instance. A deputy had a gun and whipped a man, striking him evidently in the face, for as I saw the man's face, it was bleeding. I was told that these men were going to Shields, Kentucky, to what they called a union speaking, and that the deputies were opposing their attendance at that meeting and were not permitting them to go. This happened on a public highway.

In the summer of 1934, William Turnblazer, President of District 19, to assist Dwyer, added three local organizers to the Harlan County staff. James Westmoreland, a former employee of the United States Coal & Coke Company at Lynch, was appointed to assist the locals at the eastern end of the county. Marshall A. Musick was assigned to locals in the center of the county. William Clontz, a former employee of the Creech Coal Company and a resident of Wallins Creek, was directed to assist organization work in the western end of the county. The efforts of these men to assist the local unions made them targets for the attacks of the "thugs" and deputy sheriffs. As soon as he was appointed a paid organizer, Musick was dismissed by the Cornett-Lewis Coal Company, where he was employed as a checkweighman by the miners, and was evicted from his home in the company town of Louellen. He moved his family to a house at Evarts, an incorporated town near the mines of the Black Mountain Corporation. His duties required him to travel around the county, visiting local unions and advising them on their problems. He testified that wherever he went, he was continually followed by deputy sheriffs and ordered out of company towns. At times, to avoid his pursuers, he resorted to disguises.

Musick said: "I have artificial teeth—a false set of teeth—and I carried with me in the car a bank cap (miner's helmet) and an overall jacket, and when I was trapped by a bunch of these deputies, I removed my teeth and blackened my face with some dirt off this bank cap, and put the bank cap on, in order to disfigure myself so that they could not identify me, and a number of times I slipped out of the trap because there was a bunch of deputies on either end of the highway.

"I had several occasions when I was forced to stay away from home at night. I generally stayed until along toward daylight or late in the night, until the road became clear, so that I could get back to my home. I would sometimes stay with the miners."

For attempting to assist miners to exercise their rights of self-organization for collective bargaining, guaranteed to them by a Federal statute, organizers in Harlan County were forced to steal around the public highways like hunted animals, which they were. This analogy was one which Sheriff Theodore R. Middleton himself found apt. Addressing a group of deputies and thugs at his office in Harlan, in the fall of 1934, Sheriff Middleton jocosely remarked that "it was open season on organizers." The suggestions were taken seriously. Ben Unthank contacted Larkin Baker, who was still on his payroll in the fall of 1934, and ordered him to hire a man to assassinate Lawrence Dwyer, chief organizer for the union. He gave Baker a Winchester shotgun and promised him seven or eight hundred dollars if he was able to find a man to commit the murder. Baker found a man, but he insisted on being paid in advance, so after prolonged haggling, the deal fell through.

In the fall of 1934, Unthank also offered $100 to Lawrence Howard, a grocery clerk at Wallins Creek, if he would shoot into the house of organizer William Clontz, a near neighbor of Howard's. Howard refused. The following day, George Lee, who was driving through Wallins Creek, picked him up and Lee repeated to him Unthank's proposal and offered to furnish a gun if he would accept. Howard refused again. Lee then said, "Well, we will have to do it ourselves." Howard also said that he heard a volley of shots fired into Clontz's house the following night. He went out on the porch and a car came down the road from the direction of Clontz's house and ran over and killed his dog. The occupants of the car got out and threw the dog out of the road over into the neighbor's yard. He identified the men as Unthank, Lee and Frank White.

The shots heard by Mr. Howard riddled the Clontz home. Clontz was out of town at the time, but his wife and son were sleeping in the house. On his return, he found the following damage done:

> There were ten shots fired through the house, going through the front, through the middle walls—the plastered walls—into the third wall and into the dining room; four bullets going into my boy's bedroom, one just above his body, one under his body, and one under his head, and one under his pillow, missing his head something like an inch or an inch and a half, and splitting the mattress open; and I took a .45 bullet out of the mattress under the boy's head.

Clontz appealed in vain to Sheriff Middleton for protection. His conversation with the sheriff was reported to the La Follette Committee: "I then pleaded with him to come down and help me investigate, and he refused me. I said, 'you being the High Sheriff of Harlan County and under obligation, you are supposed to give protection to the citizens of Harlan County. I am a citizen and a taxpayer, and I have never been in jail, and I think it is your duty to come down and help me investigate it.' He said, 'I am not coming.' And I said to him, 'what do you aim for me to do?—You being the Sheriff—and I just ask you, what do you aim for me to do?' He said, 'The only thing I know for you to do is to leave the County.' And I said, 'I refuse to leave the County under your authority or anyone else. I am a taxpayer and a citizen of this County, and have been here since 1913, and I refuse to leave under those orders.'

Clontz and Howard also testified that the miners at Creech mine at Twila held an election and elected Doctor Lagram as camp doctor. The Company refused to accept him because the Creech family wanted to keep the doctor they already had. A short time later, Dr. Lagram's car was blown up with dynamite. He took the hint and sought employment elsewhere.

Unthank then renewed his attacks on union locals. In the first week of November 1934, the local at the Cornett-Lewis Coal Co., at Louellen, was broken, setting a pattern, which soon became all too familiar in the County. According to James Westmoreland, the UMWA's trouble began when R. E. (Uncle Bob) Lawson, general manager of the mine, had threatened to discharge miners who were in debt to the company if they signed authorizations for checking off their union dues from their wages. At the end of October 1934, the company discharged 55 men, apparently without cause, and replaced them with new help. When he attempted to adjust the grievance, Westmoreland reported that Lawson told him: "I am not going to have anything to do with the union." The local voted to strike in protest. The following day Westmoreland drove to the mine, where he found a group of 15 or 16 deputies patrolling the company town. The Unholy Three, Unthank, Lee and White, followed his car and forced him to leave town. While driving through, he testified, he saw the deputies armed with revolvers and shotguns, dragging men out of their homes and forcing them to go to work. During the strike the vice president of the Union, John Smith, a Negro, who was also checkweighman for the miners, was kidnapped and beaten by Lee, White, and Merle Middleton.

"Uncle Bob" Lawson stated that the striking miners were attempting to picket the mine. He described the picket line as peaceful and ineffective, stating that the miners returned to work in increasing numbers. With a straight face, he denied that the men were forced back to work or that there were an unusual number of deputies present, although he recalled seeing Deputy Sheriffs George Lee and Frank White. He further testified that he was a "college chum" of Ben Unthank, having known him for 30 years, but that he did not know as a matter of fact whether or not Ben Unthank was employed by the Harlan County Coal Operators' Association, having never discussed his work with him during their frequent meetings together. The Committee's judgment of this was: "This statement is so inherently improbable as to discount the reliability of Mr. Lawson's testimony."

Failure of the strike whipped the union. Lawson summoned the men into the company theatre and had them vote on whether or not they wanted to belong to the United Mine Workers of America. He testified that the men "with a secret ballot voted 267 to 5 that they did not want any union there." He described the "secret ballot" as follows: "They were given a blank piece of paper on which they voted yes or no and then they signed their names to it."

John Smith, the vice president of the striking local, on the day following his kidnapping and beating, while still barely able to walk, came to see Westmoreland in the town of Cumberland. They went to Harlan Town together to seek justice from Elmon Middleton, the County Attorney. At the courthouse they were met by the sheriff. According to Mr. Westmoreland, this is what followed:

The Sheriff, the High Sheriff of Harlan County, called me over to him and he said, 'I know what you are looking for.' He said 'You are looking for Elmon Middleton, and he is not here.' And he says, to Jim, 'you take that damn nigger and get him out of this courthouse and out of the County.' He said, 'If you don't, he is going to be killed.' That is the words he said to me. He stated this at the same individual time, he said, 'there are about three or four of you fellows here.' He said, 'and them two long-nosed preachers (Musick and Clontz), they got to quit causing disturbances in this County.' And he said, 'I am not going to put up with no labor disturbances here.' He further said to me, 'Jim,' he said, 'You are on the spot.'

This was not denied by the Sheriff.

By the fall of 1934 the situation in Harlan County had become so serious that Governor Ruby Laffoon undertook to protect the mineworkers against the Sheriff and his deputies. When a mass meeting was called by the union at Harlan Town for November 11, 1934, Armistice Day, the Governor, at the request of the Mayor, sent four officers of the Kentucky National Guard to attend the meeting as observers. An estimated crowd of 6,000 persons attended the meeting, which passed off without incident.

Encouraged by the response at the meeting, the United Mine Workers determined to rebuild its membership and assist locals that were still functioning. "Peggy" Dwyer first went to see Sheriff Middleton and offered to limit the activities of the organizers to securing compliance with the contract then in effect between the union and the coal operators' association. If he would promise them protection, Dwyer promised, the union would not attempt to recruit new members. The Sheriff took the matter under consideration and then called him several days later and said that he was unable to agree.

On the day after Thanksgiving, November 30, 1934, A. T. Pace, an organizer for the United Mine Workers, brought a group of organizers into Harlan Town, and registered at the New Harlan Hotel with the purpose of conducting a membership drive. Pace employed a local man, Carl Williams, a former deputy sheriff in

Bell County, to act as his guide. Upon entering the County, their car was followed by Ben Unthank, who drove behind them until they reached the city. The clerk at the New Harlan Hotel was reluctant to receive them as guests, saying, according to the testimony of Mr. Pace: "You don't know where you are at. You are in Harlan County . . . They have got the biggest gang of dynamiters on earth here . . . they will dynamite this hotel."

The following day one of the organizers reported to Pace that his automobile had been fired upon from ambush. Another organizer, George Burchette, returned to the hotel covered with blood, and stated that he had been forced off the road by another car and his automobile had been wrecked. Pace then went down to the lobby with Carl Williams and noticed that a number of men with guns and sheriff's badges were entering the hotel. At that moment Lee, White and Unthank broke into the lobby. Unthank moved in the direction of Pace, while Lee seized Williams, and gave him a pistol-whipping. Lee and White then dragged Williams out of the hotel into the street, and the other deputies in the lobby followed them. Pace later learned that Williams had been hauled off to jail. Pace and the other organizers arranged with an employee of the hotel to hire a car and, slipping out the back door, drove off to Norton, Virginia.

Both Lee and White testified that White had, during this affair, a warrant for Williams' arrest on a charge of carrying concealed weapons. Lee said that he took a pistol away from Williams, who he said attempted to resist arrest in the hotel lobby. White, however, said Williams did not carry a gun. He further said that he had received the warrant for Williams' arrest "from the Sheriffs office" and had it with him "for three days." The warrant was not shown to Carl Williams and has never been produced. The Sheriffs chief deputy, Henry M. Lewis, testified that he handled all the warrants that came through the Sheriffs office and that he never saw a warrant for the arrest of Carl Williams.

After being confined in jail for three days, from December 1st to 4th, 1934, Williams was released. He was brought before Judge

Saylor on the phony charge of carrying concealed weapons but no witnesses appeared and the case was dropped. Then Williams swore out warrants to place Ben Unthank and George Lee under bond to preserve the peace. Neither man could be found in Harlan town and the warrants were not served. An explanation for the failure to locate the men was furnished by R. C. Tackett, who was once more at large, working for Unthank, after having been sent to prison for six months in connection with the dynamiting of "Peggy" Dwyer's house. Tackett testified that Sheriff Middleton had sent him to warn Unthank that a peace warrant had been issued against him, and that he was to "stay out of town."

The incident of Carl Williams' "arrest" remained closed in spite of his efforts to secure relief from the authorities. When he attempted to enter the Grand Jury room on one occasion, to present his case, the foreman after hearing his grievance, closed the door in his face. Williams brought the matter repeatedly to the attention of the circuit court judge, James Gilbert, whom he knew personally, and he was advised by the Judge "to stay out of Harlan County."

On December 8, 1934, District President William Turnblazer was authorized by the chairman of the Southern Division of the Bituminous Coal Labor Board under the N.R.A. to accompany a code authority inspector to Harlan County to investigate the amount owed the miners by the Harlan Wallins Coal Corporation for overtime, pursuant to a decision rendered by the board on October 17, 1934.

Conditions in the mines operated by the Harlan Wallins Coal Corporation were summarized in findings in a decision rendered by the Bituminous Coal Labor Board on October 17, 1934:

> All the evidence presented to the Board sustained in full the contention that the workers in the mines at Verda and at Molus were working from one to three hours above the seven-hour day, and in one instance even more than three hours, with only seven hours pay for day workers. That there is what is known as the "clean-up" system and workers are required to remain until the "clean-up" is completed, regardless of the hours spent. There was also testimony to the effect that there were times when the miners worked more than five days a week.

It was testified that no checkweighman representing the workers is allowed at either Verda or Molus. It was further testified that a notice calling for a meeting to elect a checkweighman at Verda had been torn down by foremen or watchmen of the Corporation, and that at least two men were discharged for posting such notices. Other workers expressing a desire for checkweighmen had been beaten by the deputy sheriffs.

The witnesses testified that a feudal condition exists at these mines and that it is dangerous to discuss organization or the question of electing a checkweighman. The affidavits of those not connected with the union also stated that it was generally understood that the miners of the Harlan Wallins Coal Corporation were not free to express themselves in any way, and that they were intimidated in their movements even when off the Corporation property. The testimony showed that men applying for work at the mines of the Corporation were often beaten and run off the property, particularly if there was a suspicion they were in favor of the Organization.

Relying on the authority granted by the Bituminous Coal Labor Board, Turnblazer and a group of ten other men drove into Harlan Town and registered at the Lewallen Hotel. Scarcely had the union men entered the hotel when the organized gangs in Harlan County began to converge on Harlan town. All the deputies and hoodlums were mustered together, including men even from as far as Benham, a company town operated by the Wisconsin Steel Co. Merle Middleton was there with Pearl Bassham's thug gang in full force.

"Thug" Johnson painted a vivid picture of the scene at the hotel. Forty or fifty deputies "from different companies" congregated about the hotel lobby. Some of them registered in the hotel, taking rooms adjacent to those occupied by Turnblazer and his party. Merle Middleton went away to fetch the Sheriff but stationed his men to keep watch on Turnblazer, explaining, according to "Thug" Johnson, that "we are going to take him out and bump him off tonight." The High Sheriff entered later with Merle Middleton, and after surveying the scene, turned on his heel and left.

While the deputies and thugs milled about in the lobby of the hotel, Bassham entered and looked over the crowd. He saw

"Thug" Johnson and winked at him. Testifying about the incident, Bassham acknowledged that his employees were there and that their expenses were paid by the company. He said: "Merle Middleton handled those men at that time, and if we paid for them, it was paid through him."

Turnblazer was trapped in his hotel room. The deputies set off giant firecrackers outside his room. They dragged their knuckles across the door, threatening to break in and take the union men out. As night drew on, his position became increasingly precarious. Shots were fired in the street. Turnblazer succeeded in calling Virgil Hampton, an organizer working in Bell County. Hampton went immediately to Sheriff James W. Ridings of Bell County who, with his brother, chief deputy Chester Ridings, hurried to Harlan to the office of Circuit Judge James Gilbert. Gilbert contacted the Governor by phone. The Governor issued the following order:

> Captain Diamond E. Perkins, two officers and forty-two men of Company "A," 149th Infantry, Kentucky National Guard, are hereby ordered on active duty for the purpose of maintaining law and order in Harlan County, Kentucky, and specifically for the purpose of protecting the lives of William Turnblazer and other members of the United Mine Workers of America who are now held prisoners in the Lewallen Hotel by the Sheriff of Harlan County and his deputies.

At midnight the National Guard arrived and escorted Turnblazer and his group out of the county. The thugs were reluctant to obey the orders of Captain Perkins and for a few minutes it looked as if war would start. Some of the thugs followed the National Guard and organizers to the Bell County Line. The Union officials abandoned further efforts to visit the county. In April 1935, the contract with the Harlan County Coal Operators' Association expired. It was not renewed.

10

The Sad Story of a Brave Man, Elmon Middleton

> *He died a violent death. He stepped into his car and put his foot on the starter, and a dynamite explosion ocurred that injured him sufficiently so that he lived only a matter of minutes.*

The Wagner Labor Relations Act became the law of the land on July 5, 1935. But not in Harlan County. A new UMWA organizing drive, spurred by faith in the new law, drove the operators and their tough boys to defy both the United States Government and the State of Kentucky.

For the six months prior to passage of the Wagner Act, Governor Ruby Laffoon had been trying to restore order in Harlan County. On February 12, 1935, a military commission, headed by Adjt. Gen. Henry H. Denhardt, was appointed to conduct an investigation and take evidence on the situation existing in Harlan County. The Commission held hearings in the months of March and May, 1935, and filed a report with the Governor in which it stated "there is no doubt that Theodore Middleton, Sheriff of Harlan

County, is in league with the operators and is using many of his deputies to carry out his purposes."

On July 2, 1935, on the basis of facts brought out at the hearing and affidavits filed with him, Governor Laffoon brought charges against Sheriff Theodore R. Middleton, calling for his removal from office for "neglect of official duty" on ten separate counts. However, the Governor's term expired in December, 1935, so he adjourned hearings on the charges, due to impending primaries and the election.

On July 8, 1935, William Turnblazer and Joseph John Timko, international representative of the United Mine Workers of America from Indiana, who had been assigned to assist in organizing the miners in Harlan County, visited Circuit Judge James Gilbert at Pineville, in Bell County. They asked the Judge what prospect there was for protection of the union in Harlan County if it tried to exercise rights supposedly guaranteed by the National Labor Relations Act. The Judge merely counseled them to stay out of Harlan County. In spite of this advice, union organizers determined to try to assert their legal rights.

In July, 1935, there were only three companies in Harlan County still operating under contract with the UMWA—the Black Mountain Corporation, the Black Star Coal Company and the Clover Splint Coal Company. The total union membership was about twelve hundred men. Encouraged by the National Labor Relations Act and the charges Governor Laffoon had Placed against the Sheriff, the miners once again began to join the union. By September 1935, the membership of the union had doubled, with thriving locals in thirteen mining camps.

The organizing drive was met head-on by the Harlan County branch of the Syndicate. No change in method of operation was needed. Ben Unthank, chief deputy for the Harlan County Coal Operators' Association, lavishly disposed of the Association's funds in hiring assistants to drive the organizers out of the county. Whenever union representatives entered the County, they were trailed along the highways by deputy sheriffs.

On July 18, 1935, the union finally succeeded in renting an office in Harlan Town. Timko, accompanied by two other organizers, A. T. Pace and James Allen, drove into Harlan County on the morning of July 20 to establish the office. On the way, their car was forced to halt by another automobile that blocked the road at a narrow spot. Unthank, together with two buddies, George Lee and Frank White, emerged from this car, carrying sawed-off shotguns and pistols; they approached the organizers' car and ordered them to turn around and leave the County. The union abandoned its office in Harlan County.

During the summer of 1935, the National Guard was frequently called out on active duty in Harlan County by the Governor. The home of E. J. Asbury, superintendent of the Black Mountain Corporation, which operated under a contract with the union, was dynamited. Mr. Asbury believed Harlan County deputy sheriffs committed the outrage. To guard his home, the Governor assigned two members of the National Guard on June 1, 1935, stating in his executive order:

> It having been brought to the attention of the Governor through reliable sources that a state of disorder exists in Harlan County in the vicinity of the property of the Black Mountain Coal Corporation, and that the home of Mr. Asbury, Superintendent of the Corporation, was recently dynamited, that notwithstanding this situation, the Sheriff, Theodore Middleton, refused to permit the regular Deputy Sheriffs heretofore serving as guards on said property to continue as deputy Sheriffs, having discharged them from his force and there being no other public officers available in the vicinity of the Black Mountain Coal Corporation mines other than such deputies as might be furnished by said Theodore Middleton, Sheriff of said County, and it further appearing from reliable sources that many deputies appointed by said Sheriff have been guilty of lawless acts, intimidating, threatening, abusing and beating many peaceful citizens of Harlan County, a state of lawlessness is declared to exist in the Black Mountain Coal Corporation section of Harlan County, and Captain Diamond E. Perkins, Commanding Officer, Company "A," 149th Infantry, is directed to detail two enlisted men of his Company for active duty service in Harlan County to serve in the vicinity of the Black Mountain Coal Corporation property. The said men so detailed are hereby ordered to be placed on active duty and they will serve as peace

officers for the purpose of protecting life and property in the vicinity of Black Mountain Coal Corporation.

It was quite obvious that Asbury house was dynamited in an attempt to intimidate him and force the Peabody Coal Company to operate on a non-union basis. Asbury later told me that Theodore Middleton sent him three outlaws to guard the property "without me asking for them and demanded that we pay him for their services." He said, "I sent them back to Middleton and told him to go to hell with them."

Sheriff Middleton filed suit with Judge James Gilbert to enjoin Adjutant General Denhardt from bringing the National Guard into Harlan County "to preserve the peace" on the ground that this was the function belonging to the Sheriff alone. Judge Gilbert promptly granted a sweeping injunction, which forbade the National Guard from "preserving the peace." He even enjoined them from appearing in Harlan County in uniform. This remarkable order defying the State was set aside by the Supreme Court of Kentucky on November 1, 1935, in a caustic opinion which pointed out that the Sheriff did not have a "property right in the preservation of law and order."

The ridiculous contentions of Sheriff Middleton and of Judge Gilbert that the Sheriff enjoyed a monopoly on the right "to preserve peace" in Harlan County is even more ironic when recalling the grim events that took place in September, 1935. Elmon Middleton, the County Attorney, who had made a genuine effort to redeem his campaign pledges and secure impartial law enforcement in the County, openly broke with the other members of the County Administration. He determined to lay the charges of the United Mine Workers before the Grand Jury and press for prosecution against the deputy sheriffs and thugs who were terrorizing the community. His friend and confident was the Rev. Carl E. Vogel, who was then Pastor of the Cornett Memorial Methodist Church, whose congregation included professional groups and coal operators in Harlan County. In spite of the fact that most of his flock was anti-union, Mr. Vogel had the courage to demand the rights of free speech for all Harlan County citizens. His sermons that year were filled with eloquent pleas for justice in Harlan County. It is a matter of wonder to me now, knowing the arrogance and stupidity of the gun thugs that Mr. Vogel was not shot down in his Pulpit.

In August, 1935, Joe Timko had a secret meeting with Elmon Middleton. They discussed the possibility of conducting a grand jury investigation into the methods of intimidation used against the miners. The meeting was conducted secretly at the request of the County Attorney who, according to Mr. Timko, said: "He was going to try to do all he could to help us to clear up that situation, to stop this intimidation, but that he was on the spot himself, and if he was seen talking to us, it would just put him on the spot that much more."

The grand jury investigation was never held because Elmon Middleton was assassinated on September 5, 1935. His close friend, Mr. Vogel, described the murder in the following words:

> It was the Sunday immediately preceding his death, and he remained at my home, coming in after church on Sunday night, and he remained at my home until about 11:00 or 11:30 o'clock at night, and during that time we discussed the general situation of this collusion between the coal operators and the Sheriff's office, the necessity of cleaning it up. But Mr. Middleton's statement was that he did not believe that he would be permitted to live long enough to do his job that needed to be done. His statement was that he believed himself to be a marked man, and he likewise believed that I was a marked man because of my interest in trying to clean up the situation.
>
> He died a violent death. He stepped into his car and put his foot on the starter, and a dynamite explosion occurred that injured him sufficiently so that he lived only a matter of minutes afterward. I stood with him and beside him in the Harlan Hospital, holding his hand, until he died.

Otis Noe, who had served as a deputy sheriff under Theodore R. Middleton, was convicted of the murder. The only County Official dedicated to impartial enforcement of the law had been removed from the scene. Mr. Vogel did not last long either, but at least his removal was without violence. He left Harlan County in September, 1935, shortly after the death of Elmon Middleton. He was transferred to another church as a result of "quite a sheaf of protests, chiefly from the coal operators of my own church, asking for my removal from Harlan as a pastor." He said that the only reason for his transfer was the position he had taken in opposition to lawlessness and terrorism in the county. According to his testimony to the La Follette Committee, when his new appointment had been determined, "the bishop put his hand on my shoulder and said, 'Boy, I am glad you are getting out of there without a bullet through you.'"

Miners in thirteen camps stopped work on September 22, 1935, and demanded that their employers sign a contract with the union. Armstrong R. Matthews, superintendent of the Clover Splint Coal Company, told the UMWA's Timko that he was unable to operate his mine under union conditions and compete with non-union mines in the same area. Matthews testified that he discussed the situation with George S, Ward, secretary of the Harlan County Coal Operators' Association, and then notified the Sheriff of his determination to operate without a union contract.

This strike revived the ferocity of Ben Unthank. Shortly after midnight on September 25, 1935, the third day of the strike, Ben Unthank, accompanied by his cronies Lee and White, banged on the door of Howard Williams, a Negro union member who held the office of vice president of the UMWA's local at Clover Splint. Williams opened the door, and the three thugs pushed past him into the house and ordered him to get dressed, stating that he was under arrest. Unthank and the two other men forced him into their car and drove over a mountain road leading to Virginia. Somewhere near the State line, after a brief argument as to whether or not they should kill him, they finally let him go, warning him not to return to Harlan County. Williams hid in the bushes until they left and then made his way to a coal camp at Bonnie Blue, Virginia. His wife had immediately notified her neighbors of the kidnapping and a search party had been formed to look for him. The next morning the Clover Splint camp was over-run by deputies who refused to allow the miners to leave their houses, speak to each other, or even to make purchases at the company store. The kidnapping of an officer of their local union and the presence of the armed deputies cowed the miners and the strike collapsed.

That day was described by Mine Superintendent Matthews to the La Follette Committee as follows: "On the 25th day of September, 1935, the deputy sheriff took over the camp on my orders to the Sheriff. For two hours early in the morning, they kept anyone from going into the streets. I left everything to the judgment of the Sheriff. He said the deputies were preserving the peace." Matthews admitted, however, that there had been no breach of the peace.

Strikes in the other mines were broken just as easily and in just about the same way. Williams sought out Joe Timko, and told him of his kidnapping. Reports of the activities of the deputies and of mass evictions of strikers from company towns reached Timko, and he informed Governor Laffoon of what was taking place. The Governor then called out the National Guard, proclaiming that a "reign of terror now exists in said (Harlan) County and has existed for some months." Thereupon Judge Gilbert took immediate counteraction. He announced an "inquest" in this language: "Since the adjournment of the grand jury here, it has been reported in the press of the state that some two hundred people have been evicted from their houses, and that there has been a reign of terror and lawlessness in Harlan County; that people have been taken in charge, whipped, and driven out of the County, and based on said reports, as shown by the newspapers, the Governor has sent troops into Harlan County for the third time, and that the Court has had no information or knowledge, direct or indirect, of any such conditions existing in Harlan County, and in order to satisfy himself a man by the name of Timko and others have been summoned in here, who, it is reported, have circulated these reports, and this investigation is held for the purpose of finding out whether there is any justification in these reports."

What the hell kind of an "inquest" was that? These unusual proceedings had no basis at law, yet Judge Gilbert issued summonses for Joseph John Timko and Robert Childers, the latter also an organizer for the UMWA, to appear at the Courthouse in Harlan Town on September 30 and October 1. Timko came, bringing with him thirty witnesses to tell the story of violence in Harlan County.

Before the very eyes of Judge Gilbert, heavily armed deputy sheriffs pursued union witnesses around the Courthouse and openly menaced and threatened them. Physical violence was prevented only by the presence of National Guard officers. Timko described the proceedings to the La-Follette Committee: "I was not able to get around in the Courtroom to talk to these witnesses, as I was constantly being pushed around by the deputy sheriffs. I also saw there and particularly recognized one who seemed to have much pleasure in following me around in the Courthouse, with the exception of going into the Courtroom, and that was George Lee."

Howard Williams was placed on the stand to testify about his kidnapping. His kidnappers were in the Courthouse play-acting as peace officers. In spite of Williams' testimony, the Court would take no action to bring the kidnappers to justice; however, Judge Gilbert figured out a way to send the complaining witness to jail. He was held as a material witness, needed for the grand jury. His bond was set at three hundred dollars, a little beyond the means of a coal miner making four dollars a day. So they locked him up. Nor was he the only union man thrown in the calaboose. Two other witnesses who described details of the "reign of terror" were similarly treated. Williams testified about this as follows:

> Mr. Adkins, Mr. Jones and I were confined in jail for the lack of $300 bond. We had testified at the request of Judge Gilbert about the violence in Harlan County. We were supposed to be held as material witnesses. I testified about being kidnapped by the deputy sheriffs. Mr. Jones testified about so many deputies being on the streets of Clover Splint in the morning. Mr. Adkins testified about the deputies kicking and cussing him and forbidding him from going to the post office. We remained in jail from 7 P.M. Tuesday. We later testified before the grand jury but it took no action.

This brand of "justice" was challenged in a damage suit against Judge Gilbert for false imprisonment, filed in the Federal District

Court of London, Kentucky, by Howard Williams. Judge H. Church Ford, of the Federal District Court, in instructing the jury, stated that: "These men were not legally committed to jail." But he added: "Judges are not held civilly liable in damages for exceeding jurisdiction, nor for making orders or requirements that are merely beyond their jurisdictions, if they have jurisdiction of the subject matter."

This latter bit of double-talk merely said in the ceremonial language used by lawyers that nothing could be done to Judge Gilbert. Judge Gilbert's so-called "inquest" again temporarily blocked efforts of the union to operate in Harlan County. The Black Mountain Corporation was the sole union-operated mine in Harlan County.

11

Happy Chandler Muddies the Waters

> *He described Sheriff Middleton as "competent, efficient and energetic," neglecting to add that these sterling duties were all directed toward his true job, supervising the killing and beating up of union miners.*

Unfortunately for the UMWA, the Kentucky gubernatorial campaign in 1935 resulted in the election of Albert Benjamin Chandler. A portly, fast-talking, hymn-singing character, Chandler was widely known as "Happy," a nickname that wrongly describes his pseudo-pious personality. In 1935, he had promised union miners the moon. They wound up without even a piece of green cheese. Timko said that early in his administration, in spite of the fact that the UMWA had supported him during the campaign, "we have not gotten any real protection from the Governor as long as he has been in there." This remained true during his entire term of office. It did not take Chandler long to show his true stripe—the big white one down the middle of his back. Among the honored official guests at his inauguration was none other than High Sheriff Middleton of Harlan County, complete with deputies. Middleton still faced charges placed by outgoing Governor Laffoon for malfeasance in office and neglect of duty.

After Governor Chandler took office, the union temporarily withdrew from Harlan County. Its representatives did not even enter the county for the purpose of negotiating legitimate matters arising under the contract, which was in effect with the Black Mountain Corporation. E. J. Asbury, superintendent at Black Mountain, had to go to Bell County if he wanted to talk to union representatives.

But the UMWA had not given up. It tried a new technique by turning to the courts and newspapers to publicize the hell that was Harlan. In 1936, Judge Henry Warrum, the UMWA's chief counsel, arranged with John Young Brown, Speaker of the House of the Kentucky Legislature and former Congressman-at-large from Kentucky, to organize a radio program to "let the public know what was going on in Harlan County." Brown, one of Kentucky's great orators, prepared a series of speeches using as his source material the record of hearings conducted by the investigating commission appointed by Governor Laffoon in the spring of 1935. He arranged for a series of speakers and delivered the first address himself over Radio Station WHAS, Louisville, on the subject of the "Feudal Lords of Harlan."

Following the program, Harlan County authorities stated that speakers on the program who had dared to criticize conditions in Harlan County would be summoned to appear before the Harlan County grand jury. Brown received a telegram from Daniel Boone Smith, Commonwealth Attorney, directing him to appear before the grand jury. He received a similar summons from H. H. Fuson, County Attorney of Harlan County, who had succeeded Elmon Middleton following his assassination. Fuson, it will be remembered, was the attorney who had been hired by the Harlan County Coal Operators' Association to appear in defense of Ben Unthank and his four accomplices in the proceedings brought against them in connection with the 1933 dynamiting of "Peggy" Dwyer's home. Brown testified before the La Follette Committee that speakers on his program were afraid to appear before the Harlan County grand jury "because once they get you in Harlan County—at least the general impression over the State is that they can do most anything they want to in Harlan County."

Fear of physical reprisal by Harlan County authorities caused the scheduled speakers on the program to beg off. Brown testified: "The effect of it was to destroy our program."

In the spring of 1936, James Westmoreland, who had been obliged to take up residence in Virginia because of a well-founded fear he would be killed by the deputy sheriffs, brought suit for damages against High Sheriff Middleton in Federal District Court for a false arrest in Cumberland in February, 1935. In December, 1936, the jury found in favor of James Westmoreland and rendered the verdict for damages in the amount of fifteen hundred dollars. Elated by the outcome of the trial, the union determined once more to organize Harlan County. The two lawyers who successfully represented the union in the Westmoreland damage suit were T. C. Townsend and Ben Moore. Moore later became Federal District Judge in West Virginia.

In preparation for the new drive, Bill Turnblazer addressed a letter to Sheriff Middleton on December 29, 1936, advising him that it was the intention of the United Mine Workers to hold meetings in Harlan County and requesting "that our people be given every degree of protection under the laws of your Commonwealth." The

"HAPPY" CHANDLER (1898-1991) *garnered UMWA support in his gubernatorial campaign. It must have been disappointing for organizers to see Sheriff Middleton and five of his Harlan deputies serve as Chandler's official escort in his inaugural parade.*

letter was returned with a notation upon the envelope, "Refused, not opened."

Turnblazer's unopened letter to the Sheriff said that the first UMWA organizing rally would be held in Evarts on January 3. Harlan County officials prevented that particular meeting by placing the County under quarantine from January 2 to February 6 because of an alleged meningitis epidemic. All public meetings were banned. UMWA organizers opened their drive on January 9 under orders not to hold meetings but rather to talk to individuals. A District convention at Middlesboro January 4-5 authorized the new drive to organize Harlan and placed District Vice President L. T. "Tick" Arnett in charge.

The operators again prepared for battle. The Association doubled its assessments in January, 1937, as it had done during the organization drives in 1933 and 1935. Association Secretary George Ward explained the increase to the La Follette Committee. He said two things were responsible for the increase—freight rates and the organization situation. He said the minutes of the Association provided for the one cent per ten assessment to continue until further notice.

The gang of deputies led by Unthank was again mobilized for action. At this time the Harlan Wallins section of Murder, Incorporated, was without a leader. Merle Middleton, "chief thug" of Harlan County while he was employed by Pearl Bassham, had left Harlan Wallins in February, 1936 to manage a bus company that he largely controlled. When the union drive opened, an effort was made to persuade Merle Middleton to abandon his peaceful ways and again take over direction of the "thug gang" at a salary of five hundred dollars per month. He refused the offer and lucky Ben Unthank got the job. The talkative "Thug" Johnson later reported this little deal to the La Follette Committee.

This made Unthank, with a raise in salary and the large slush fund of the Association at his disposal, generalissimo of the anti-union forces in the county, leading not only his own band of deputies but also the "thug gang" formerly led by Merle Middleton and separately financed by the individual coal operators. He had become what big city mobsters would call "The Chief Enforcer."

On January 16, 1937, Governor Chandler, by executive order, dismissed the charges against Sheriff Theodore Middleton, which had been instituted by his predecessor, Governor Laffoon, in July 1935, as a result of the investigation conducted by the Denhardt commission. The executive order stated: "The records in the said action had been lost or destroyed . . . and no records or charges can now be found in any of the offices of the State government."

Chandler also went out of his way to attempt to whitewash Laffoon's charges. He described Sheriff Middleton as "competent, efficient and energetic," neglecting to add that these sterling qualities were all directed toward his true job, supervising the killing and beating up of union miners.

But Happy was not only guilty of an attempted whitewash. He was soon exposed by the La Follette Committee as a plain, everyday type of liar. The papers detailing the Laffoon charges weren't lost at all. They were in the Statehouse in Frankfort in a locked drawer.

Allen R. Rosenburg, a La Follette Committee investigator, told the true story. He testified he went to Frankfort, Kentucky, to secure records from the Adjutant General and Secretary of State's offices in the State Capitol. "In contacting the Secretary of State's office, I had occasion to inquire into the records of the charges that had been filed during Governor Laffoon's administration against Sheriff T. R. Middleton. In the latter part of March and the first of April, I got access to the records and the charges in the dismissal proceedings against Sheriff Middleton. Miss Ora Adams, assistant Secretary of State, furnished me with an executive journal containing the charges in the civil proceeding against Sheriff T. R. Middleton. There was also a record of the hearing held in the pursuance of these charges."

The Louisville Courier-Journal on April 28, 1937, carried an Associated Press dispatch, dated April 27, 1937, from Frankfort, Kentucky, which read: "The transcript of evidence taken during the Laffoon hearing was found locked in a desk drawer in the office of the Secretary of State today. Employees in the office said it had been available for some time."

The La Follette Committee reported it had been unable to find out "how careful a search was made for the lost records." Happy undoubtedly carefully searched the ceiling of his office, and then issued his executive order.

Meanwhile, back in Kentucky's own Siberia, the man who had been complimented by the Governor as a "competent, efficient and energetic official," proceeded in his usual way to "maintain law and order" in Harlan County. He augmented the number of deputy sheriffs, until by April 15, 1937, there were 163 on active duty, only three of whom were paid from public funds. In January 1937, Sheriff Middleton also recalled Frank White from South Charleston, West Virginia, to resume active duty as deputy sheriff. White, the often-mentioned henchman of Ben Unthank, had unceremoniously left Harlan County in the fall of 1936 after being involved in the shooting and gassing of Chad Middleton, an uncle of the Sheriff, at Evarts. White was not prosecuted for his part in the attack. The killing was reported to have been the culmination of a personal feud between the two men. White and his playmates used tear gas to flush Chad out of hiding, and then riddled him with bullets. Kelly Fox, a former deputy, had witnessed the murder. At the preliminary examination held in Judge Saylor's court, Fox was summoned to identify Frank White. When he took the stand, a member of White's gang stood at the entrance of the courtroom with his hand on the butt of his revolver. Fox failed to identify White; he was one of the wise old foxes. He did not want to leave the courtroom in a box.

Following Fox's ordeal, no witness stepped forward to identify White and no warrant was issued against him. White left the county two weeks after the shooting, fearing the personal vengeance of the Sheriff. He said he thought it would save trouble for himself and others. He fled to South Charleston, West Virginia, where he remained four months. When the union drive began in January 1937, the High Sheriff summoned him back to Harlan County.

There would be no blood feud. Whate's highly specialized talents were urgently needed.

On his return, White immediately was appointed deputy sheriff and placed on the payroll of the High Splint Coal Company at a hundred and sixty dollars per month.

Hugh Taylor, a deputy sheriff, stated that Sheriff Middleton gave him an explanation for bringing Frank White back to Harlan County. Taylor testified that Middleton told him "White was a machine-gun man and an amateur gas man, and that is the reason he got him back the other time when he left here and ran off. He had been working for the High Splint Coal Company with Ben Unthank and his gang."

Sheriff Middleton had the necessary equipment to utilize Frank White's talents. On September 21, 1934, he had purchased a Thompson submachine gun and two "Type L" magazines. He testified that "I felt like I wanted one, and I purchased one." But he said himself, or his deputies had never taken it out. He also had purchased a tear-gas riot gun and twelve tear-gas projectiles and six "Triple- Chaser" tear-gas grenades on September 23, 1935, during the Clover Splint strike. From whatever source it was obtained, a machine gun was part of Frank White's regular equipment after his return to Harlan County in January 1937. Taylor also testified that White regularly carried a machine gun and pistols in the back of his car.

Among the many deputies appointed by Sheriff Middleton after the beginning of the union drive were Robert Eldridge, appointed January 11, 1937, and Hugh Taylor, appointed January 13, 1937. Sheriff Middleton paid their salaries of a hundred and twenty-five dollars per month, but five coal companies that utilized their services repaid him in full. These two men were assigned to the company town of Shields, owned by the Berger Coal Company, and were given free board and lodging at a boarding house operated by the company for its deputies, popularly known as the Clubhouse.

Eldridge had worked from August 1933 to January 1936 for Pearl Bassham as a "peace officer" in the company town of Molus, owned by the Harlan Wallins Coal Corporation. His career was typical of Harlan County deputy sheriffs. On September 9, 1930, he had been convicted of voluntary manslaughter in Harlan County, and had been sentenced for a term of five years at hard labor, of which he served twenty-one months. On later occasions, he was also convicted of carrying concealed weapons and of assault and battery. Two indictments against him, one for assault and battery and one for malicious striking and wounding had been dismissed on the motion of Commonwealth Attorney Daniel Boone Smith.

Taylor's background differed from that of Eldridge. For six years he had worked as a miner for the United States Coal & Coke Company, and later as a miner for the Bardo Mining Company and the Harlan Wallins Coal Corporation. In 1933 he joined the United Mine Workers of America and was promptly fired by Bardo, the reason given being that he was a member of the union. He also attributed his discharge by the Harlan Wallins Coal Corporation to discrimination against him because of his union membership. He supported Middleton in his campaign for Sheriff in 1933, and on January 6, 1934, the Sheriff appointed him deputy sheriff, and he obtained a job with the Harlan County Coal Operators' Association riding as a guard on coal trains. He then secured employment intermittently as a deputy sheriff, participating in some of the thug-gang activities. In September 1936, Taylor was indicted for the murder of a man named Robert Moore who, according to Taylor's testimony, had been drunk and had drawn a pistol in resisting arrest.

In spite of the extensive experience of his deputies, High Sheriff Middleton took precautions to instruct them specifically what they were to do. Taylor was to report to Eldridge at Shields where the coal companies would give him further orders. The High Sheriff personally directed him, according to Taylor, "to police the camp and move the organizers along" and particularly "to keep them from talking to the men." Taylor said, "He told us to follow them around. I asked him what good it would be to follow them and he said see who they talk to—what men they talk to—and report the men to the company.'"

Sheriff Middleton likewise armed his deputies so that they could carry out their duties effectively. Taylor said, "He asked me how many guns I had. I told him I had one and he told me he would give me another one. He said 'carry two; carry them out where they could see them. The organizers hate the looks of two guns. Carry two where they can see them.'" Hugh Taylor carried out his instructions to the letter. He cruised about the coal camps in his car, armed with his two revolvers and a 30-30 Marlin rifle. Eldridge confirmed the testimony of Taylor with respect to their duties as deputy sheriffs at Shields.

Ben Unthank, in addition to his expanded activities as "chief thug," still continued his leadership of the army of deputies appointed by High Sheriff Middleton. Accompanied by his lieutenants, Unthank made regular tours of the coal camps and coordinated the efforts of the deputy sheriffs who were assigned to specific posts, promising them assistance when needed. Taylor described the visits as follows: "He would go up and down on occasions and stop. The first time I saw him stop there, after I went up there, he stopped and said he would see if he had my pay. He ran through his pay envelopes and did not have it, and he went on by, went on to town, I guess."

Taylor continued, "Unthank told us if we needed to do anything in the camp that we did not want to do ourselves, to call him and he would send somebody up there to do it. I understood if they wanted somebody whipped or kicked out of there, to call him."

It was into this lair that the union organizers entered. On January 11, 1937, "Tick" Arnett, in charge of the organization drive, decided to establish headquarters in Harlan Town and secured rooms in the New Harlan Hotel. In the hotel, Allen Bowlin, a deputy sheriff whom he had known as a boy in his hometown, Jellico, Tennessee, immediately approached Arnett. Arnett testified that Bowlin gave a friendly warning, saying: "These fellows up here will kill you, they will dynamite, they will shoot, they will burn you." Arnett asked, "What fellows? and Bowlin answered, "This outfit you call thugs up here." Bowlin then offered to work secretly for the organizers but his offer was not taken up.

For a few days nothing occurred to substantiate Bowlin's warnings. For a short while the organizers made their way about the county with relatively little difficulty, speaking to the miners. On January 15, 1937, Arnett met George Ward on the street in Harlan and stopped to greet him, congratulating him on the "nice treatment" the union organizers were receiving in Harlan County. According to Arnett, Ward said, "Well, we are not all bad." Arnett stated that if the peaceful conditions continued he would publish an advertisement publicly retracting the charges that had been made against the Association. Arnett reported that Ward enigmatically replied, "You stay on awhile and you will find out."

The following day, January 16, 1937, Governor Chandler issued his executive order dismissing the charges against Sheriff Middleton. In an instant the situation in Harlan County was completely transformed. The deputies and thugs who had been relatively restrained in their conduct came out in the open and swarmed over the county. In effect, Happy had let the mad dogs out of their kennel. Arnett described the change as follows: "We had been followed continuously and hounded, and so forth, wherever we would go and made to move on in a quiet manner, and then immediately after the 16th, speaking in our language, they began to tighten up awful on us and it seems to me there were more of them than we had miners in Harlan County. We saw more of them than we did the miners. They just got thick everywhere and they would come up to our people and jump out of their cars and come around and pull their guns from their hips around to the front, and talk rough and mean to them, and tell them to get out, get going, get on the highway and keep moving, and so forth."

Disturbed by these occurrences, Arnett tried to confer with Sheriff Middleton, but his messages were not answered. An attorney who went to see the Sheriff on behalf of the union reported back that the Sheriff had said, "to hell with the damned United Mine Workers, they have got me indicted with everything in the calendar of crime and I ain't got any counsel for them." The union was never able to see the Sheriff. The Sheriff did not contradict this testimony, and admitted that he refused to accept letters sent to him by registered mail by the union. He merely commented: "Well, they never came to my office."

The day clerk of the New Harlan Hotel, Dan Breck, became concerned about rumors that were circulating in the town and warned Arnett that trouble was brewing. The rumors proved well founded. At three o'clock in the morning on January 23, 1937, dynamite explosions in front of the hotel rocked the building. Awakened by the detonations, the guests rushed out of their rooms and found themselves engulfed in clouds of tear gas that came through the hallways. Arnett described to the La Follette Committee the panic that ensued: "Well, of course, in a couple of minutes we were all crying, and there was quite a lot of commotion and in some three or four minutes after this explosion there was commotion all over the hotel, and I decided if they were trying to decoy us out, they would kill everybody, and I ventured out into the hall and when I went into the hall women and children and cripples and everybody was coming down half dressed and screaming and crying. I had failed to dress at this time and I saw all of our people come out of their rooms except one. They turned this gas loose on the second floor of the hotel, and people were coming down the third and the fourth, and all of them trying to get down together at the same time.

Breck confirmed Mr. Arnett's testimony:

> At approximately 3 o'clock in the morning there was a terrific explosion somewhere in the neighborhood of the hotel. It woke up everybody but possibly two or three guests who were on the extreme back of the house, and at the same time I heard someone in the hall. I was on the fourth floor in the rear, on the side. Somebody yelled 'fire.' I jumped out of bed and grabbed some clothes and stuck my head out of the door and could not see down the hall for smoke that I found out had come from tear gas bombs. I still did not know but what the house was on fire, so I rushed on down the steps afraid of the elevator if there was a fire, and when I got to the third floor the gas just about choked me up. I could not see and I could hardly breathe. So I stepped into a room standing open which somebody had vacated and grabbed a towel and wet it and put it over my

face and went down to the lobby. I was one of the last ones to get down to the lobby. There were some fifty people, I suppose, milling around the lobby, men and women and one or two children, all very excited. And about that time I noticed quite a bit of laughter, and I looked down and I had not completed my dressing, so I went on out. Some of the guests checked out immediately, a few of them went back to bed, but a great number of them left.

George M. Jenkins, the night clerk of the hotel, stated at three o'clock in the morning two men came running down the steps wearing masks on their faces. One of them drew a pistol and waved it in the direction of Jenkins. He remained at his desk as they went out the door and immediately afterward fumes of the tear gas came down and blinded him. He was unable to identify either of the men. The proprietor of the hotel, Victor H. Hooper, called the home of Sheriff Middleton but was unable to reach him. The sections of the containers of a tear gas bomb were found in front of the organizer's room. Arnett and his companions went outside the hotel and found that two of their cars had been completely destroyed by dynamite. He telephoned "Peggy" Dwyer at Pineville and at 5:45 a.m. Sheriff James Ridings of Bell County and one of his deputies came with an escort to take the union men safely out of Harlan County. Clinton Ball, Harlan County jailor, arrived about the same time.

The two masked men who set off the tear gas bombs were not apprehended. George Jenkins, the night clerk at the hotel, had examined the pieces of the tear gas bomb. He described them as being reddish brown in color, in small sections. From the description, it appears that the bombs were "triple chaser" grenades, manufactured by Federal Laboratories, Inc., which are painted red and separate into three pieces when exploded. Earlier I pointed out that Sheriff Middleton had purchased six "Triple Chaser" grenades on September 23, 1935, probably for use by Frank White. Middleton testified before the La Follette Committee on April 26, 1937, that he no longer had these gas grenades in his possession. "I don't know whether they have been used," he said. "I haven't got any of them in my possession at this time." With a straight face he said he believed that shortly after he purchased them, his deputies had discharged the grenades on a hill to experiment with the use of gas.

The tear gas containers that had been taken from the New Harlan Hotel were turned over to Sheriff Middleton. On March 26, 1937, investigators of the La Follette Committee subpoenaed the containers from the Sheriff for the purpose of securing the serial numbers that are stamped on the bottom of the containers by the manufacturers. The manufacturer kept a record of the serial numbers of the grenades that were sold to each customer. The High Sheriff told Committee investigates that the containers were in a safe in his office, but he refused to allow them an examination. On April 14, 1937, Sheriff Middleton testified in response to the subpoena that he no longer had the used tear gas containers in his possession, offering as an excuse, "I think they were supposed to have been delivered to the grand jury for their investigation and they were never returned to my office."

He later testified, "Some of the representatives of this committee came to see me about those gas bombs, and I thought I had them in my possession, but I later learned that they had been turned over to the grand jury for investigation."

However, the Commonwealth Attorney Daniel Boone Smith denied seeing the tear gas containers in the course of the grand jury inquiry into the gassing of the hotel. He expressed surprise that such evidence had existed: "I never saw them; and until I heard some evidence here, I assumed that they were a thing that disappeared when they went off. I thought they vanished. I didn't know that there was anything left."

Senator La Follette pressed Sheriff Middleton for an explanation of why he had failed to secure the serial numbers from the tear gas containers while they were in his possession and why he had not availed himself of this clue to discover the names of the persons to whom the gas bombs had been sold by the manufacturers. Middleton explained his failure in this respect by claiming: "They were burned so badly that I could not tell whether there were any serial numbers on the grenades or not."

Expert opinion impeaches the testimony of the High Sheriff. Thomas F. Baughman, a special agent of the Federal Bureau of Investigation for over seventeen years and a firearms-identification expert, described for the La Follette group the operation of the "triple chaser" grenade and exhibited sections of a bomb that he had exploded to serve as an illustration. The serial number on the bottom of the container was not obscured in anyway, nor were the sections of the container perceptibly distorted. The Committee concluded: "Mr. Baughman's testimony casts doubt on the credibility of Mr. Middleton's excuse.

The Committee also said: "Throughout the inquiry held by the Committee, the Sheriff maintained a sullen and hostile attitude, replying to questions with evasive answers. He refused to answer certain questions, which he conceded were pertinent on the grounds that by testifying, he would tend to incriminate himself under Federal law. This attitude on the part of a peace officer would be strange if it were not for the fact that Sheriff Middleton had had a court record.

"The Sheriff was grossly negligent in failing to conduct a proper investigation himself of the gassing of the New Harlan Hotel on January 23, 1937, and in permitting valuable evidence to disappear so as to prevent a proper investigation to be made by others. These circumstances, the evasive character of the Sheriff's testimony, and the tenuous nature of his excuse for failing to make a proper investigation of the crime do not clear him of the suspicion that he knew more about the incident than he cared to divulge."

On January 25, 1937, "Tick" Arnett and his assistants returned to Harlan Town and again applied at the New Harlan Hotel for rooms. The management of the hotel refused to permit them to register as guests. The manager, Victor H. Rooper, stated: "During the time they stayed at my hotel, the members of the United Mine Workers of America were at all times peaceful and desirable guests." His refusal to furnish them with rooms was solely due to loss of business arising from the "fears of violence and disturbances caused by those opposed to the organizing of the mine workers."

The organizers were forced to set up temporary headquarters at Pennington Gap, Virginia, near the Harlan County line. Shortly after they arrived there, Frank White and another thug came into the hotel where the organizers were staying. White, according to the testimony of Theodore Roosevelt Clarke, warned one of the union organizers that if they persisted in coming into Harlan County, they would be "bushwhacked." White, a "poor" witness, at least as far as the operators were concerned, went home after testifying briefly before the La Follette Committee, but never returned. On April 26, 1937, Drs. Jones and Crouch sent a telegram to Senator La Follette stating that White would be absent on April 26 and 27 "on account of serious illness of baby daughter." That was the last word from Frank White. The Dr. Jones who signed the wire was a crony of Frank White and was observed many times by United Mine Workers organizers accompanying White in his car when White was thugging. I do not know whether or not he ever carried a medical kit, but I do know he invariably toted a pistol.

In any event, A. B. Chandler's public endorsement of Theodore Middleton marked the beginning of a new era of violence in Harlan County. Union organizers had been chased out and there were still worse things to come.

12

Even Little Boys Weren't Safe

> *I thought they would try to scare us and frighten us in every way they possibly could, but the next day we went in and discovered that Bill and I were wrong, because they shot me.*

On February 6, 1937, the Harlan Courthouse gang lifted the quarantine for meningitis that had banned all public meetings since January 2. The following day, United Mine Workers of America organizers gathered in the Continental Hotel, Pineville, Kentucky, and debated the advisability of returning to Harlan County. Some urged caution while others dismissed the threats of gassing and bombings as mere bluff. The bolder councel prevailed. Thomas Ferguson, a veteran of thirty-seven years in the United Mine Workers of America, had been newly assigned to act as an organizer in Harlan County. He described the union conference as follows: "All of the fellows who were organizers, along with William Turnblazer who is the president of District 19, were present.

We discussed the advisability of all of us fellows going back into Harlan County and staying there and trying to reestablish headquarters until we could organize. Bill Turnblazer made this statement, 'they ain't going to shoot you organizers' and Mr. Arnett spoke up and said, 'the hell they won't. They shoot governors in Kentucky'. (He was referring to Governor Gobel who was assassinated on Inauguration Day.) Well, I agreed with Bill that I did not think they would. I thought they would try to scare us and frighten us in every way they possibly could, but the next day we went in and discovered that Bill and I were wrong, because they shot me."

Two days later the organizers drove into Evarts where they rented a plot of ground to be used for holding an open-air meeting on the following Sunday. Then they proceeded to the mines of the Black Mountain Corporation, which was under contract with the UMWA, and attended a local union meeting. The meeting was held in the afternoon in order to permit them to be out of the county before nightfall. At 4:30 p.m. they returned on the road from the Black Mountain Corporation's coal camps to Harlan Town.

Thomas Ferguson and "Tick" Arnett were riding in a car driven by William Milton Hall. Three other organizers followed in a second car. Between the towns of Verda and Ages, they came upon a car parked by the side of the road. Frank White was seated in the car behind the driver's wheel. As the cars bearing the organizers drew near, two blasts on the horn came from the parked car. Instantly bullets rained onto the two cars as they drove by, damaging the front car and wounding Ferguson in the shoulder. The drivers stepped on their accelerators and careened down the highway at a speed of more than seventy miles an hour, swerving past obstacles that had been placed across the road by the bushwhackers. Arnett later described this wild ride to the La Follette Committee:

> Just as we got about even with the car, the driver, who was later identified as Frank White, gave two blasts on the horn. We were approximately twenty feet past his car when a rain of bullets began to hail in and around our car. There was one bullet came and penetrated the radiator and there was another bullet came through over my head and knocked off my hat and exploded, and a fragment of it struck Ferguson in the shoulder. Another came through the back of my neck, the best I could tell, because the window was rolled down, and there was a hole in the car, and also struck him (Ferguson) in the shoulder and exploded and tore an awful nasty hole in his back. He was seriously injured.

Matt Bunch (UMWA International Representative from Illinois) was following. He was following in his car and I felt awful uneasy. I felt an awful uneasiness for him but he got through the rain of bullets with only one bullet hole in his car. I ducked down when all of this shooting took place. And when I raised up, I looked ahead and I saw another car parked on the side of the road with a menacing look of a gun inside which I saw after I got up to it; and we began to run into brush and rocks and obstructions on the road, and finally at last, right even with the car, there was a wagon hub lying on the road endways to us. We were making something around seventy or seventy-five miles an hour, as much as we could make in that length of time, and we hit this wagon hub, nearly wrecking us. They were very menacing with their guns, and I could not identify anyone in the car.

No shots were fired. Then we proceeded down and just after we passed through Coxton, there was another car with one man standing on the outside and another man at the wheel, and something that looked like a gun up against the wheel, and we went so fast there I don't think his marksmanship could have allowed him to shoot us. The radiator had been blown up and we had to leave it in a Chevrolet garage.

We were being followed by two carloads of men that acted suspicious, and we went in a circle, just around through Harlan, trying to lose them as we were coming through, and when we got to the Chevrolet garage on the outskirts of Harlan, we had to leave this car in the garage. The six of us got into Matt Bunch's car. The injured man got in with us, and we were so crowded there, we drove over across the bridge . . . I believe to the town of Baxter, but as you cross the bridge, there is the State Highway Garage there, and I saw two State patrolmen that I did not know nor I cannot name.

The organizers appealed to the two State patrolmen to give them safe conduct out of the County. The patrolmen drove into Harlan town to obtain permission from their superiors, leaving the organizers at the garage. Fearful for their safety and concerned over the wound received by Tom Ferguson, the organizers did not wait for the return of the State police, but boarded a bus, which took them out of the County. The bus was followed by two carloads of men who had pursued the organizers into Bell County.

Ferguson was seriously wounded. The bullet, which had struck him, tore a three-inch hole in his shoulder. He was hospitalized in Pineville, Kentucky. After an operation, he was removed to the hotel occupied by the organizers so that he could be guarded against further attack. On April 27, 1937, when he appeared before the La Follette Committee as a witness, he was still being treated by a doctor for his wound.

The army of deputy sheriffs and thugs were highly pleased with the success of the ambush that had been laid for the organizers. The evening of February 8th, Hugh Taylor testified, he saw Frank White. "He called me up there and told me not to tell Bob Eldridge, and that Bob Eldridge talked too much. He said they caught hell a while ago, he said the organizers, or the agitators, or something like that. I don't know what they called them. I believe he said agitators. Anyway, he was referring to the organizers. He said, 'they got hell a while ago. We fired into them a while ago.' Then I went on to ask him who had fired into them and he said he and Wash Irwin and Lee Hubbard. He said there was some fellow that blowed the signal, that was in the car with him. He said they gave blows on the horn."

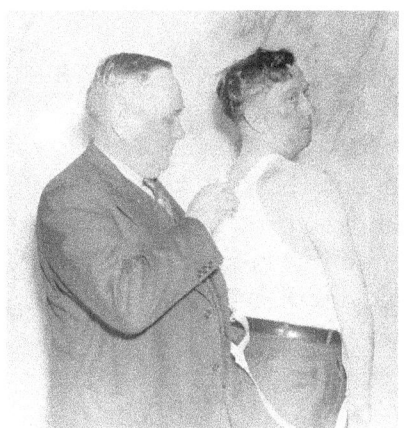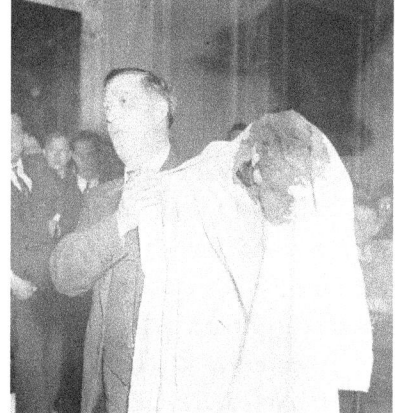

THOMAS FERGUSON *testifying before the La Follette Committee a few months after the ambush. Left, UMWA representative A.T. Pace reveals the wound for photographers. Right, Ferguson shows the shirt he was wearing.*

Three small boys witnessed the ambush and lived to regret their presence upon the scene. John Clouse, age 13, and his little brother, Jasper Clouse, age 9, were sons of Lloyd Clouse, a miner employed by the Harlan Wallins Coal Corporation, who lives at Ages. Markham Clouse, age 12, was a half-brother of Lloyd Clouse who had been staying with him for a year. The three boys had been "hunting scrap iron on the river bank" and they were returning home along the road when the shooting took place.

Markham Clouse testified: "There was a black two-seated car came on the road and that car blowed two times and people on top of the cliff started shooting." According to the boy's testimony, one of the men on the cliff shouted: "Look out!" Markham Clouse said bullets struck at his feet and ... "I started running across the road, started off on the railroad, and I turned around and I saw the cars, and on top of the cliff they were standing up behind the trees, I could see their heads."

He identified the men on the cliff as Bill Lewis, Melvin Moore, Luke Hubbard and Lee Hubbard, all of whom "worked" for Pearl Bassham.

John Clouse and his little brother Jasper also ran for safety. John, the thirteen-year old, testified: "I heard the car a-blowing. Then when the front car got about even with us, the hind car blowed about three times, and then the shooting began. I ran on the cliff, me and my brother, and Markham was trying to run toward the railroad, and then he came back from the railroad to us. One of their bullets struck right in the middle of the road and one of them hit that front car."

The terror-stricken boys remained hidden in a ditch until a miner named Isaac Eversold came down the road. John Clouse testified, "I thought he would keep them from shooting me, and I went home with him. When we got home, I told my mother and daddy what we saw. We were told not to talk to anyone about it or name that we saw or our house might be blown up. Mother said, 'there is a lot of them, Lee Hubbard, Luke Hubbard, Wash Irwin and others.'"

That same evening two deputy sheriffs, Sherman Howard and Charlie Rose of Brookside, a nearby mining camp, called at the Clouse home. Mrs. Clouse said, "they told my husband to ask the kids if they seen anybody. The kids weren't at the house. They told my husband to ask the kids if they had seen anybody that did the shooting and my husband told them if they did, there would not be anything said and it wasn't any use for to talk any further about it."

A week later, in spite of the precautions taken by Mr. and Mrs. Clouse, the boys were subpoenaed to appear before the Harlan County grand jury. At five o'clock in the morning of the day that the boys were to appear before the grand jury, Lloyd Clouse left to go to work at the mines of the Harlan Wallins Coal Corporation. When he entered the mine, he told his brother, Jasper Clouse, according to the latter's testimony to the La Follette Committee: "that Pearl Bassham seen him and told him to be damn sure that he did not let those kids go before the grand jury."

Mrs. Clouse sent the three little boys down to the neighboring town of Brookside to take the eight o'clock train into Harlan town. After they had left, Mr. Clouse returned. (At this point in her testimony Mrs. Clouse broke down weeping). "When he came back he said Mr. Bassham told him if he let the kids go and testify it would cause trouble."

Lloyd Clouse brought the children back from the station without permitting them to go on to Harlan town. His son, John Clouse, testified that shortly thereafter two deputies called at the house.

On Saturday evening, April 24, 1937, during the La Follette Committee hearings, Lloyd Clouse was shot and killed by Bill Lewis before the Committee had a chance to obtain Mr. Clouse's testimony. Bassham, testifying on May 4, 1937, after Clouse's violent death, denied telling Lloyd Clouse that he wasn't to let the boys testify before the grand jury. Bassham said, "I would be glad to repeat just what I did tell him. Lloyd Clouse came to me and I did not know the man at the time. He came to the office and I had not been in the office but a few minutes in the morning, and he said that some man had come and summoned his two boys to go down before the grand jury. He said he was not an officer and that he was afraid to send them that they might get their testimony twisted up. I said, "If they had not been summoned, why send them?' That is what I told him."

Bassham was told by Senator La Follette: "I want to tell you that my experience with you on the witness stand convinces me that of all of the evasive witnesses this Committee has had to deal with, you are the worst. You had an interest, did you not, in seeing to it that these men who were in your employ were not identified as having taken part in the shooting?"

Bassham replied, "I certainly did not back them up in any shooting."

Senator La Follette asked, "Well, but if they were in your employ, they were your agents, weren't they?" And Bassham replied, "I did not assume any responsibility for them going out and breaking the law, and they were off of my property."

They were not cut off his payroll, however.

13

Murder of an Innocent

> *I shook Bennett, and he was dead. We did not have light in the room, and Pauline and I just drug him to the door where that light shined in from the living room and seen he was dead.*

The ambush of "Tick" Arnett was only part of the thugs' renewed campaign. Their fury was also aimed at UMWA organizers who lived in Harlan County. Marshall Musick, who was organizer for the central part of the county, was living with his wife and children outside the village of Evarts when the union drive began in January, 1937. William Clontz, organizer for the western part of the county, resided at Wallins Creek with his wife and son. In January, 1937, when the union resumed activity, Musick and Clontz became once more targets for attack.

Musick was selected as the first victim. During the last week in January, Ben Unthank tersely ordered Hugh Taylor: "Get Musick whipped. He had a ten dollar bill to give the man to whip him," Taylor testified, and "he said to get some coal digger to whip him up." Taylor arranged for the beating with Ase Cusick, who operated a beer stand at Shields. On Sunday afternoon, January 31, Mr. and Mrs. Musick left their home at Evarts and strolled toward

Ridgeway to visit with two deacons of the Baptist Church, James H. Brewer and a Mr. Adkins. Along the highway above Lejunior, they walked past a car in which deputies Hugh Taylor and Robert Eldridge were sitting with Tom Holmes, a coal operator who was manager of the Cooke & Sharpe Coal Company. Nearby was another parked car in which deputies Frank White and Lee Fleenor were seated. As the Musicks proceeded down the highway, the car bearing Taylor, Eldridge, and Holmes cruised back and forth. Taylor testified as to their conversation:

> Mr. Holmes and I were sitting up there talking. While we were sitting up there talking, along came Musick and he says, 'there goes Musick and his wife now,' and he stood around and talked a while about it. He said, 'go on down and see Ase. Ase said he wanted to whip him. If Ase is going to whip him, now is the chance. Let's go down and tell him about it.' We turned around and went down to Shields.

At Shields, they notified Ase Cusick where Musick was going and according to Taylor, Cusick said "he would see him when he came back down the railroad" and "he would whip him when he came back." They then returned down the road and followed the Musicks until they entered the Adkins house. Tom Holmes then left to visit his brother-in-law, James Brewer, stating that he was then going to Clover Splint to meet his wife. Eldridge and Taylor waited on the highway in their car. At that point Frank White drove up in his car and asked where the Musicks had gone. He told Taylor and Eldridge to keep watch on the Musicks and drove off to the town of Ages. There he picked up two members of his gang known as the "Sargent boys," and returned close to the spot where Taylor and Eldridge were parked and left the Sargent boys on a hill behind the road (The Sargent boys were employed in the shooting and gassing of Chad Middleton at Evarts in 1936, along with Frank White). White then drove off again and returned a short time later with Allen Bowlin. Bowlin and White went down the road in the opposite direction from the hill on which the Sargent boys had been posted.

While they were visiting with Adkins, Mrs. Brewer and her ten-year old son came to the Adkins house in a state of great excitement. They were concerned over the safety of the Musicks because deputies had been cruising about the neighborhood. While Mrs. Brewer was out of the house, Tom Holmes visited Brewer and told him, according to the latter's testimony, "that he (Brewer) was not to be excited about anything," adding, "stay in the house" and "not see anything." Holmes said that Musick was going to get a "chouncing." After the warning from Mrs. Brewer, Mrs. Musick came over to see Brewer and he warned her of impending trouble.

Mrs. Musick returned to the Adkins home and she and her husband, thoroughly alarmed, thought it best to go back to Evarts before dark. They walked down a railroad track leading toward the main highway in order to take a bus. When they were several yards from the highway, they heard a horn blow. Thinking it was the bus, they turned and saw two cars screeching to a halt on the road nearby. Suddenly they were caught in a crossfire of bullets. Musick later described it in this way:

> While I had stopped to turn, she had advanced possibly three feet ahead of me, but she was yet holding my coat. I had on a raincoat, and shots began to fire from two angles. The second shot that was fired, I felt the sting of something on the back of my neck, and my hat left my head. I caught my hat as it fell and I touched my wife's arm, in grabbing at my hat to put it back on my head, and under the excitement, she rather turned around in front of me. Some of the bullets were striking in the edge of the highway where there was loose gravel and it was throwing this gravel on me, and some of the bullets were striking the field of the main-line railroad on my left and striking in a hole of mud and water there, and it was a continual stream of bullets.
>
> There was a car being driven up meeting me and he stopped and reversed his car to get out of the way of this rain of bullets, and he ran his car into the ditch and stopped, and I looked back again and the two cars were still standing on the road. I was under the impression from the direction that part of these bullets was coming, that possibly it was coming out of the hill. There was a little elevation that came down into the highway just at the point I was when the shooting started up, and I did not see anything with the exception of the men that were in the car. A number of people came out from the houses on the left-hand side of

the main line of the railroad, and on the side of the highway possibly 200 people, men, women and children, came out into the highway.

My wife said, 'Let us wait here for the bus,' and I told her I did not think it was best, but let us walk on. She apparently could not—she was so nervous she was not able to walk, and we rested for possibly a minute until she rather came to her composure, and we walked down the pike for a short distance, down the crossing where we had left the highway possibly a thousand feet to where this bus that we were expecting overtook us and we loaded up on that bus and drove down to this White Elephant saloon. The bus stopped to pick up passengers, and the same two cars that were there as we passed by came back and parked by the side of the saloon again near the point that they were as we went by. We went on home on the bus.

At this time, Taylor and Eldridge were still parked on the road. Taylor described the shooting as follows: "I did not see any shots fired. All I saw was where the bullets had hit. You could look at the road and see the smoke rise up from the gravel. It was a gravel road and tar put on it. You could see the smoke rise from it where the bullets hit. The bullets were coming out of the hill around there to the right; coming down or off of one of them spurs up there. It sounded like it was up there somewhere. They were using high-power rifles."

According to Taylor's testimony to the La Follette Committee: "Frank White went to Ages and picked up the two Sargent brothers who would do anything for a few dollars, and sent them around a knoll to bushwhack Mr. and Mrs. Musick; White then ran up and down the road in his car where he could watch their performance."

The following morning, Taylor met White, who was laughing about the incident. He also met Wash Irwin, whom he had not seen the night before at the scene but who appeared very well informed about what took place. Irwin said that White had given the signal for the shooting from the hill, and again according to Taylor, "He said if it had not been for Musick's wife getting over there, he would have gotten a bullet through him." He said, "She got on the wrong side of him, between the shots and Musick."

Tom Holmes, who had been present during the testimony of the other witnesses, had no comment to make other than he had not told Brewer "that he had a choust" for Musick, or that "my gang had a chousting for Mr. Musick." He admitted cautioning Brewer to stay in the house. He had no comment to make on Taylor's testimony that they had arranged with Ase Cusick to beat up Musick.

The net tightened around the UMWA, Musick and Clontz. On February 2, 1937, Marion Howard, nephew of Ben Unthank, came to see Clontz and delivered a warning from Unthank that he would not be safe if he went out after dark. On February 4, Homer Clontz, his son, drove into the town of Wallins Creek to attend band practice. As he passed by a dark alley beside the Baptist Church, a spray of bullets struck the car, eleven bullets piercing the left rear fender. Other bullets missed the car and hit houses on the other side of the street. The persons who did the shooting were never apprehended.

At the same time, Musick was receiving warnings from his friends that he should leave town. On February 2, 1937, James Brewer warned Musick that he should leave the county. Brewer testified: "I thought he would be killed, everything looked that way." For his part in the Musick affair, Brewer did not escape the attention of the deputies. Ben Unthank's chief assistant, George Lee, Lee Fleenor and Allen Bowlin, visited his house on February 4th to search for "a thousand pounds of meat supposed to be stolen."

Brewer said, "I asked them to show me a search warrant. They refused. They were looking in the dresser drawers and chifferobe. Yes, they were looking for a thousand pounds of meat in the dresser drawers. I think they were looking for United Mine Workers literature, but they found neither meat nor literature. Then they went away." The visit of the deputies was a silent warning to Brewer not to interfere with the Musick affair.

On the evening of February 8, when White was describing to Taylor the ambushing of the organizers, he brought up another matter for discussion. According to Taylor, White said: "We will go down and shoot up the Musicks' house and run him out." I asked him what he would do and he said, "We will go and shoot it up." I asked White who was going and he said there was a "bunch of them."

Taylor further testified that White had told him that there would be money in it for those taking part, at least a hundred dollars more in their pay. Taylor said he promised White he would take part in this, but did not do so.

Taylor then went to stay with Robert Eldridge to avoid meeting White again. Later the same evening, Wash Irwin came to Eldridge's house looking for Taylor. The Sargent boys and nine women accompanied him. He sent the women and the Sargent boys out and told Taylor that Ben Unthank would finance the raid. He also told Taylor that they would get a hundred dollars each for the job. Taylor further testified: "Irwin did not say exactly that he would pay it, but he inferred that Unthank would be the rudder of it—he did not exactly say it that way either, but that was what he was referring to; I can tell from his talk."

Taylor made a noncommittal reply to Irwin. He said he turned down the proposition because he was afraid of dying but gave his noncommittal reply because he was afraid to refuse, was afraid he would be killed. White was absent from the Committee's hearings without leave and was unavailable for comment. Wash Irwin, who followed Hugh Taylor to the witness stand, left his testimony unchallenged.

On February 9, 1937, Musick heard of the ambushing of the organizers with "Tick" Arnett that had taken place on the previous day. Shortly thereafter on the street in Evarts, he met George Middleton, an uncle of the High Sheriff. He told Musick, according to the latter's testimony: "I have always took you to be a good man. You have lived in my property for a year and a half and I think you are a good man. I feel like I ought to advise you that your life is in immediate danger and I want to advise you as a friend that you had better get out of town, and out of the county before you are killed."

On the same day Musick encountered John Clemm, police-court judge of Evarts, on the street. Musick reported the following conversation:

Immediately after noon that day, I met John Clemm, the police judge of that town, and he gave me almost exactly the same advice, with this exception: 'My life has been threatened just like yours.' And I said, 'Judge, what is your trouble?' And he said, 'Well, I am in trouble with the same gang.' And I said, 'How come you to break with them? You and they have been good friends.' 'Well,' he said, 'Merle Middleton, the president of the bus company, I decided some cases against him here in the city and he has been angry with me and my life is in jeopardy, just like yours.' He said, 'Possibly both of us will have to leave the county.'

The attempt on his life and the repeated warnings from friends convinced Musick he had to leave the county in which he had lived for over fourteen years. His decision was reinforced by the fact that Unthank, White, Fleenor, Lee and Irwin, together with three car-loads of deputies, were stalking him in Evarts "where they could see what I was doing, where I was going and what buildings I was going into." He was finally convinced by his wife's argument that his family would be safer if he were away from home. He parted with his family, believing that his absence would avert the menace against his wife and children. But to no avail. Musick's story of the big tragedy of his life begins about three o'clock in the afternoon of February 9th.

> I stayed home and sat around with my wife until very late, and the train that went up the head of the hollow and back generally went out about nine o'clock. I called my boy Bennett just before I started to the train and after dark, and I related to him the warning that we had had, and when I started to leave the house I said, 'Bennett, I want you to stay here tonight and try to take care and watch your mother and the other children.' And he said, 'Pop, I will do that.' And that is the last words I ever heard him speak.
>
> I left on the train and when I got off that train at Pineville about nine o'clock there was a message in the hotel that my boy was killed in the home. As soon as I came to the lobby of the hotel, Mr. Arnett was in there, and he came over from the clerk's office and he said, 'Brother Musick, I have some sad news for you. Your son was killed in your home in Evarts.'

The murder of Bennett Musick occurred at about 8:30 p.m. on February 9, 1937. Mrs. Musick and her three sons were sitting about the fireplace and her daughter was busy at the household tasks when a shower of bullets tore through the walls of the house. Mrs. Musick described what took place:

> Well, I could not tell how many shots, it was so excitable and unexpected. The first shot that I heard, I was reading the paper next to the baby boy who had just come back from Evarts and brought the day's paper and handed it to me. I was reading the paper and the first shot, I thought just for a second that it was something that had exploded in the grate. I was sitting in front of the grate and I looked down. By that time there was another one, and at that time, of course, I did not remember seeing Bennett go out of the room. It was a week before it came to me that I never did think I saw him leave, but in a week I remembered seeing him just kind of crawl to go into the bedroom, but he must have fell. This boy that is 14 was sitting on the studio couch at the end that came around to the door to go into the bedroom, and he said Bennett just rose out of his chair and went in the front room and just fell into the bedroom, but he had turned. He was lying right around a trunk, just to the left of the door. He crawled around and his feet were past the door.

After the shooting had stopped, Mrs. Musick called the roll of her family: "We hushed for two or three seconds, or two or three minutes maybe, then the shooting stopped, and I thought... well, I said, 'Are any of you shot?' And the baby boy said, 'I am shot in the arm', and Pauline said, 'I am not shot,' and Virgil went behind the door. The fourteen-year old boy got behind the door, and two bullets went in just above his head. He just scattered down behind the door that stood open just a little, and I took Bennett by the shoulder."

It was then that Mrs. Musick discovered that Bennett was dead. She recalled: "I shook Bennett, and he was dead. We did not have light in the room, and Pauline and I just drug him to the door where that light shined in from the living room and seen he was dead. She unbuttoned the clothes and felt his chest, and he was already dead."

The fourteen-year old Musick boy ran to the house of a neighbor, Floyd Creech. Creech was already getting out of bed, having been alerted by the fusillade of shots. Mrs. Musick continued her narrative: "Mr. Creech came over and said that Bennett was dead, and I asked him if he would go and call my husband, and he said he would. Pauline washed Bennett's face and some more neighbors came too at that time, and they helped us. We laid him out on the studio couch."

Mrs. Musick was unable to fix the direction from which the shots had come, but she believed they came from the road:

> I thought at the time they were just somewhere right around the house. They made such a ring. The first one went just like something exploded. It seemed like I could not hear it for a long time, but it just deafened me, and I thought it was right around the house. I did not have any idea they were shooting from the road. I just had an idea that we had the window shades down, and it was cream colored window shades, and I had an idea that they seen the boy—that someone looked in and thought it was his daddy. That is what I thought. But I reckon they must have come from the pike.

The night of February 9th, after hearing of the murder of his son, Marshall Musick frantically sought to return to Harlan County from Pineville and bring back his family and the body of his son. He spoke to Sheriff James Ridings of Bell County and appealed for an escort. He was told that it was too dangerous. Musick testified:

> I asked the Sheriff to take me home, and Sheriff Ridings said, 'Mr. Musick, I cannot afford to do that. Possibly you and I both would be killed,' and he said, 'I will do this. I will get some of my deputies' and he told me of some brave men that he had, deputy sheriffs in that county, that he would gather them up and get a couple of cars and go to an undertaker and get the ambulance and the two cars, and they would bring my wife and the other children out, and the undertaker would bring the corpse out. I talked to a number of men there, and they all told me that they could not afford to take me up there, that possibly they would be killed. Sheriff Ridings left, and I waited until late in the night, possibly four o'clock or approximately three o'clock, and one of Ridings' sheriffs, I don't know whether it was the High Sheriff or his deputy, came in and

told me that he had been up there and how the house was shot full of holes, and that after he went to the home and the condition thereof up there, that it was too dangerous for him to undertake to take my family out. He was unable to get an undertaker to go in there owing to the fact that they were afraid of being killed, and he told me that the doctors up there would not go to the home, that they were afraid.

The following day, the Musick family left Harlan County, taking the dead body of Bennett Musick with them.

There was an eyewitness to the shooting into the Musick home. Kelly Fox, a former deputy sheriff, was employed as an automobile mechanic at the Black Motor Company at Evarts, Kentucky. He lived near the Musicks. On February 9, 1937, the night of the shooting, he was returning home, crossing a footbridge over the river that ran below the road where the Musick house was located. As he left the bridge to go up toward the highway to his house, he saw these cars coming down the road. As they passed the Musick house, shots were fired from the three cars. Fox stopped behind several large rocks that lie between the river and the highway. One of the cars drew up opposite the Musick house. The other two cars drove up the road and circled the road returning slowly to join the other car. There were three men in the parked car. Two of the men placed their guns out of the windows and continued shooting into the house. The headlights of the cars that were moving back down the road illuminated the parked car. Kelly Fox recognized one of the men in the parked car as Frank White. Fox reported the incident to Bryan Middleton, brother of the High Sheriff, who was a personal friend of his. However, he did not report it to the authorities. He had vivid memories of the time in 1936 when he had appeared as a witness against Frank White in connection with the shooting of Chad Middleton. The recollection of armed gunmen eyeing him in the courtroom was sufficient to seal his lips.

The series of crimes which had followed in close succession after the tear gassing of the New Harlan Hotel and the dynamiting of the organizers' cars on January 23, 1937, culminating in the murder of Bennett Musick on February 9, 1937, forced the county authorities to appear to take action. A special term of the Harlan County grand jury met on February 15th, 16th, and 17th to investigate the outrages.

Grand juries in Harlan County were selected by three Jury Commissioners who were appointed by the Circuit Court Judge. In January 1937, Judge James Gilbert summoned Bassett Warren to his office. Warren was a businessman who had formerly been a miner and a member of the United Mine Workers of America. According to Warren's testimony, Judge Gilbert told him that he wanted him to serve as Jury Commissioner "and get it out of politics if he could; that his dockets had been delayed or something like that." Warren accepted the offer and according to his testimony, Judge Gilbert said, "I will call you sometime in February." Later Warren was notified to appear at the Courthouse and be sworn in as Jury Commissioner. However, he did not take office. "A day or two before the date came," he said, "I got another call which said for me not to come, that Judge Gilbert was sick."

On February 15, 1937, Warren received a letter from Judge Gilbert telling him that he would not head the grand jury. The

MARSHALL MUSICK *testifying about the killing of his son.*

letter was merely a series of excuses given in an attempt to justify the fact that it was planned to appoint a coal operator as head of the grand jury instead of an impartial citizen.

In place of Warren, Judge Gilbert selected for Jury Commissioner W. Thomas Holmes, manager of the Cooke and Sharpe Coal Company at Lejunior, Kentucky, who was certainly involved to some extent in the plots against Musick. He was the man who had arranged for a thug to attack Musick on the highway on January 31, 1937, and who had warned his brother-in-law, James Brewer, on that day, to remain in his house in order not to see what was going to take place outside. To what extent Holmes was involved in the shooting at Mr. and Mrs. Mustek's home on January 31 was not clearly established. It is clear, however, that a grand jury selected by Holmes and his fellow commissioners would not be likely to inquire deeply into Holmes' own connection with the crime.

Obviously, even an impartial grand jury would have operated under severe handicaps. The Commonwealth Attorney, Daniel Boone Smith, was nothing less than an employee of the coal operators. And the High Sheriff was Theodore Middleton. Both wanted only to cover the truth about the slaying of the Musick youth.

The Sheriff blandly informed the Grand Jury that there had been no disorders "of any importance during the last two years." He added: "I think murders and crimes and unlawfulness of all kinds has been reduced as much as it is possible to do here in this county, considering the number of people and the class of people we have here in the coal mines." Middleton did not refer to the "class of people" who were deputy sheriffs, nor did he state what he considered to be a "crime of importance." It was certain that murder was not an "important crime" insofar as the Sheriff was concerned.

The Grand Jury Commissioners left nothing to chance in selecting a grand jury. The foreman of the special grand jury in February was Homer Highbaugh, son-in-law of A. B. Cornett, vice-president of the Cornett-Lewis Coal Company. Highbaugh had served as a deputy sheriff under Theodore Middleton since December 4, 1934. The foreman of the regular grand jury in March was

Hans Bennett, whose brother, C. V. Bennett, was a coal operator interested in the Dixie Coal Company, the Harlan Central Coal Company and the Rex Mining Company. The foresight of Judge Gilbert in substituting Holmes for Warren was rewarded. Neither the special term February grand jury nor the regular March grand jury returned any indictments.

However, a feeling of revulsion swept Harlan County as a result of the cold-blooded murder of Bennett Musick by Ben Unthank's night riders. Voices were raised in protest, even among the deputies. Henry M. Lewis, chief deputy under Middleton, resigned February 20, 1937. He explained his action by saying, "Well, there were things going on all over the County that I did not approve of." He later amplified this statement, "Well, lots of things had happened that I did not know how they happened or who done it. You take killing the Musick boy in Harlan County was a bad piece of work by somebody. I don't know who did it, or anything about it. It was about as bad a crowd as ever happened to be in our County. That house being shot up in the night and that boy killed, that was a bad piece of business."

Hugh Taylor was so shocked by the murder of young Musick that his emotions overcame his caution. The day following the attack on the Musick home, he was warned not to talk about the affair. Ben Unthank himself ordered Taylor to keep his mouth shut.

Taylor said, "I first heard of the murder of the Musick boy on the morning of February 10th and I heard it in Harlan town. I first heard it from Lee Fleenor. He asked me had I heard about it. I told him no, I had not. He turned and walked off, left me. Then Ben Unthank came up and asked me if I heard anything. I said I heard Musick's boy was killed and he asked me who told me and I told him Lee Fleenor. He says, 'Well, don't talk any more about it.' He said, 'Let them get the news out.' He said, 'don't say anything more about it.'"

After the Musick murder, which the special term February grand jury was holding its inquiry on February 15th, 16th and 17th, Taylor permitted himself to protest against the violence of the gangs.

He unwisely confided in Frank White. Taylor said: "I was talking to Frank White in the Harlan courthouse, in the Sheriff's office. We were talking about the special grand jury that was called there. I says, 'It is a shame,' I says, 'that the County gets into such a damn shape like this, the deputy sheriffs getting out of here and doing all of this, most of this being done by them, it is a disgrace.' I says, 'You fellows are going to get us all put in the penitentiary, or right in hell somewhere, maybe where we all belong,' I says, 'the way you are doing it.' He said I had better keep my mouth shut or I might go down too. I told him I might go down too, but somebody would go right down with me."

On February 20, 1937, White made good his threat. That evening Taylor was in a saloon with David Sullenberger, whose father operated the Clubhouse at Shields, where the Berger Coal Company deputies stayed. Wash Irwin noticed him and said, according to Taylor: "You don't belong here" he says, "You better go back down to Shields." Taylor and Sullenberger left the saloon and drove back in the direction of Shields. They were overtaken by a car driven by Frank White, who had with him Irwin and a third man. Taylor described what followed:

> The car came up behind me. His car came up behind me and he blowed his horn for me to stop. I told the boys I better stop and see what he wants. I stopped and Frank got out. I saw him getting out. I waited for him to come up there. He says, 'Where are you going?' I says, 'I am going to bed.' I cast my eyes to the side and I saw somebody else walk out from the car. I saw Wash Irwin and somebody else right alongside of him. Wash Irwin had a pistol; it looked to me like a bright-looking automatic. Frank says, 'You will like hell.' He stuck the pistol alongside of my head, and when he stuck the pistol alongside of my head, I grabbed the pistol with my left hand and jerked it up. When I jerked the pistol up, he fired on me. I was hit in the fingers of my left hand. That is the hand I grabbed it with.

Taylor then reached for the pistol with his right hand, and White fired through the knuckles, breaking the hand. Taylor was left helpless. He managed to struggle out of the car and ran for the side of the road.

Taylor later told the La Follette Committee: "The door of the car came open; I don't know how I could get it opened but I got it open, I don't know how, but anyway, the door came open and I had two 45's and I reached for them, but I could not do anything with them. I could do nothing with my hands to get them, and then I turned to run. Just as I started, he shot me through the hip, out through the groin, and that run me down."

As he lay helpless on the ground, White and Irwin drew close to deliver the final blow. But they decided it was not necessary. Hugh Taylor told it this way:

> Then I laid down. They came to examine me. I laid there flat dead. Wash Irwin got to me there. My right hand was spurting blood; the artery was cut, and the thought struck me that I could not run, I could not get away, and I held my arm up to my breast, and I held it up so that blood got on my breast so it would look like I was shot through the chest somewhere, so he would not shoot me again. I laid there, letting the blood come down on my chest, and they turned me over and examined me. He says, 'He is as dead as he ever will be.' Frank White said, 'Let the damn son-of-a-bitch lie there. He will quit talking.' Then he took my two pistols. I was afraid to wiggle my head, so I lay down there and every once in a while he would reach over there and see the blood spurting, and then he came back down again and turned me over and examined me again, and he said, 'He is as dead as he will ever be.' I lay like a possum again, and he looked at me and examined me again, and then he took my flashlight, my blackjack, my fountain pen, and stuck them in his pockets and went on.

David Sullenberger was also wounded. He confirmed Hugh Taylor's testimony and added, "And when the shooting started, I got hit five times. Mr. Taylor got out of the car door. Mr. Taylor jumped out of the car Some way or other and when he done that, I fell over in the seat like I was dead. I had been hit five times and I was shot from both sides of the car. I was hit on both legs, both arms and through the right shoulder."

The man who was with White and Irwin dragged Sullenberger out of the car and took away his wallet. Sullenberger testified that White "spoke up then and said, 'I ought to shoot you again.'" At that point, a car came along the road and the three gunmen quickly drove away. The passengers in the car took Sullenberger and Taylor to the hospital at Harlan. Later, fearing for their lives, they were transferred to the hospital at Pineville. Hugh Taylor identified the third man as Luke Hubbard.

Wash Irwin had only the following comment to make to the Senate Committee on Taylor's and Sullenberger's testimony, "I ain't got no compliments to say about it."

Irwin and White had taken Hugh Taylor's guns from his apparently lifeless body. They carried the guns back to the chief, Sheriff Middleton, and presented them to him as trophies. Middleton himself described their visit, "Well, sometime after I returned from the hospital, these two men came down to my home and reported on the trouble they had had, and they returned these two 45 automatics over to me there. They said they had taken the two guns from Hugh Taylor." The High Sheriff accepted the pistols and let the culprits go free.

HUGH TAYLOR *showing the La Follette Committee the bullet wounds to his hands.*

Senator La Follette asked Sheriff Middleton, "Have you removed Frank White as a deputy?" And Sheriff Middleton replied, "I have not." Senator La Follette then asked, "Is it your habit to have deputies who have been charged with crimes of violence bound over for trial or appearance before a grand jury, continue to serve as 'peace officers' in your County?"

Mr. Middleton: "I think, as a rule, we do not dismiss an officer or cancel his appointment until he is convicted."

Senator La Follette: "Even though he came to you and surrendered the weapons he had taken off the man who had been shot and left for dead?"

Mr. Middleton: "Yes, sir."

After these events, organizers for the United Mine Workers stayed out of Harlan County. On March 22, 1937, District 19 Vice President "Tick" Arnett went to Frankfort to appeal to Governor Chandler for assistance. With Arnett was Thomas Ferguson, whose shoulder was still bearing a wound from the dumdum bullet fired by Harlan County "road killers." The Governor refused to talk to them. They met with the Adjutant General of Kentucky who, according to Arnett, " advised us that he could not do anything for us in Harlan County unless he was called on by the local authorities up there."

Ferguson blurted out: "It was the local authorities that shot me, the deputy sheriffs . . . They have declared open season on us organizers for the United Mine Workers organization."

The Adjutant General repeated, according to Ferguson: "Well it is strictly up to the local authorities and unless they ask for help, we can do nothing."

The "local authorities" belonged to the Harlan County Coal operators. No help would be forthcoming from Happy Chandler or his henchmen, so the coal miners of Harlan County had to depend solely for help from their union and the Federal Government.

14

The La Follette Committee Sums Up

> *One man, if he will, can do the things most necessary to civilize Harlan County. He is the Governor of Kentucky. They call him "Happy" Chandler.*

It was about this time that I came into Harlan County. What took place then makes up the rest of this true account of "Hell in Harlan." This chapter summarizes briefly a fast moving two years. Written in prosaic "Federalese" prose, it is directly quoted from the report of the LaFollette Civil Liberties Committee.

George J. Titler joined the organizing force January 1, 1937, and was made chief organizer June 1, 1937.

On March 22, 1937, this committee opened its hearings on conditions affecting the civil liberties of citizens in Harlan County. The hearings were concluded on May 5, 1937.

On July 12, 1937, the National Labor Relations Board, by order, permitted District 19 of the United Mine Workers of America to file with it charges under the National Labor Relations Act against the Harlan County Coal Operators' Association and the following companies operating mines in Harlan County:

Harlan Collieries Co., Crummies Creek Coal Co., High Splint Coal Co., Southern Mining Co., Creech Coal Co., R. C. Tway Coal Co., Cornett-Lewis Coal Co., Mary Helen Coal Corp., Mahan-Ellison Coal Corp., Harlan Central Coal Co., Harlan Fuel Co., Bardo Coal Co., Blue Diamond Coal Co., Berger Coal Co., Three Point Coal Corp., Black Mountain Corp., Black Star Coal Co., Clover Splint Coal Co., King Harlan Co., Southern Harlan Coal Co., Elkhorn Piney Coal Mining Co., Clover Fork Coal Co., Harlan Wallins Coal Corp., Kentucky Cardinal Coal Corp., Kentucky King Coal Co., Perkins Coal Co.

On November 27, 1937, the National Labor Relations Board issued a decision and order in the matter of Clover Fork Coal Co., and District 19, United Mine Workers of America. The Board made the following finding with respect to the activities of the Harlan County Coal Operators' Association: "The evidence in the record clearly indicates that one of the major functions of the Association is to exert the combined power of the coal operators of Harlan County against the organization of the mine employees, and to interfere with, restrain, and coerce the workers in the mines of Harlan County in the exercise of their right to self-organization, and to form, join and assist United Mine Workers of America."

The Board struck boldly at the Harlan County Coal Operators' Association and ordered the company to:

> Cease and desist from contributing to, cooperating with, or assisting, through membership therein or otherwise, the Harlan County Coal Operators' Association or any other organization engaged in interfering with, restraining, or coercing its employees in the exercise of the right to self-organization, to form, join or assist labor organizations, to bargain collectively through representatives of their own choosing and to engage in concerted activities for the purpose of collective bargaining or other mutual aid or protection, as guaranteed in Section 7 of the National Labor Relations Act.

In addition the Board ordered the company to reinstate, with back pay, 60 men whom it found to have been unjustly dismissed because of their membership in or activities on behalf of the union.

On June 8, 1938, the Circuit Court of Appeals for the Sixth Circuit upheld the order of the Board in full.

As a result of this decision, the other coal companies of Harlan County, which had not yet abandoned their unyielding attitude toward the union, settled their disputes with the union. On August 19, 1938, the Harlan County Coal Operators' Association signed an agreement with the United Mine Workers extending the terms of the Southern Appalachian contract to the Harlan County Coal Operators' Association. Shortly thereafter a contract similar to the general Appalachian one was signed between District 19 of the United Mine Workers of America and the Harlan County Coal Operators' Association, which was to be effective September 1, 1938. At the same time an agreement was reached between the union and the association whereby members of the association agreed to reinstate a total of 243 men who had been discharged because of union membership and to pay these men varying amounts of back pay, depending on the circumstances of each individual case.

The facts disclosed at the hearings held by this committee resulted in the entry of another Federal agency into Harlan County. The Federal Bureau of Investigation carried on an inquiry for the Department of Justice which on September 27, 1937, resulted in the indictment by the Federal grand jury of the eastern District of Kentucky under section 51, title 18 of the United States Code, for conspiracy to deprive citizens of the United States of rights secured to them by the Constitution and laws of the United States. The defendants indicted consisted of three groups, as follows:

> COMPANY DEFENDANTS: Mary Helen Coal Corp., Harlan Fuel Co., Bardo Coal Mining Co., Berger Coal Mining Co., Black Mountain Corp., Blue Diamond Coal Co., Clover Splint Coal Co., Clover Fork Coal Co., Cornett-Lewis Coal Co., Crummies Creek Coal Co., Harlan Wallins Coal Corp., High Splint Coal Co., Kentucky Cardinal Coal Corp., Mahan-Ellison Coal Corp., Southern Mining Co., R. C. Tway Co., Three Point Coal Corp., Creech Coal Co., Black Star Coal Co., Harlan Collieries Co., Harlan Central Coal Co.Southern Harlan Coal Co.

OPERATOR DEFENDANTS: Silas J. Dickinson, Charles S. Guthrie, George S. Ward, Kenes Bowling, Charles E. Ralston, Elbert J. Ashbury, William H. Sienknecht, Armstrong R. Matthews, Denver B. Cornett, Robert E. Lawson, George Whitfield, Roscoe J. Petrie, Lewis P. Johnson, Pearl Bassham, John E. Taylor, James Campbell Stras, W. Arthur Ellison, Elijah F. Wright, Jr., Robert C. Tway, Elmer D. Hall, Robert W. Creech, Charles B. Burchfield, C. Vester Bennett, Bryan W. Whitfield, Jr.

LAW OFFICER DEFENDANTS: Theodore R. Middleton, Ben Unthank, Brutus Metcalfe, George Lee, John P. Hickey, Frank White, Moses Middleton, Sherman Howard, Lee E. Ball, Earl Jones, Charlie Elliot, Merle Middleton, Ballard Irwin, Avery Hensley, Bob Eldridge, Hugh Taylor, Perry G. Noe, Lee Hubbard, Homer Turner (alias D. Y. Turner), Lee Fleenor, Bill Lewis, Allen Bowlin, Fayette Cox.

On May 16, 1938, the trial of the case was begun in the United States District Court for the Eastern District before Judge H. Church Ford. The case went to the jury on July 30, 1938. On August 1, 1938, the trial ended with a hung jury and the judge declared a mistrial. The case has been set for retrial in the forthcoming May term of the court.

On May 31, 1938, there went into effect a statute adopted by the Kentucky legislature forbidding the appointment of strikebreakers or men with criminal records to the office of deputy sheriff. It prohibited also the private employment of deputy sheriffs.

As a result of these developments, conditions in Harlan County appear to be ameliorated, at least for the present. According to a telegram from George J. Titler, Secretary-Treasurer of District 19 of the U. M. W. in Harlan County, to Senator La Follette, chairman of this committee, dated January 3, 1939, peaceful enjoyment of civil liberties in Harlan County may at last be restored to its residents. The telegram states: "Miners of Harlan County thank you and your Committee for bringing peace to Harlan County. 10,000 men under contract, 2,000 in one local union at Lynch, Ky. U. S. Coal and Coke Company dissolved company union and cooperating fine. This is direct result of your efforts."

After the La Follette hearings were complete, newspapers from coast to coast-started giving Chandler hell. He was caught between a rock and a hard place. The Memphis Press-Scimitar on August 11th, 1937, addressed an editorial, "Spotlight on Kentucky," to Governor Chandler. The editorial said in part:

> One man, if he will, can do the things most necessary to civilize Harlan County. He is the Governor of Kentucky. They call him 'Happy' Chandler.
>
> He has seemed strangely indifferent to what went on in Harlan. But if Governor Chandler cares anything for public opinion, if he has any interest in protecting the good name of his State, he can hardly ignore what the La Follette investigation has brought to national attention.
>
> He can remove the notorious Sheriff Middleton. He can disband that army of company-owned deputies and 'gun thugs.' He can compel the mine owners to obey the laws of Kentucky. He can demand that the courts of Harlan County function honestly. He can give the miners and their families protection against violence and oppression.
>
> The spotlight is centered now on 'Happy' Chandler.

The editor of the Memphis Press-Scimitar received a reply from "Happy" that read in part as follows: "Thank you for your letter of the eleventh. I appreciate the interest in good government which prompts such a message...may I call your attention to the fact that practically all of the acts of violence in Harlan County, which have been so greatly publicized, took place under a previous administration? Whenever called upon by labor leaders or others to provide protection for organizers, I have sent as many members of the highway patrol (the only State constabulary under my control) as have been requested. I need not remind you that all of the representations that have come to your attention are not based on actual facts."

Happy's alibi was puny and did not contain the facts that had been recorded in the official records in blood. It had been less than five months since "Happy" had said Theodore Middleton was a competent, efficient, and energetic Sheriff and had dismissed the charges against him instituted by "Happy's" predecessor, Governor Ruby Laffoon. Cold-blooded murder had been the order of the day in Harlan since "Happy" had taken office.

15

The "Bull of Harlan" Gets to Work

Half an hour after the explosion, two deputies, John Hickey and Frank White, came into the hotel lobby. It was later learned that they were the men who committed the crime. It was also revealed that the bombs came out of the Sheriff's office.

What has been narrated before is entirely based on written, official records. It brings the sad story of Harlan County's downtrodden coal miners to the chronological point where I was assigned to organizing duties in Harlan.

Mentioned earlier was a District 19 convention called by District President William Turnblazer. Its purpose was to plan and organize a renewed campaign to bring the benefits of unionism to the drudges who slaved in Harlan County coal mines.

I was working in Chattanooga, Tennessee, at the time, field man for the UMWA in charge of the coal mine workers in the Sequachia Valley and Tracy City Areas. I asked Bill Turnblazer to assign me to Harlan County. He said he thought I was nuts. He said: "The men who go into Harlan County will probably come out feet first." However, he finally yielded and put Tom Jones in my place in southern Tennessee while I joined the forces in Harlan County.

The convention was an enthusiastic one. The International Union pledged its support through various speakers, including several District officials—Pat Pagan, District 5 (Pittsburgh); William Blizzard, District 17, (Southern West Virginia); William Mitch, District 20 (Alabama); Ed Morgan, District 23, (Western Kentucky); John Saxton, District 28 (Virginia); Sam Caddy, District 30 (Eastern Kentucky); and Fremont Davis, District 31 (Northern West Virginia).

Each of these Districts loaned one or more organizers to work in the drive, which was to be headed by District 19 Vice President "Tick" Arnett. The list of their names almost constituted a UMWA "Who's Who" of that day and time. By Districts, this militant group was: District 2, George Green; District 5, Pete Jackson; District 6, Tom Ferguson (who was shot) and Shorty McIntyre; District 12, Paul K. Reed and Jim Mitchell; District 17, George Blizzard and Millard Cassidy; District 19, L. T. Arnett, Bill Clontz, Marshall Musick and George Titler; District 20, Melton Youngblood; District 23, Matt Bunch, International Representative; District 28, Fred Scroggs; District 30, Frank Hall, Milt Hall and Ted Clark; and District 31, Fred Stubbs and Ray Kelly.

As a first step we planned to load up in cars and go to the forty-eight mining towns in Harlan County to enroll UMWA members. It was mentioned earlier that we were thwarted by a so-called quarantine, which the La Follette Committee believed had been imposed by Harlan County officials to prevent us from holding large-scale organizing rallies. I believe that Committee was one hundred percent right. The County Health Officer, Dr. William P. Cawood, imposed the quarantine. He said there was a polio epidemic but an investigation revealed there were only five polio cases in the entire county. I believe the Harlan County coal operators made a deal with Dr. Cawood, promising their political support for his nephew, Herbert Cawood, a candidate for High Sheriff, in return for a quarantine that would slow up the union's organizing efforts.

Under this edict not more than two people could congregate. The churches and movie houses were closed. The schools were not, nor were the saloons and beer joints, because the Sheriff and his henchmen had a vested interest in the sale of liquor.

All was quiet until January 22, when we moved into the New Harlan Hotel. On that date, we met in one of the hotel rooms until midnight, discussing our plans for the next day. Whatever plans we made were radically changed almost immediately because we had scarcely gotten to sleep when the hotel was tear-gassed. This renewal of the thugs' "reign of terror" has already been mentioned. The La Follette Committee recorded "Tick" Arnett's version of it. I remember it well, myself.

I shared Room 214 with Arnett. He awakened me and said "Buddy, they are dynamiting the hotel." The first thing I heard was a sputtering that sounded like a fuse spitting. I jumped out of bed and ran to the window to see if there was any method of escape, but there was not. It was sixteen feet to a brick-covered alley and no fire escape. Arnett then got his lungs full of smoke and realized it was tear gas. He opened the door and kicked the bomb down the hall. The bomb looked exactly like a torch used to show a dangerous place on the highway, or a mark to show a standing truck at night, but the smoke from the bomb was another thing entirely.

Fifty hotel guests, men, women and children, rushed from the top floors to the lobby. Many of the women were hysterical and crying from the tear gas. The day clerk was sleeping in the hotel and wore a wooden leg. In his hurry to get out of his room and see what was the matter, he got his wooden leg on backward and it wouldn't tract. Shortly McIntyre came out of his room and filled his face with Five Brothers (tobacco). He looked like a chipmunk in chinkapin time. Matt Bunch pulled his trousers on over his nightshirt and looked like a ghost. Melton Youngblood came running out of his room with a Luger in his hand.

Five minutes after the tear gas bombs exploded outside our rooms, two hand grenades were thrown between the fender and the hood of two automobiles parked in front of the hotel across the street from the L & N depot, breaking all the windows in the depot. The two cars, both new, were demolished. One was a Dodge, belonging to Frank Hall; the other a Buick, owned by Milton Hall. The blast sounded like an earthquake.

Half an hour after the explosion, two deputies, John Hickey and Frank White, came into the hotel lobby. It was later learned that they were the men who committed the crime. It was also revealed that the bombs came out of the Sheriffs office.

When Arnett found the bomb, he turned it over to the chief of police, Avery Hensley, who in turn gave it to Sheriff Middleton, who destroyed the bomb so that the evidence could not be used against him. He contended that the bomb was given to the prosecuting attorney to take before the grand jury but the prosecuting attorney denied seeing it.

I was subpoenaed to appear before the grand jury in the matter and Daniel Boone Smith, the prosecuting attorney, was presenting the case to the jury. Hs asked me if I knew what blew up in the cars and I said they were blown up by hand grenades. He asked me how I knew and I told him I had used them in the army. Parts of the outside of the grenades were picked up on the street.

Anyone appearing before the grand jury could see that Attorney Smith was not interested in indicting anyone. He seemed intent on whitewashing the matter, if possible, which was exactly what happened.

After this whitewash, we were unable to operate from headquarters in Harlan County. Some of us worked out of Pineville, Bell County, while others lived at Pennington Gap, Virginia. Sheriff Middleton had told the boss thug, Ben Unthank, that it was "open season on union organizers." Their thuggery immediately proceeded at an accelerated pace, acts of violence coming thick and fast until the La Follette Committee moved in. The list of violent acts below, all of which have been described earlier, shows just how frenzied the operators' thugs became in their campaign to destroy the UMWA:

January 31—Marshall Musick and his wife ambushed at Lejunior, Kentucky.

February 6—Polio quarantine lifted by Dr. Cawood.

February 7—Young Bennett Musick murdered by killers who were paid $100 each by Ben Unthank.

February 8—Tom Ferguson wounded and three cars shot full of holes when deputies ambushed UMWA organizers near Verda.

February 20—Hugh Taylor and Dave Sollenberger shot, robbed and left for dead by Frank White and Wash Irwin.

April 24—Lloyd Clouse murdered by Bill Lewis to prevent him from testifying before the La Follette Committee or in court.

From March 22 until April 9, little organizing was done in Harlan because both organizers and operators were in Washington testifying before the La Follette Committee. On April 21st, President Turnblazer called me to Jellico and told me that the ordeal in Harlan had made a nervous wreck of "Tick" Arnett. The tear gas in the hotel had also seriously affected the lungs of Melton Youngblood, who never saw another well day. However, he stayed on until the county was organized.

Bill Turnblazer gave me a check for $3,000 to establish a payroll and told me to go into Harlan County, establish headquarters, pick up half a dozen local organizers, and go to work. I hired Bob Hodge, Matt Hollars and Bob Owens, all from Morley, Tennessee, and Virgil Hampton, Ed Beane and Jim Westmoreland. Hampton and Beane were from Black Mountain and Westmoreland was from Big Stone Gap, Virginia. Matt Bunch stayed on with us.

We established headquarters in the Turner Building in Evarts. This building covered a whole triangular block with a road all the way around it. (The Turner Building served as part of the fortress in the battle of Evarts in 1931.) Evarts is an incorporated town. The Chief of Police, Floyd Lewis, a coal miner, was prounion. He deputized all organizers as city police. Every night from midnight until morning, one man stood guard watching out of the windows on each side of the building to see that no one blew it up.

We were there just a few days when we saw a young fellow riding into town one night with gun thug Frank White. When he got out of the car, we saw that he was drunk and had four sticks of dynamite and some fuses and caps in his pocket. The city police picked him up and threw him in jail for intoxication and Ed Blue, a union coal miner from Black Mountain, was put in jail with him to see what he could find out. Because he had come to town with Frank White, we supposed that his intentions were not honorable.

The story the boy told was that he worked at the Cook & Sharp mine at Shields; that the commissary closed at five o'clock in the evening and it did not open until after he went to work in the morning. He said he needed the dynamite for a rock shot and after he bought the dynamite, he decided to come to Evarts, so he brought the dynamite with him. I think the boy's story was correct because in those days in Harlan County, miners had to purchase with their own money explosives used in their work.

The next morning I met Bryan Middleton on the streets of Evarts. In spite of the fact that he was Theodore Middleton's brother, he was friendly to the union. He asked me: "Why don't you keep that fellow in jail?" I said: "We have nothing on him. We must turn him loose." Bryan then made me an offer. "I'll hire you a witness," he said.

That was the first time I had a proposition made to me to suborn perjury. Witnesses could be hired for five or ten dollars to testify to anything you wanted. I was shocked by his statement and so told him. This was just an example of how men were "railroaded" in Harlan County by the Sheriff and his deputies when they wanted them out of the County. They could hire a witness to testify to anything they wanted. Another gimmick was to plant moonshine whiskey in a car, get a search warrant to search the car and send the owner to jail for moonshining or handling moonshine liquor.

Three days after we had established headquarters in Evarts, Virge Hampton and Ed Beane reported to me that they had organized all the mines on the Clover Fork and on Yokum's Creek above Evarts, and set up local unions. They had organized Gaino, PVK, Cook & Sharp, Bergers, High Splint, Louellen, Clover Splint and Woods. To get into these camps, they had to avoid such thugs as Bob Eldridge, Frank White, Lee Ball, Wash Irwin and a dozen others, including Ben Unthank and his road runners.

We held a big rally the following Sunday in an orchard at the same spot where Peggy Dwyer had a meeting shot up three years before. About five thousand men, women and children turned out to hear the speeches. In order to keep the place from being shot up, we sent miners into the mountains overlooking the meeting place, with high-powered rifles and shotguns, to stop any thugs who might try to repeat what had been done to Peggy Dwyer earlier. We intended to stop them before they got started. While I was speaking at the rally, our men on the mountain made themselves visible on top of some large rocks. Some of the women panicked until they were told they were union men, placed there for our protection.

A few days later, Earl Houck and T. C. Townsend, United Mine Workers attorneys, came to Evarts on legal business for the organization and asked us where the thugs were. I told Ed Beane and Virge Hampton to show them around and as they left the office, they were followed by two carloads of deputies. They were not stopped, but when they returned to our office, they jokingly said the Sheriff made sure they were well protected.

Another thing we had to overcome in our organizing drive was the accusation by our enemies, who constantly depicted us as red-necked Communists, atheists, and everything else that was distasteful to the Mountaineers' code. But we overcame this. We had in our group four ministers of the Gospel, and as we billed our mass meetings, the circulars used in advertising the meetings always announced the speakers as Reverend Matt Bunch, or Reverend Matt Hollars, or Reverend Marshall Musick or Reverend William Clontz.

In one meeting at Lynch, we advertised all four of these preachers as speakers. It was very effective and spoiled the propaganda that the union organizers were evil men. In fact, it drove them nuts. One of our circulars read as follows:

TO THE MINERS OF BENHAM AND LYNCH ORGANIZATION CAMPAIGN UNDER NEW MANAGEMENT

By orders of the International Officers of the United Mine Workers of America, the organization of Benham and Lynch has been turned over to International Representatives Matt Bunch and George J. Titler, who have been in charge of organizing the commercial mines of Harlan County, under the jurisdiction of District No. 19. An entire change in policy will be inaugurated and the policies of the International and District Organizations will be carried out to the letter.

Local unions at both Benham and Lynch will start holding secret meetings and a new tabulation of our membership will be taken. If you are in favor of a bona fide Labor Union, join the UMW of A.

The personnel of the new organizing staff will be: Rev. R. A. Music, Rev. Wm. Clontz, Rev. Matt Bunch, and others who are well-known and highly respected by the people of the community.

If you have not joined this great organization, get in touch with Matt Bunch and his bunch of organizers who will explain the principles and benefits of the world's largest and greatest labor organization.

The only bona fide collective bargaining agency for the coal miners of America.

Get on the band wagon of the union that has brought 7 hour day, 35 hour week, time and a-half for overtime and 200 percent increase in wages to 97 percent of the coal miners in America in the last 4 years.

WILLIAM TURNBLAZER, President of District No. 19

GEORGE J. TITLER, International Representative in charge of Organization in Harlan County.

Too much credit could not be given to these four preacher-organizers, Marshall Musick, a Missionary Baptist; Matt Hollars from the Church of God; William Clontz, a Methodist, and Matt Bunch, a Presbyterian. Each one preached a different religious doctrine but all preached the same union doctrine. These men had a way of blending the emoluments of collective bargaining with the spiritual benefits of being a Christian. The Missionary Baptist teachings of Marshall Musick and the Church of God's version of Matt Hollars appealed to me most strongly. They preached short sermons. Bill Clontz was too long-winded. William Turnblazer said of Clontz: "Never expect to hear all of Clontz' sermon if you are going to catch a train."

A. T. Pace was making the arrangements for a convention banquet in Middlesboro in 1936. He reported to Turnblazer that he had a problem—if he asked Clontz to speak, he would talk too long, and if he didn't, Clontz would be offended. Turnblazer suggested that they call on Clontz to ask the blessing. Clontz prayed so long that the food got cold. Yet it was strange how some of our members thrived on long speeches. After Clontz talked for two hours, they would holler for more. Clontz missed his calling—he should have been a United States Senator. He was a natural for a filibuster.

Matt Bunch, an ordained Presbyterian minister, came from a different bread of cats. Matt was long, tall and lean, and smooth as a school marm's elbow. He married Laura Smiddy when they were both kids and had a large, fine family. They were inseparable. When the campaign started and we (seven men) moved into the Turner Building on the square in Evarts, Matt and Laura moved into an apartment close by, also owned by the Turners. When a wave of terror would break out and it became necessary to stand guard at night, Mrs. Bunch stood guard with a shotgun while Matt slept.

Matt was the only preacher on the staff who always packed a gun and a Bible. When he was not making organizing speeches, or in the pulpit preaching the Gospel, he was doing missionary work attempting to convert some heathen like me.

One evening we were going down the Cumberland River from Harlan to Wallins Creek to relieve an organizer who was trapped by some thugs. I was carrying a shotgun, Matt a 38 Colt. As we traveled along the road at sixty miles an hour, Matt proceeded to give me a lecture on how I was neglecting my spiritual life. In fact, he told me I was plumb wicked. What Matt was telling me was probably the truth, but I was a trifle nervous, heading into a probable gunfight, and his advice did not appeal to me at that time.

I said to Matt: "What are you going to do if we get into a fight and you are forced to kill a thug in self defense? You go around with a Bible in one pocket and a pistol in another. If you are forced to kill a thug, you will sit down on a stump and search your Bible for a way to justify your deed. If that happens, and I was you, Matt, I would search in the Old Testament. You might find something comforting under the Mosaic Law." Matt never converted me but at least he started me thinking in a different direction. Some day his preaching might bear fruit.

Once when Matt was addressing a large mass meeting on Sunday at Evarts, I was out mingling with the crowd, attempting to find out how effective his talk was, and I asked Luke Slavey and Dewey Hensley what they thought of it. Dewey said: "That's a damn good sermon" and Luke said: "He is a hell of a good preacher."

These four preachers, along with Virgil Hampton, Ed Beane, Jim Westmoreland, George Gilbert, Bob Hodge and Melton Youngblood, were all dedicated men who had decided to give the miners of Harlan County an opportunity to be free. They valued the union as greater than their own lives. They had all worked in the mines under the mailed fist and the Iron heel of the feudal barons.

Matt Bunch always contended that the organization of Harlan County was under Divine Guidance because in eighteen months, no mass meeting was ever rained out. Mass meetings were held on every Sunday. This is the record. It always rained in Harlan on the Sunday we held a mass meeting in Black Star, and vice versa. Or so it seemed.

The organization grew by leaps and bounds. Around May 1st, the organizers went to work on the mines between Evarts and Harlan. They did well except at the Brookside and Kitts mines, which were owned by the Whitfield family. We organized the large mine at Verda owned by Harlan Wallins Coal Corporation. The general manager there was the now famous, or infamous, Pearl Bassham. Pearl had had his claws clipped in Washington by Senator La Follette and his thugs were not so vicious as they had been previously.

When we started up Martins Fork and Caterns Creek, we first came to the Elcombs mine run by an obese MD by the name of Doctor Buttermore. He liked the Union like a bee likes vinegar. A thug named George Shepherd guarded the bridge across the creek. When we got to Tway, we found the gate guarded by other thugs: Russ Collins, Tom Gibson, Lee Fleenor, and at Mary Hellen was "Big Ugly" glass-eyed Earl Jones who had the disposition of a gila monster. In the neighborhood of Lenarue and Crummies Creek, the organizers would encounter D. Y. Turner. Early in 1938, George Shepherd killed Turner. The organizers regarded this as progress—one bad thug less to deal with. Shepherd was acquitted. He pleaded self-defense.

Our headquarters in the Turner Building had two large rooms, one of which was used for an office. In the other room where the organizers slept were seven army cots. The first three and a half months in Harlan, no union organizer was allowed to carry a gun or a jack knife although it was not against Kentucky law to carry a gun, as long as you did not conceal it. We had been an unarmed platoon. This was to change.

16

A Gun For Every Man

> *These crooks in Harlan County were cowards and were reluctant to get into a gunfight with anyone and would never start trouble unless they had the odds in numbers in their favor. They preferred bushwhacking.*

We soon came to the conclusion that we could not fight convicts with powder puffs and kind words. We decided to carry guns in accordance with the laws of Kentucky, and every man was allowed to carry a pistol so that he could face as an equal the convicts parading as minions of the law. Our men were instructed that if the thugs attempted to stop them in the lawful pursuit of their duties, they were to meet force with force, but that they should use their guns only in self-defense. This also was a deterrent to bushwhacking. We called George Ward, secretary of the operators association, and warned him that the organizers were armed and intended to defend themselves when necessary. However, no one asked Turnblazer's approval of the change for fear of a veto.

Men who were hired as organizers were hired for their courage as well as for their ability to organize. Only one man on the force, Matt Hollars refused to bear arms. Matt was a Holiness preacher who had plenty of courage but depended on accomplishing his end by passive resistance and by preaching the Gospel as he went. Matt fit into the picture very well. He was absolutely fearless and went anywhere he pleased in the county and was not molested. We had observed that most of these crooks in Harlan County were cowards and were reluctant to get into a gunfight with anyone and would never start trouble unless they had the odds in numbers in their favor. They preferred bushwhacking.

We organized Verda and bought a hall along the highway just outside the camp. Every time we had a local union meeting, the hall was filled with from three to four hundred miners. Harlan-Wallins employed seven hundred fifty men at Verda.

In 1934, an incident occurred in the Hazard coalfield of Eastern Kentucky that returned to haunt me and UMWA organizers at Verda. At that time the reckless mountain men from Hazard began to flex their muscles. They began to realize the strength of the union. They had been plagued or harassed for years by a company doctor who, in their opinion, was a quack. After the field was organized, the mine committee at one of the mines in the Hazard field notified this company doctor to leave town because the men wanted to hire a real doctor. (Before the union was organized, the company hired the doctor and the men paid him.) He refused to obey and some one, or a group of men, placed a cow bell around his neck on a chain, put a padlock on it and told him to cross the mountain and never come back. The coal operators in the Hazard field, who also controlled the press, turned the incident into a national calamity. The same operators who had no compunction about hiring a man killed, used the newspapers to make the belling of the doctor a national scandal. This incident was a joke among coal miners all over eastern Kentucky for many years and was often talked about.

As the miners of Harlan County began to grow in strength, they occasionally became over-anxious to break their shackles and wanted everything done over night. Members of the Verda local union bought four cowbells and short chains and locked them to the seats in the local union hall. They said they had no intention of putting cowbells on anyone who did not join the union but only used them as a means of applauding when a speaker made a good point. I went to the hall one night and it was crowded. Much to my surprise, when I started talking I was applauded not only by human hands, but also by these four cow bells. The noise was deafening. I remember it as the greatest burst of applause ever given me anywhere. Pearl Bassham heard about this through some stooge he planted in the local union, and the next day deputies Lee Fleenor, Allen Bowling and Charles Elliott with Perry G. Noe, broke down the doors in the hall and tore the cowbells off the seats and arrested the officials of the local union. A week later I was indicted by the grand jury, charged with banding and confederating, and it was alleged that the cowbells were brought in to be put around the necks of the company officials and those of our own miners who violated the union rules.

I had been on fairly good terms with Pearl Bassham for about two weeks, so I went to see him. I told him what I thought of his under-handed action of having deputy sheriffs raid the hall and take the cowbells. He declared that he had nothing to do with it and to prove it he would bail the men out of jail. Their bail was $1,600. He told Ray Cornett, company clerk, to go to the company store, get $1,600 and give it to me to take down to put up as bond. I refused to do this, but Cornett went with me and put up the bond with Judge Ball, the County Judge. Ball at first refused to take the $1,600 because he said he had no safe strong enough to hold that much money; that if some of the thugs found out it was there, they would blow the safe and he would be holding the sack for the bond. However, he finally took the money and deposited it in the bank. The local union officials were then released.

On April 1, 1938 the cow bell case came up for trial. On April 2, the Knoxville News Sentinel carried the following story:

> The jury today acquitted all of the "belling" charges. They were John Gross, Henry Gross, Pearl Pace and George Savior. A directed verdict of acquittal was ordered by Judge Gilbert for George Titler, International Representative of the UMWA, in charge of Harlan County activities,

and Lee Mitchell. They have been accused of plotting with others at Verda to chain cowbells around the necks of nonunion miners or rule violators. The court declared there was no evidence to connect Titler and Mitchell with the others. Attorney James Golden arguing for the defendants charged there is somebody in back of this case, feeding money into the prosecution of these union men because they are members of a legal organization. He termed the bells as innocent reminders of liberty and charged the deputy sheriffs had raided the hall and confiscated the bells, chains and locks and then framed a case against the defendants. Joe B. Snyder, attorney for the prosecution, argued that it was a queer thing that the chains they declare represented unionism and liberty were but just the right length to go around a man's neck.

The success of our organizers in Harlan County became a topic of interest to many newspapers. A lady reporter, representing the Louisville Courier-Journal, came to my office to get the facts for a story about our success in organizing a large part of Harlan County in just a few weeks. She came into the office unannounced and, while she was there, the organizers kept reporting in. As they came in they unstrapped their gun belts and threw them on the beds. Rifles and shotguns were hanging on the walls. The following Sunday, the Courier-Journal rotogravure section featured pictures of mine workers headquarters and "arsenal" at Evarts. This was a great help to us because the Courier-Journal is widely read in Harlan County and all of the thugs could see what they would be up against if they came looking for trouble.

While the story written was not very complimentary to the organizers, it was certainly an asset to the organization as a deterrent to violence by the deputy sheriffs. This seemed to me to be proof of the theory that if we, as a nation, are prepared, we are not so apt to be attacked—that prepared-ness brings peace. It was certainly true in Harlan County.

17

Organizing Benham and Lynch

> *By July 1937, organizing was progressing in Harlan County, progressing so well in fact that several abortive attempts were made to murder me.*

Our next step was to organize the mines from Harlan town to the Bell County line. This was done in very short order. The organizers were then recalled and began to organize from Harlan town to the head of Martins Fork and Catrons Creek. This job was simple. When we got to the United States Coal and Coke Company's mine, at Lynch, we knew management had set up a company union, the Union of Lynch Employees. Bill Hollins, president of the organization, and a company stooge, headed this organization. He was a big, six-foot-two, hillbilly from Clay County, Kentucky, with plenty of courage and not much gray matter.

The organizing of Benham and Lynch was at that time under the jurisdiction of UMWA, District 30, who sent a crew of organizers in there to sign up the employees. The working conditions at Benham and Lynch were better than the other part of Harlan County and it was, therefore, more difficult to organize the miners. They had already begun making good money and working shorter hours. Of course, our efforts in other sections were responsible for the better pay and hours.

District 30 called for an NLRB election at Benham and lost by thirty-one votes out of about four hundred. They were about to demand an election at Lynch (because District 30 President Sam Caddy had been advised by his organizers that two-thirds of the men had signed United Mine Workers membership cards.) Bill Turnblazer asked me to make a survey. I did and reported back to him that if an election were held, it would probably be lost just as at Benham. I was then instructed by Turnblazer to file an unfair labor practice charge against the United States Coal and Coke Company. U. S. Steel did not know what we had for a hole card and apparently became worried.

During the time we were trying to organize Lynch, U. S. Steel threw every roadblock possible in our way. For instance, they used the Union of Lynch Employees as a front to try to stop the UMW organization at this mine. Sheriff Middleton sent them a little red-cherub-faced deputy by the name of Dan Cloud, about twenty-five years old, who worked around Lynch exclusively. His greatest stock in trade was planting moonshine whiskey in union men's cars. He would then have some one get a search warrant, search the cars and throw the owners in jail. Many a union man working in the mines at Lynch was arrested for bootlegging and moonshining through Dan Cloud's efforts.

Another man U. S. Steel used was a fellow who worked in the Lynch mine, part of the time as a classified worker and at other times as a boss. His name was Preacher Johnson. Preacher Johnson had been a deputy sheriff for Theodore Middleton, and also for John Henry Blair. He was a big, ugly, sandy-haired fellow who looked something like a gorilla and who could not be trusted as far as you could throw a bull by the tail. Many a man was beaten up and kicked around in the Lynch camp by this so-called preacher. Johnson apparently was getting his advice and orders from somebody at the head of the United States Coal and Coke Company police force.

A boy by the name of Elbert Witt, who was discharged at Lynch because he was helping to organize for the union, was put on the organizing force and sent to Lynch to line up the people he had worked with. Witt was a courageous individual who would go any place, regardless of the danger, in order to contact mine workers.

The slowest group of people at Lynch to join the union was Negro miners who had been imported to Lynch, mostly from Alabama. When U. S. Steel recruited these colored coal miners from Alabama, it thought they couldn't be organized, but it was our experience in Harlan County that the best stickers we had, after they were organized, were the colored men. They would not worry about getting fired as long as they had assurance that there would be corn bread and beans furnished them by the organization.

While working with these people, Witt had arranged a party, or a dance, at the home of Amanda Davis, wife of a union miner. The organizers furnished the music and refreshments. Everybody was having a good time and Elbert Witt was signing up cards right and left when Dan Cloud and Preacher Johnson came into the hall and pulled guns. They claimed they had a search warrant for moonshine liquor. Several shots were fired and a bullet grazed Witt's head and knocked him to the floor. While he was on the floor, he shot and killed Johnson. The case was tried in Harlan County before a jury brought in from Wayne County. Witt was acquitted because the coroner's evidence was to the effect that the bullet that killed Johnson ranged upward and hit him in the stomach. The proof was that Witt was lying on the floor, after being knocked down by Johnson's bullet, and fired at the latter from a lying position. The case was tried on April 6, 1938, and Amanda Davis, a co-defendant, was also acquitted.

Lynch was then a town of more than ten thousand persons, 4,500 of who were employed in the U. S. Steel mining operation. As stated above, the company used all of its power to try to beat the union down. On our part, we had to use every ounce of our strength to fight back and to organize its men who were of almost every conceivable creed and color. Among our greatest strengths were the rank-and-file members working for union organization. I remember two men particularly.

One was a colored moderator of the Baptist church whom I hired to help to organize his congregation. He went to a Sunday mass meeting in Lynch and when he came back he was so high he could not hit the ground with a handful of shot. I bawled him out for getting high and said: "You are a fine Baptist. You cannot organize church people with your snoot full." He replied: "Brother George, you don't know what you are talking about. You just don't know your Baptists. They have no faith in anyone who does not take a little nip."

The second was the man who became president of the Lynch local union, Hamp C. Wooten. He was a small motorman in the mine with the strength and courage of a wolverine. He furnished strong leadership to our largest local union for two years. In addition to this, he gave us yeomen service in other parts of the County. He later engineered the building of the Lynch local union hall that was dedicated January 1, 1940.

U. S. Steel was not the only company operating in Harlan County using the subterfuge of company unionism to fight the UMWA. Other Harlan County coal operators had found it legally dangerous to use killers to stop union organization so they held a meeting and decided to organize as many company unions as possible. Lynch had already organized the Union of Lynch Employees; Wisconsin Steel, at Benham, formed the Benham Employees Association; Harlan Central, at Totts, formed the Poor Fork Employees Association (with only twelve members); Harlan Fuel Company, at Yancy, formed the Yancy Workmen's Association; another company union was formed at Cardinal Coal Company, near the Harlan-Bell County line; and the Insul Employees Association, at Insul, in Bell County.

Kitts and Brookside, of the Whitfield Company, outsmarted themselves. Instead of forming company unions, they hired Red Anderson, a renegade machine runner, to form what they called an anti-union group. This group struck against working with union men. After the strike, the company bought them six kegs of beer as a reward for the demonstration. This was later revealed in the National Labor Relations Board hearings.

U. S. Steel seemed for a time to become almost deranged in its efforts to use the company union system to break the United Mine Workers. On June 18, 1937, the Union of Lynch Employees staged a rally at Lynch with W. F. Corn, chairman of the company union's board of directors, as principal speaker. All other company union members in Harlan County were invited to attend the "picnic," Corn made an immoderate attack on the CIO and its "six hundred international unions" which he said were trying to impose "Red Russian leadership on American Workers." He alleged that the UMWA was behind this so-called movement in spite of the fact that the UMWA had long denied the privilege of membership to communists. Other speakers at this rally were W. B. Russell, Gus Moister, Harvest Goodgame, R. H. Lock of the Lynch company union, and Swamp John, a Negro clown from Benham.

All reports as to membership in these company unions were inflated. For instance, it was said that the following representations were present at the June rally: Benham Employees' Association, three hundred; Yancy Workmen's Association, two hundred; Insull Employees Association, one hundred. The true figures were much lower. The companies also made much of the fact that company unions had 3,100 members in Harlan County while the United Mine Workers had only 1,500.

Whatever the membership figures may have been, it is true the Harlan operators worked hard to form company unions and most of them were successful in coercing at least some of the men to join. In addition to those already mentioned, a company union was set up at Louellen, with a man named Van Cupp as president. The High-Lo Association, at High-splint, was organized for the company by a fellow, imported from Illinois, named George Hudson. All but one of these phony organizations was short-lived, however.

The National Labor Relations Board soon stepped in and conducted hearings on company unionism in Harlan County.

Evidence showed they were clearly under control of management and in violation of Federal law. A July 19 hearing at Pineville, Kentucky, brought out the fact that employees of the Straight Creek Coal Company were asked by company officials to join something called the Southern Miners Union. In a hearing at Yancy, Charles Guthrie admitted that his company brought in strip teasers from out of the County to entertain the employees attending company union meetings. He stated the show cost $100. With the company paying half and the Yancy Employees Association paying the other half.

The operators often made headlines in their attempts to defend company unions, at NLRB hearings, but they lost anyhow. In one Labor Board Hearing, where Cleo K. Calvert was the defense attorney, Calvert came into the hearing room walking with his gold-headed cane. He needed it. He was weaving from side to side. Both he, and his court reporter, a middle-aged widow, were higher than a Georgia Pine. However, he made newspaper headline by accusing the Union of putting $500,000 in President Roosevelt's campaign in 1936 and by alleging that the Department of Justice and the National Labor Relations Board were now paying a political debt by harassing the Harlan operators.

He also accused the Delano family, relatives of President Roosevelt, of owning controlling interest in the Kentenna Land Company (which owned coal lands in Harlan County leased to certain of the Harlan operators). Leonard Shore and Charles Ryan were attorneys for the Labor Board. After listening to Calvert's harangue for twenty minutes, Shore moved that the hearing be recessed until Calvert sobered up, and it was so ordered by the trial examiner, Mr. J. G. Ewell.

All of these company unions amounted to about as much as a snowball in perdition. In almost every case, before the National Labor Relations Board got through with the hearings, the operator had admitted under oath that it had a hand in organizing the independent union as a deterrent to the organization by the Union Mine Workers of America. Except the company union at Benham, all were ordered to dissolve. In order to keep from being considered illegitimate, they affiliated with the Progressive Miners of Illinois. While the illegitimate child was given a name, it still continued to function as a company union.

U. S. Steel could see the handwriting on the wall. When District 19 filed the unfair labor practice charge against the United States Coal & Coke Company, Harry Moses came to Lynch and called my office, saying he wanted to get in touch with Matt Bunch. Bunch had worked for him, as a cutting machine operator, in Illinois when Moses had been a superintendent at the Bunsonville, Illinois, mine. When the two men got together, Moses asked Bunch to get in touch with Bill Turnblazer, saying he was ready to sign a contract.

We met in the hotel in Middlesboro, Kentucky, and Moses signed a contract with the United Mine Workers for its membership at Lynch. He signed the same contract with the Union of Lynch Employees for the members that it had signed up. This was September 17, 1937.

At that time both organizations had about the same number of members. However, as soon as the contracts had been signed, members of the Union of Lynch Employees started flocking to the United Mine Workers until our membership was double that of the company union. Then Bill Hollins, of the company union sent word to me, through Mike Carroll, labor relations man for U. S. Steel, that he would like to liquidate the Union of Lynch Employees. He said he would recommend to his membership that they join the United Mine Workers. We reached an agreement with Hollins and he went to his local union and notified the men that they were dissolving the company union. He recommended that everybody join the United Mine Workers. When I left Harlan January 1, 1941 I took a transfer card from Lynch Local Union 7425. It had become the largest local union in the United Mine Workers of America, with approximately 3,400 members.

The operators' company unions drive and its eventual failure did not mean the complete repudiation of thuggery and murder. Activity in this field was merely quieter for a brief period of time.

A symptom of this was the attitude of County Judge Morris Saylor, who began to court the UMWA after he had won the nomination for County Judge on the Republican ticket. This "new look" was not caused by any love for the union, however, but by dissension and murder within the ranks of the thugs themselves. The murdered man was the notorious Wash Irwin. His buddies feared that his loose tongue and heavy drinking would land all of them in the clink. He was "taken for a ride" in typical Harlan County fashion. A carload of deputies, with jugs, decided to ride to the top of Pine Mountain, where radio reception was better, to listen to the broadcast of a heavyweight championship fight. Irwin, who was in the front seat, was plugged through the right ear by one of the men in the back seat. Deputy Perry G. Noe was charged with the murder, and Judge Saylor discharged him as deputy sheriff. In addition to Noe, he also released Leonard Creech and Roy Metcalf. Two other deputies, Henry Metcalf and John Hickey, resigned to protest at this "injustice."

To replace the discharged deputies, Saylor appointed six men to the County patrol—William Clontz, Melton Youngblood, Robert Hodge, George Green, E. C. Mullins and Sam Brown. All except Brown were members of the United Mine Workers. The naming of five members of my organizing staff in the County patrol gave us additional protection, but did not disguise Saylor's true feelings. He kept on many deputy sheriffs who were operators' thugs, stating that some of them were good officers, whose services were an asset to Harlan County. In addition, he feared for his life, a fear so strong that he asked for protection of the State Police during his purge of the deputy sheriffs. A three-man detail headed by Clyde Jones was assigned by the State to guard Judge Saylor's office.

By July 1937, organizing was progressing in Harlan County, progressing so well in fact that several abortive attempts were made to murder me. Someone paid two brothers, by the name of Huskey, living at Evarts, to assassinate me for $700. The boys took the money and went over to St. Charles, Virginia. After they loaded their cars with shotguns, rifles, and pistols, they proceeded to get intoxicated. They were picked up by the State Police and given a year in the penitentiary for having an arsenal in their car. It is quite obvious that I was sitting in the lap of Lady Luck because while the Huskey boys did not know me, they would certainly have tried to carry out their mission if given the right opportunity. The year incarceration they received in the State of Virginia probably saved my life.

A little later in the year, we learned through the grapevine that another attempt was going to be made on my life, and the life of an organizer named George Gilbert. This time the payoff was to be $2,500. The job was to be done by Lee Fleenor. Fleenor had been convicted and sentenced to fifteen years in the penitentiary for killing a deputy sheriff named Bige Howard on the courthouse steps in 1934. However, he spent only a few months in the penitentiary and was then paroled. As soon as he got out of the penitentiary, he was appointed deputy sheriff. Prior to the killing of Bige Howard, he was credited with killing two men who were in a soup line on the outskirts of Harlan for no apparent reason. No one ever was indicted or tried for these killings although it was shown the victims were doing nothing more than standing in a line waiting for something to eat.

In July 1938 when Fleenor was on his way from a hearing in London, Kentucky, he shot and killed Charles Reno who had killed Fleenor's father and had served time in the penitentiary for doing so. When I got the information that Lee Fleenor would probably be the triggerman, I went to Frankfort to see Happy Chandler. Chandler said: "He should be in the penitentiary anyhow. Ever since he has been on probation or parole, they have used him as a deputy sheriff in Harlan County and he has continued his murderous ways. I will send the State Police down to pick him up and put him back in the penitentiary where he belongs." Fleenor was picked up at Tways where he was serving as a deputy sheriff or a watchman. When they picked him up, he was carrying two pearl handled .38 pistols in shoulder holsters.

Joe Allen and Carl Scott were then hired to bump us off. These two men had seven killings as a part of their record. Allen had been convicted by the Harlan County Court and sentenced to life imprisonment for murder and had served one year in the Harlan jail while waiting a decision by the Kentucky Court of Appeals. The court granted him a new trial on a writ of error. The Commonwealth Attorney and Circuit Judge decided not to try him again and turned him loose.

After Allen and Scott had been paid half of the bounty ($1,250) they went to Brookside, along with a section foreman named Sizemore, to enlist the help of Lee Hubbard. A quarrel ensued between the conspirators and Allen and Scott were killed with a blast of buckshot. $1,250 was found in Allen's pocket. The next morning Lee Hubbard gave himself up and pleaded self-defense. He was put under a $5,000 bond. At a preliminary hearing, Hubbard was turned loose by the court. These were the murder attempts that I knew about. There may have been others.

It was during this period in the early summer of 1937, that I got a call from Elmer Hall, coal operator at Three Point, inviting Mrs. Titler and me to Three Points for a conference. Hall was one of the friendly minority members of the Harlan County Coal Operators' Association, and he did not like the vicious policy of the Association. He abhorred violence but could not do anything about it. He was one of those who had tipped me off to the attempts on my life.

When we got to Three Point he told me that the coal operators and thugs were speculating as to whether I was brave or dumb. He said he thought I was too dumb to know the danger I was in else I would leave the county.

Before we left Three Point, about ten o'clock p.m., he traded pistols with me. He traded me Bill Randolph's pistol, a .44 pearl-handled Colt, for a .38 Special. After we had traded, he gave the .38 special to Mrs. Titler. I did not know it at the time but I found out later that the .44 Colt, according to legend, had been used to kill five men. A superintendent at Three Point had shot and killed his wife and himself with it. This entitled the pistol to seven notches. I decided the gun carried a curse and decided to get rid of it. I gave it away and it eventually wound up in the hands of Hugh Jones who used it in an attempt to kill Merle Middleton. Instead of killing Merle Middleton, Jones killed Ernest Rose by mistake. Jones, a restaurant owner, and his father, John Jones, were charged with the crime. It was assumed that Hugh Jones, who carried a .38 pistol, had shot Rose with his father's .44 but John Jones was released after ballistic experts found Rose had not been shot with John Jones' .44. Hugh Jones was tried and acquitted.

After his acquittal, I asked him if he had killed Ernest Rose and he told me the following story:

> I had decided to kill Merle Middleton and I met Claude Benfield on the street carrying the Bill Randolph .44. I asked to borrow it and he agreed. It was snowing a little and I was following Merle Middleton but somehow I got off his trail and started following Rose, a man about the same build and dressed like Middleton. I shot Rose at the bus depot, and there I found I had shot the wrong man. I went to the State Police and offered to give myself up but was advised not to do so. A State Policeman, a close friend of mine, emptied the cartridges from the gun and threw them in the commode and kept the gun.

The gun with a curse had killed for the eighth time. I think the incident upset Jones psychologically. He became restless and was killed two years later in a gunfight with a tavern keeper in Middlesboro, Kentucky.

18

Elections and Harlan Democracy

> *Yes, life was cheap in Harlan. Using the Klondike massacre as a yardstick, you could figure that one human life equalled twelve-and-a-half votes.*

Earlier in this book I described "Harlan County justice" as defined by the La Follette Civil Liberties Committee. It was pointed out that most coal miners lived in company towns and were forced to depend upon elected county officials for what little protection they received under the law. The manner in which these officials were elected during my stay there could be made into a college textbook with the title *How to Steal Elections*. Every necessary method was used. Both political parties were guilty and practices instituted by the Harlan coal operators forced their opposition to use similar unsavory methods. What follows is a partial record of an unbelievable era, but which is made up of incidents I know of personally and can prove.

For instance, at Mary Hellen in 1937, the same man cast four hundred twenty-two votes in one precinct. This was revealed when the election was contested and Judge Sanders E. Clay, a special judge brought in from the Bluegrass section to decide the contest, ordered a hearing. The proven testimony on the Mary Hellen incident was that the company clerk had cast the votes of everybody on the election roster the night before and put them in the ballot box, and that no election was held at Mary Hellen on election day because all the bonafide ballots were thrown away. The company clerk had an odd way of making an "x." A hook was put on the end of each "x" and all of the ballots were marked in this exact way. The election records also showed that voters had been voted alphabetically.

At other places in the county, voters were brought and "chain ballots" were run. Four organizers went to Molus to help with the election and found Sheriff Theodore Middleton back of the commissary running a chain ballot. This was done by giving a man a ballot already marked and having him put it in the ballot box. He then had to bring out his blank ballot to be marked by the Sheriff to give to the next voter. When the voter brought out the blank ballot and turned it over to the man running the chain ballot, he was given $2.00 for his vote.

When the election contest came up, Clint Ball, running as Sheriff on the Democrat ticket, charged the Republican Party and Herb Cawood with corrupt practice. Cam Ball, who had been successful in winning the county judgeship on the Democrat ticket from Morris Saylor, was contested by the Republican party and the coal operators.

Cam Ball was an old settler who was born and raised in the mountains of eastern Kentucky and had hundreds of kinfolk in the county. He was a wealthy man who was highly respected. Judge Clay threw out the Republicans' contest against Cam Ball. During the trial, witnesses were brought in to testify that Judge Ball had given them money to buy votes. Ball testified that he had never seen the two men who had been imported from High Splint. After the lunch recess, these witnesses came back and told Judge Clay that they wanted to change their testimony and that they had been paid $25 each by Jack Taylor, mine superintendent at High Splint, to come in and perjure themselves. To Judge Clay, who came from a relatively law-abiding part of Kentucky, this was a great shock. He told me that never in his life had he seen such corruption and such contempt for law and order. The Republican Party was found guilty of corrupt practice and Herb Cawood's election as High Sheriff was thrown out. County Judge Cam Ball appointed the defeated Democrat candidate, Clint Ball, to be Sheriff until the next regular election, which took place in November 1938.

This election was a recurrence of the first fiasco, with the exception of the fact that we had a Sheriff in office that was enforcing the law and attempting to keep the voting reasonably straight. Both parties spent plenty of money in order to win the Sheriff's powerful job. The Democrats gave John W. Gross $300 and a case of whiskey to work the polls at Verda, where he was president of the local union. He drank a pint of whiskey, put the money in his pocket, put the case of whiskey under his bed, and slept all day. The next day he picked up a girl and went on a two-weeks vacation in Tennessee. When he came back, the local union fired him and put Floyd Catron in his place as president of Local Union 3892. Catron gave the local strong leadership and served several years.

However, there was nothing even faintly humorous about a clash that took place during this election at Klondike, a little coal camp near High Splint. It began when Charlie Rose and Sherman Howard, both watchmen and operators' gun thugs, attempted to steal a ballot box. The ballot box was in the custody of two deputy sheriffs and the president of the UMWA local union at Clover Splint, who were taking it in a car to the Harlan Courthouse. All three men—good UMWA members—were killed like sitting ducks when Rose cut loose at them with a tommy gun. One of the deputies, however, somehow found time to fire one shot that killed Howard. Over this ballot box, which turned out to hold a Democratic majority of fifty votes, four men lost their lives.

Nothing was ever done about the murder of the three union men guarding the ballot box from Klondike. A token investigation was made but the Harlan County coal operators had retained control of the courts because their candidate for Sheriff was elected.

There was no question among the people as to who controlled the Republican Party. The coal operators in Harlan County were responsible for the killing of these coal miners, and it was they who sent Charles Rose and Sherman Howard to steal the ballot boxes from a small precinct at the cost of their lives.

Yes, life was cheap in Harlan. Using the Klondike massacre as a yardstick, you could figure that one human life equaled twelve-and-a-half votes. The really important thing to the coal barons of Harlan was power and prestige, which they were unwilling to return to the people to whom the American Constitution said it belonged by right.

Another ballot box dispute that ended with murder occurred in 1933 before I came to Harlan. It happened during Theodore Middleton's primary campaign for Sheriff at Kenvir, the Post Office at Black Mountain. Theodore and his brother, Clarence, said they went to the home of Bill Parley where they caught Parley and Robert Roark stuffing a ballot box. A first-hand story I heard later was that the two Middletons surprised Roark and Parley stuffing the ballot box. Clarence Middleton then shot Roark, put his body in the car, and hauled it back to Harlan Courthouse where he dumped the corpse in the yard. Clarence then yelled to the incumbent Sheriff, John Henry Blair, who was opposing brother Theodore for Sheriff, "Come on out you dirty SOB's and I'll kill you all." Blair and his deputies watched discreetly but did not venture into the courtyard. Clarence Middleton was then considered to be the toughest man in Harlan County by everyone who knew him, which made him a very tough character indeed.

This incident was still hanging over Theodore Middleton when he was about to go out of office in 1938. He could still be tried for Roark's murder and astutely he judged it would be better to undergo trial while he still controlled the machinery of "justice" than to take a chance on a new administration. If acquitted, of course, he could not be tried again on the same charge, regardless of guilt. On December 2nd, a handpicked grand jury indicted the Sheriff for Roark's murder, a quick trial before another carefully selected jury was staged, and the expected "not guilty" verdict was handed down. The "judge" at Middleton's December 16th trial was J. B. Snyder, Attorney for the operators and also for Theodore Middleton. Judge Gilbert had disqualified himself because he was a candidate for office when Middleton was elected in 1933. The jury took less than five minutes to reach their verdict of acquittal.

In the November, 1938 election the seventh precinct at Verda was run by Logan and Merle Middleton, Theodore's first cousins. They started stuffing the ballot box early in the morning and nobody was allowed to come into the polls except their father, Morgan Middleton, an honest, long-whiskered mountaineer who lived out on top of the mountain between Verda and Evarts. When he came down the two boys let their father into the polls and allowed him to vote. When he came out of the polling place, he remarked to somebody standing nearby vainly trying to get in to vote: "They sure must have voted heavy this morning already for the ballot box is full." The fact was that Morgan Middleton's was the only honest vote that was cast that day and it is quite possible that his vote was discarded if after he left his offspring decided he had voted "wrong."

In the same election at Yancy, four election officers, two Republicans and two Democrats, refused to perform their duties after they had been appointed, but did not advise anyone in authority that they were not going to serve. They merely waited until the election was over, and then took the ballot box back empty. They were indicted and tried for violating the election laws but were freed by the courts.

In 1938 when Clint Ball was running for Sheriff, the coal operators put up a fabulous sum of money to buy votes at Lynch for his opponent. The Republicans put the money up to buy Negro votes in the hands of a diminutive colored fellow who always wore a derby hat and went by the nickname of "Cigar." Cigar was ordered to buy votes for $2.00 apiece. It was known that Negro miners at Lynch would not vote until they were paid. The Democrats, in order to keep the Negro Republicans in Lynch from voting, spread a rumor in the camp that "Cigar" had money enough to pay them $5.00 a vote and they should not vote until they got $5.00. "Cigar" didn't have enough money to pay them and refused to give them any more than $2.00. They went on strike and before they knew it, it was time to close the polls and none of them got to vote. And none of them got paid anything either. The three hundred votes that were not cast were all solid Republican votes.

Stealing votes in Harlan County was so commonplace that honest politicians, if any, were forced to resort to purloining in order to have a chance in an election, if both sides purloined the same amount of votes, then the honest votes became the balance of power.

When Clinton Ball ran for election in 1938 for Sheriff on the Democratic ticket, he asked me to recommend a man to go to Blackstar to work at the polls. I recommended a minister of the Gospel. Clint gave the minister $500. He bought votes all day and had $120 left over. He returned the money to Clint who declared that it was the only case in history in Harlan County that election money was ever returned to the candidate. Votes sold for $2.00 each so the minister evidently bought 190 honest votes; that was a good days work.

In the town of Harlan they hired professional voters who went from precinct to precinct and voted several times under the names of absent voters. A poll clerk would give a confederate a list of names of registered voters who were absent or dead. The confederate, in turn, would distribute the names among the professional voters. They voted in each precinct under a different name.

We had a Negro maid who asked to be off on Election Day in 1938. Permission was granted, and on returning to work the day after the election, she declared she had made $14.00. She had voted seven times at $2.00 per vote and she had been hauled from precinct to precinct in a limousine. This was known as the sneaky approach.

The subtle approach was where the poll clerks voted all the absent voters. From 1920 until about 1942, when the Federal government came into Harlan County and sent a number of election officers to the penitentiary, I am of the opinion that there never was an honest election held in Harlan County. It was not unusual to appoint as election officers two or three gunmen who refused to let a voter into the polls, but voted everybody on the voting list themselves. And prior to 1938, the voting list had not been purged in Harlan County for ten years, and in every election there were voting people who had been dead for as long as ten years. Even fictitious names were carried on the voting lists. Many of these were names of mine mules, pit cars or family pets. Our big city political bosses could have learned a few tricks in Harlan in those days.

19

Coal Operators Indicted

> *A G-Man told me the whiskey contained enough strychnine to kill an elephant. Thank God our organizers weren't elephants.*

An action taken by the Federal government on September 27, 1937, seemed to goad the operators and their thugs and killers to step up their acts of violence and senseless brutality. On that date a blanket indictment charging violation of the National Labor Relations Act was returned by a grand jury in Federal District Court at London, against twenty-two Harlan County coal companies, twenty-four company executives and twenty-three deputies or former deputies. A full account of the "conspiracy" trial is in the next chapter. One might believe that this would have made the Harlan Hillbilly syndicate more cautious. Exactly the contrary was true.

Things got particularly rough in the spring of 1938 when it was known that the trial would be held in May. Ben Unthank began a real war of nerves and sorely tested the courage of every union man in Harlan County. He would send two or three carloads of company-paid deputies to surround a local union hall where a meeting was being held, or to sit in parked cars along a nearby road, prominently displaying rifles, shotguns and pistols. Someone would then be sent into the meeting to spread the story that when a speaker or local union officer came out he would be killed.

It was during this time that Ed Beane and Jim Westmoreland were bottled up in a boarding house in Evarts by three carloads of thugs. They phoned to the headquarters in Harlan for help. All the organizers, including myself, were out at local union meetings. Mrs. Titler, who was a valuable asset to the organization staff in Harlan, attempted to get in touch with Sheriff Clint Ball who had just been appointed. He also was out of his office. The governor had fifty or more State Police in the County but they were all out on duty. So Mrs. Titler, who did not know the meaning of the word "fear," got a car, drove to Evarts, picked up Ed Beane and Jim Westmoreland and drove them through the picket lines set up by the thugs. Her actions in matters of this kind were on the reckless side and people who knew that she was flirting with the undertaker notified her. She merely laughed and said that she did not think even the thugs would kill a woman in broad daylight and that the records would show they never had.

About a month later, a similar incident happened at Wallins Creek when Melton Youngblood was addressing a large local union from Twila in the Masonic Hall. A phone call came to me in Harlan that three carloads of thugs, including Frank White, George Lee, Perry G. Noe, Allen Bolen and others, were waiting outside the Masonic Hall for the meeting to break up, at which time they planned to assassinate Melton Youngblood. I got hold of Matt Bunch and a shotgun. While Matt drove his Ford I sat in the back seat with the shotgun, loaded with buckshot, sticking out the window. We drove into Wallins Creek and the three carloads of thugs took off "in high." We had left word in the State Police headquarters in Harlan that if any officers came in the office to send them to Wallins Creek. Five minutes after we landed and had everything under control, three carloads of State Police came into Wallins Creek but the thugs had flown. This was the first time we realized the thugs hated buckshot.

About a week later a stone was thrown through my window with a note tied around it warning me to get out of town. By the time I got my shotgun and got out on the porch I saw the car two blocks away going down the street passing the Courthouse.

A few days later, Mrs. Titler took Mrs. William Clontz and Mrs. Matt Bunch to Knoxville shopping. When they returned to Wallins Creek, and after letting Mrs. Clontz out of the car at her home, Mrs. Titler started crossing the railroad tracks and her right front tire and left rear tire blew out. After examining the tires, we found that all four had been slashed with a knife. A blowout at another place could have sent them over a high bank and all three women to their death. We never found out who slashed the tires but we had a sneaking suspicion it was somebody who didn't like us.

Ben Unthank was not the only one who was nervous about the upcoming conspiracy trial. The High Sheriff Theodore Middleton, called a meeting in the "whispering" room of his office and, according to a deputy who was present, issued orders to liquidate all witnesses who might be dangerous to the defendants. This meant that deputies, thugs, or retired thugs, who knew too much, had better not talk at all—or else. The heat was also on union men.

By June and July, 1938, all organizers in Harlan were on the spot. Gun thug Bill Lewis attempted to kill George Gilbert, but Gilbert beat him to the draw. Lewis was wearing a bulletproof vest. The bullets from Gilbert's gun only knocked Lewis down. Gilbert was then forced to shoot Lewis through the shoulder. Gilbert was shot in the leg. Lewis swore out a warrant for Gilbert charging him with malicious wounding which carries a five to twenty-five year penitentiary sentence if convicted. Lewis was induced by a friend to withdraw the warrant in consideration of $200 and the case was dropped.

This shooting started in Sally Howard's restaurant on Main Street in Harlan. Lewis declared he was the toughest man in town. He bragged that he had killed Lloyd Crouse and three others and he would kill Gilbert if Gilbert kept working for George Titler. Gilbert retorted that Lewis was not nearly as tough as he thought he was. Then Lewis went for his gun.

Lewis wound up his career four years later in another blaze of gunfire. On April 2, 1941, during the opening days of a strike called by the union because Harlan operators refused to sign a contract, he was stationed behind a machine gun "emplacement" on the meat counter of a company store at Crummies Creek. Four UMWA pickets, who were tired and thirsty, walked into the store to buy a coke. Lewis cut loose with the machine gun and killed all four of them. The victims were Virgil Hampton, the brave organizer who began working with me in 1937 at Evarts; Oscar Goodlin, of Lynch, and Charles Ruth and Ed Tye, of Kenvir. Lewis wounded five other men with the same savage burst from his machine gun.

Fate finally caught up with Lewis in the form of a young mountaineer named William Deane. He walked up to Lewis in August, 1941, when he was guarding ballot boxes in the Courthouse, and shot him dead. This took place after I left Harlan County and the only reason I can think of to account for this young fellow's action was that he just plain did not like Bill Lewis. When Deane was asked why he killed Lewis he said he was trying to win a medal.

These fellows would try anything. It was in July, 1938 when Luke Hubbard, a peg-legged taxi driver, attempted to poison a group of organizers. He spiked a pint of whiskey with strychnine and offered them a drink. Ed Beane, George Gilbert, Jim Westmoreland and Virgil Hampton refused. Virgil Hampton's brother, Henry, who worked at Black Mountain, took a drink. It knocked him cold but he got quick medical attention and recovered. A G-man told me the whiskey contained enough strychnine to kill an elephant. Thank God our organizers weren't elephants.

Earlier, on May 25, 1938, prior to the opening of the conspiracy trial, John Kmetz, International Board Member of UMWA District 1, Pennsylvania, and Harmon Kelly, International Board Member of District 11, Indiana, came to Harlan. They were met at Pineville and escorted into the county by two carloads of armed union miners. Kmetz was cognizant of the lurking danger that threatened "furriners." Kelly was contemptuous of the precautions and accused us of putting on a show to scare him. They arrived at District Headquarters just in time to see a deputy sheriff kill a man in cold blood for resisting arrest. The next day Kelly reluctantly made a speech at Lynch surrounded by guards and when Kmetz and Kelly were escorted out of the county by two carloads of protection, Kelly said: "I am glad to be out of the county. It is dangerous to be in Harlan but more dangerous to attempt to leave." Kmetz seemed to enjoy the experience.

A colorful character that was friendly to us was Sally Howard. She ran a restaurant on Main Street, sold package whiskey and beer, and was the widow of the Bige Howard who was shot and killed on the Courthouse steps by Lee Fleenor. She hated thugs with a passion and was a friend of the union, and a good cook. She made biscuits as light as swansdown that would melt in your mouth. I ate her biscuits and fried chicken when I was in jail in 1939, and relished them. Sally also hired several good-looking waitresses who drew miners like bees to honey. It was a good place to eat and a likely place to get shot. One of the waitresses in the summer of 1938, while standing behind the counter was accidentally shot through the heart by a thug playing with his gun. The coroner declared it death by accident.

Sue Nancy, a waitress in Sally's restaurant, dated Lee Hubbard and kept us advised, through Sally Howard, of the Sheriff's next move. She was later found shot to death along the highway. The murder was not even investigated by the authorities.

In the fall of 1938, just before the election, my wife and I were invited to the home of Sheriff Clinton C. Ball for Sunday evening dinner. Ball lived three blocks from our house so we decided to walk. Things in Harlan town were tense and everybody was expecting a lot of assassinations just before the election. The tension was so thick you could feel it everywhere. When we got to the Sheriff's home, I knocked and when he opened the door, he greeted us with a gun in his hand. He asked us how we had gotten there and I told him we had walked. He told me that I should have better sense than to walk on the street of Harlan at night when there was a price on my head and his, too. After we had eaten a turkey dinner prepared by Mrs. Ball, the Sheriff would not let us walk home, a mere three blocks in the town of Harlan, for fear of our being killed, and hauled us home in his car.

A few days later, the election took place. It was a duplicate of the previous elections. The ballots were not counted nor estimated, they were weighed, as usual, and the operators' candidate for Sheriff, Herbert Cawood, won by about fifty pounds.

The new Sheriff, Herbert Cawood, ran one of the two funeral homes in Harlan. The Smith brothers owned the other. A true story involving the keen competition between the two undertaking firms may be typical of that lucrative business and is certainly typical of Cawood's attitude while he was Sheriff. Two men got into a gunfight at the town of Cawood and killed each other. The Smith brothers arrived at the scene first and removed the bodies. A relative of one of the deceased men called the Sheriff to ask him why he did not come to Cawood to investigate the shooting. The Sheriff, obviously vexed because he had lost the fees for two funerals, replied: "To hell with the investigation. Let the man do the investigating who got the bodies."

When he was not busy undertaking, Cawood did another chore—to pay off the coal operators by harassing the United Mine Workers. This was not easy because the union was entrenched in Harlan and the National Labor Relations Board had outlawed all but one of the company unions. But he tried. He sent to Illinois for some so called organizers for the Progressive Mine Workers union, a weak, puppet, dual organization that had a brief moment of glory when the leadership of the Illinois miners split in the late 1920's and early 1930's. These organizers were supposed to take over whatever structure was left of the company unions in an attempt to give them legal status. About half-a-dozen organizers for the "Proggies" came to Harlan but they did not venture into the coalfields. They spent their time lying around their rooms in the Lewallen Hotel, playing poker and fighting among themselves. This effort by Cawood was a miserable failure.

These incidents, however colorful, were a mere sideshow. The big drama was being staged in a Federal courtroom at London, Kentucky, where the Harlan hoodlums again became the objects of nation-wide scrutiny.

20

Big Coal on Trial

> *It became difficult for outsiders to believe that Harlan County was a part of the United States of America.*

The big courtroom drama of 1938 really began on September 27, 1937, when a blanket indictment charging violation of the National Labor Relations Act was returned by a grand jury in Federal District Court against twenty-two Harlan County coal companies, twenty-four executives of those companies, and twenty-three deputy sheriffs, or former deputies.

The defendants were accused of having, since July, 1935, "unlawfully and feloniously conspired to intimidate employees of the aforesaid defendants in the free exercise and enjoyment of certain rights and privileges" guaranteed by the Federal Constitution, "to-wit, the right and privilege of the said employees to self-organization and to form and join and assist labor organization and to bargain collectively through representatives of their own choosing and to engage in concerted activities for the purpose of collective bargaining and other mutual aid and protection, and secured to the said employees" by the National Labor Relations Act.

U. S. Attorneys who developed the charge were Amos W. W. Woodcock, of Baltimore, and Special Assistant Attorney General George P. Jones, of Washington. The indictment was returned after a parade of more than one hundred witnesses, most of them Harlan County coal miners. This was the first criminal case prosecuted by the U. S. Government against persons charged with depriving workers of the rights guaranteed by the National Labor Relations Act, better known as the Wagner Act. The indictments were based not only on evidence submitted by witnesses, but also on investigations made by the Federal Bureau of Investigation and the La Follette Committees.

Thus the stage was set for the great conspiracy trial that opened in May, 1938. Before beginning to describe that fast-moving drama, perhaps it would be best to describe briefly the legal experts who were arrayed to do battle.

Chief prosecutor for the government was Brian McMahon, a thickset, black-haired Irishman who was then head of the Criminal Division of the Justice Department. He was famous for having successfully prosecuted several gangsters and was the same Brian McMahon who was later elected to the U. S. Senate from Connecticut. At the time of his death, during the Truman Administration, he was chairman of the Joint (House-Senate) Committee on Atomic Energy.

McMahon's first assistant was Welly K. Hopkins, a Texan who was chief of the Department's Trial Division. He later became Senior Counsel for the United Mine Workers (a post he held until 1966) and was chief legal adviser to the union during many of its legal fights in the 1940's and 1950's.

Other government assistants were Harry A. Schweinhaut, of Washington, D. C., (now a Federal judge), Walter Gallagher of New Haven, Connecticut, Richard Shanahan of Chicago, and John T. Metcalf, U. S. District Attorney of Lexington, Kentucky.

The newspapers headlined "defense has wiley foxes who have come through many battles." The defendants were ably represented, that's for sure. Their battery of barristers was clever, eloquent, and most of them were experienced at doing legal battle with labor organizations.

The list of defense lawyers was headed by Charles I. Dawson, of Louisville, Kentucky, and Forney Johnston, of Birmingham, Alabama. They were general counsel for all defendants except Hugh Taylor, former deputy sheriff, who was arrested as a fugitive after the trial started.

Dawson was a former Federal judge who resigned three years before the conspiracy trial to enter private practice. He had spent most of that period in court fighting New Deal legislation and had also acted as defense counsel for Harlan County coal operators in several NLRB cases. After the conspiracy trial he continued to practice law and was one of several men who led the coal industry's fight against the UMWA Welfare and Retirement Fund. He is now an immensely wealthy man, having struck oil on his Western Kentucky farm. He is also president of several insurance companies.

Forney Johnston was a pint-sized dynamo whose primary job was chief counsel for the Alabama Power Company. He had also argued the first court case against the New Deal's Tennessee Valley Authority. He tangled with UMWA President John L. Lewis during an argument over promulgation of a code for the bituminous coal industry under provisions of the 1933 National Industry Recovery Act. During a heated debate Lewis roared that Johnson had become "inebriated with the exuberance of his own verbosity."

Cleon Calvert, of Pineville, Kentucky, was one of the more colorful lawyers lined up for the defense. He was the gentleman with the gold-headed cane who had disrupted an NLRB hearing earlier. He told a newspaper reporter before the trial opened that if necessary some "graduate witnesses" (professional perjurers) would be brought to court.

Other defense attorneys and firms included: Ray Lewis, who was appointed by the court to act for Hugh Taylor; Ray Lewis' father and law partner, William R. Lewis, former circuit judge; Reid Patterson, of Pineville; the law firm, Tye, Gillis & Siler, of Williamsburg, Kentucky; J. J. Greenlee, of Richmond, Kentucky;

William Sampson, of Harlan; Judge Casper C. Williams, of Mt. Vernon, Kentucky; T. E. Mahan, of Williamsburg; B. M. Lee, of Harlan, and Charles Dayton, of Harlan. These represented various individual defendants.

The judge was H. Church Ford, of the U. S. District Court for Eastern Kentucky. He holds this post today. He was fair and impartial all the way through a trial that can only be described as one of the most tortuous and difficult in the history of American jurisprudence. The case was opened on May 16 and lasted until July 30. Each day brought forth almost unbelievable evidence. There was testimony as to perjury and subornation of perjury by the defense. Witnesses were murdered during the course of the trial to seal their lips. The trial consumed fifty-seven days in eleven weeks. The record totaled more than 2,225,000 words. By the time the case was turned over to the jury on July 30, it had cost the government $350,000.00. On August 2 the jury reported to Judge Ford that it was unable to reach a verdict. It would seem that all of the time and money involved had been wasted, but this was not completely true because the Harlan County Coal operators had been unmasked to the American people. They did not like what they saw.

The trial opened in a dramatic way. Judge Ford ordered the U. S. Marshall to search everyone going into the courtroom for firearms in order to curb violence. It had been strongly rumored that gun thugs would try to intimidate witness in the court. After this, Charlie Dawson "staged" his opening argument for the defendants. He denied that they had any connection with the atrocities in Harlan County and repeatedly pointed out that the trial was a trial for conspiracy, not murder.

Dawson spoke with such heat and paced so vigorously before the jury box that on one occasion his sock garter came unfastened and he had to pause to fix it. He told the jury that after the Evarts massacre in 1931, "the whole county became inflamed against those outside labor agitators, a feeling that exists down to this very day. You'll probably hear a lot of testimony about alleged outrages against some of these labor organizers," he said, "but I don't care if the record is full of that sort of testimony. The Wagner Act guarantees no such rights to a bunch of union organizers. Keep in mind that this law only concerns employees of the company."

The government's first witness, FBI Agent George A. Stevens, testified that George S. Ward, secretary of the Harlan County Coal Operators' Association, admitted he destroyed association records "in anticipation of a Federal investigation." Stevens also testified as to details of assessments paid by the operators to the Association, numbers of deputy sheriffs paid by the operators and Ward's activities as a lobbyist. This merely confirmed what the La Follette Committee had discovered about the Harlan County Coal Operators' Association and its role in fighting the UMWA.

The defense fought every inch of the way to keep the testimony from getting into the record. Both Dawson and Johnston kept up a constant stream of objections, all based on the reason that the questions and answers showed no conspiracy. Judge Ford instructed the jury that the testimony was admissible as to Ward but was not to be considered as against other defendants.

The first break in the ranks of the coal operators occurred early in the trial when the Clover Splint Coal Company signed a contract with the UMWA changed its plea from "not guilty" to "nolo contendere" and put itself on the mercy of the court. A second break occurred when E. J. Asbury, superintendent of the Black Mountain Coal Company at Kenvir, did the same thing. He testified as a government witness on May 25. He told the court he had attended most meetings of the operators' association and that Ben Unthank, captain of the thug-killers, also attended the meetings. He said his company's assessment was $600.00 to $750.00 per month the previous year, and double the normal assessment because of the activity of the union.

"In these executive sessions of the Harlan County Coal Operators' Association, was the subject of the efforts of labor union organizers ever discussed?" asked Welly K. Hopkins, chief examiner for the Department of Justice.

"Yes", Asbury replied, "I remember on one occasion Elmer

Hall, of Three Point Coal Company, protested against the use of association funds to fight the union."

"Did anyone reply to that?" Hopkins asked.

"Bob Tway told Elmer Hall that he was too thin-skinned."

Part of the rest of the story of the trial can be told in the words of day-by-day newspaper accounts. Some of the events they reported were merely colorful; others were unbelievable; the total effect was shocking. It became difficult for outsiders to believe that Harlan County was a part of the United States of America. We'll begin with a typical report out of London, Kentucky, dated May 27.

> The star witness of today was a little 57-year-old lady in a polka dot dress, by the name of Bell Lane, who told of her experiences at a union mass meeting on the first Sunday in July, 1935. She was cursed and struck by an armed deputy sheriff when she screamed a protest at another deputy who was beating the speaker. She said the meeting was held at Evarts and Preacher Marshall Musick was the speaker. She said the deputies were blowing their car horns to drown out the speaker's voice.
>
> "I saw Merle Middleton, George Lee, Frank White and John Hickey beat up 'Rock House' Mullhollen (a big, but outnumbered, loyal union coal miner from Evarts, Kentucky)."

Charles Scott, a bass-voiced Negro, said that he was working at Verda and when he became sick, Lee Fleenor evicted him from his house. "Threw my furniture and stuff out in the road. I asked him why and he said 'Goddamn you, we got orders from Mr. Bassham.'" After he got well, he went to work at Green Silvers Mine, owned by Sheriff Middleton.

"When I signed up with the union, Sheriff Middleton asked me why I had signed up with the union and I told him I thought it was a free country. He threw back his coat and showed his badge and said, 'I am the rule in Harlan County. If my baby would speak to a damn union man, I would take my pistol and blow its brains out. You get out of here and don't look back.' I asked him if I could get my tools and he said, damn you and your tools, too. Get on across that foot log.'"

"Did you ever go back after your tools?" asked Brian McMahon.

"No, that was the law talking," said the witness.

On cross-examination, Dawson asked the witness: "Did the officer serve you with a forcible detainer?" Scott looked up and said, "Forci-which?," and everyone in the courtroom laughed, including the judge.

John Severa, a miner at Jack Taylor's mine at High Splint, testified that he went to a union meeting and was kicked out of the hollow by Frank White. He said that White kicked him and told him if he ever came back in the hollow, he would kill him. Timothy Huff testified that he worked at Louellen from September, 1936, to January, 1937. He said the cut boss (section foreman) came around and asked him to sign a paper. It was a company union paper, Huff said. Subsequently he said that R. E. (Uncle Bob) Lawson addressed two meetings and told the men if they stayed at Louellen they would have to join the company union. Mr. and Mrs. George Gilbert testified about threats at Totz and shots being fired into their house, and being fired and evicted by the Harlan Central Company. All of these were government witnesses.

On June 11, Mrs. Marshall Musick retold the story of the murder of her son, Bennett, by gun thugs. Kelly Fox testified that he was an eyewitness to the February 9 shooting and identified Frank White as one of the men who did the shooting. Dawson asked Fox if he had not told Slemp Middleton that George Titler had paid "you $200.00 to testify before the La Follette Committee," and that he would leave the county and not testify for $1,000.00. Fox answered, "No, sir."

The government closed its case on June 17. A newspaper account related the sensational events of that day. It reported:

> LONDON, KY. June 17—The closing minutes filled with stories of an alleged "perjury factory" where prospective witnesses were asked to make false affidavits, and marked by a short clash between opposing counsel, the government has reached the end of its long conspiracy case against Harlan County coal companies, operators and deputy sheriffs.

The prosecution rested at 3:30 Thursday afternoon after delivering the long awaited "knockout punch" with the testimony of Ernest Huff and Avery Eggers, both of Ages. Huff is a young miner employed by the Harlan Wallins Coal Company and Eggers is a youth of 14.

Both Huff and Eggers said they were taken to the little office in Merle Middleton's garage and asked to make the false affidavits. Huff said he refused to sign. Eggers said he signed but didn't think he made an oath that it was true because "I didn't hold up my right hand."

Eggers said he signed the false affidavit because he was afraid not to, while Huff said he had been kept in jail here in London at his own request for fear "something would happen to him" if he were on the streets.

Huff told of being halted in front of Lee Hubbard's poolroom at Ages and asked to go inside to a back room where Hubbard wanted to talk to him about some "important business."

In response to questions by Brian McMahon, chief of government Council, Huff told this story:

On Sunday, May 29, my wife and I walked down to Ages to do some trading. As we passed Lee Hubbard's poolroom, Luther Hyde called to me and said Lee Hubbard wanted to see me inside. I went in and Hubbard said, 'Jack, I've got some very important business to talk over with you. Can you come back down here a little later?'

I said I didn't think I could and he said he would come up to the house after me. About ten minutes after I got back home Hubbard drove up with Luther Hyde and some others. They asked me to go back down town.

On the way we stopped at Eddie Brackett's house and Luther Hyde went up to the house. While he was gone Hubbard said to me, 'You remember the night you were in my pool room, the night when the Musick boy was killed?' I said I didn't remember it.

Luther Hyde and Eddie Brackett came down in the car and then we drove to the garage of Merle Middleton's and went in. Lee Hubbard said to Middleton, 'Well, we've got five—what will we do with them?'

Middleton said: 'Take them out and get them to make the affidavits and then we'll take them over and swear them.'

A few minutes later Hubbard called me back into the office. Middleton was sitting at the desk and Hubbard was standing up. They filled out a paper and handed it to me. I said I couldn't read.

'Can you read?' broke in McMahan.

"No, sir' Huff replied. He then continued:

Hubbard said 'I'll read it to you.' Then he started to read the paper. It said that I was in Lee Hubbard's poolroom on the night of February 9 from about six o'clock and got in a nine ball game with Frank Allen.

Then, it said, Lee Hubbard got in the game and played with us a while and then Wash Irwin came in and got in the game.

After a while, the paper said, a big black car drove up and the horn blew. Wash Irwin went outside and we held up the game until he came back. He came in and hung up his cue, so when we played on without him, the game going on until about half past ten.

'I asked them what the paper meant and Middleton said 'Well, you have heard that Lee Hubbard killed the Musick boy. This just says you know he didn't because you were playing pool with him that night.'

'I said that couldn't be so because I didn't play pool.

'I laid the statement down on the desk and said I wanted to step out and buy some cigarettes. I went out and tried to get a taxi, but I couldn't find one. So, I started to walk home and a man came along and picked me up. After I got home I started to think about it and got scared, so I went over to my brother's house and told him about it.

'Was there any truth at all in the statement they wanted you to sign?" McMahon asked.

'No, there was not,' Huff answered.

Later he saw Hubbard again, Huff said, and Hubbard asked: 'Where did you go when we wanted you to sign the affidavit?'

I said: 'went home.'

He said: 'you didn't even sign the paper.'

I said: 'No, and I'm not going to.'

Then Hubbard said: 'If you don't believe Pearl Bassham and Mr. Cornett are with us on this just get in the car and I'll drive you over there. You can have anything you want.'

I said: 'Mr. Bassham and Mr. Cornett haven't got anything I want!

Eggers was first asked to tell of an incident at the home of Ben Wilburn, next-door neighbor of the Eggers, more than a year ago. He said Wilburn came home from work one afternoon and a few minutes later Wash Irwin and Lee Hubbard followed him. They soon reappeared, Eggers said, bringing Wilburn along. They pushed him off the porch and then Lee Hubbard kicked the fallen man several times in the back, saying: 'Get up from there, you sorry S.O.B. You can't lay that on me.' The officers then put Wilburn in a car and drove off, Eggers said.

Following his account of this incident, young Eggers was asked if he had seen Lee Hubbard recently. He said he had, about two weeks ago. This is what he said occurred at that time: 'Sammy Thomas came and got me and said Lee Hubbard wanted to see me. He took me to Hubbard's house. His wife and a girl were there. Hubbard asked me if I remembered the time when he arrested Ben Wilburn and I said I did and told him all about it.

'Then he said he wanted me to say Mrs. Wilburn had run out on the porch right after Ben came home and called for the law and that I went and got the law. Then he said he wanted me to say I overheard Wash Irwin ask him to go along when he went up to see what the trouble was at the Willburns.'

'Was any of that true?' asked McMahon.

'No, sir,' the boy answered.

"Did he ever say anything to you about money?'

'Yes. Lee Hubbard said he would give me a job at $5.00 a day if I'd tell them lies for him.'

Eggers said Hubbard took him, Eddit Brackett, Luther Hyde and Jack Huff to Merle Middleton's garage, where Middleton wrote an affidavit. Eggers said every time he tried to tell what actually happened at the Wilburns, Hubbard would break in and dictate to Middleton what to write.

After the affidavit had been prepared, Eggers said, a man whom he did not know took him to the Black Motor Company office where he signed the paper.

'But I didn't hold up my right hand,' he said.

Asked if he thought he had to hold up his right hand before the oath would be legal, he said he did. Mr. McMahon then asked Eggers why he had signed.

'I was afraid not to,' the boy answered.

On cross-examination defense counsel Dawson said: 'You said you signed because you were afraid. You're pretty scared, aren't you?'

'You're dad-gummed right. I'm afraid of all of 'em,' the boy replied.

Both Huff and Eggers underwent stiff cross-examination but both stuck stoutly to their stories.

I personally attended many sessions of the conspiracy trial. The newspaper stories already quoted tell many of the highlights of the incredible events that took place. It is impossible to print in this book all of my recollections but I do remember bits of testimony that were particularly vivid.

Henry Lewis, Chief Deputy for Sheriff Middleton, testified that the Sheriff had asked him to go with him one Saturday night to Verda to keep some miners from speaking. He said he refused to go and on Monday the Sheriff asked him why he did not show up. "You could have made a little extra money," said Middleton.

Lewis said the Sheriff had a private room back of his office that was known as the "whispering room" where the Sheriff and his deputies met to make plans. The room known as the "whispering room" contained a big safe filled with high-powered rifles and shotguns.

Clinton C. Ball, Jailor, testified that in the four years he was Jailor the Sheriff had jailed about 14,000 persons. He said that shortly after "I took office, the Sheriff called me down to the whispering room and complained that the assistant jailors are testifying against his deputy sheriffs in swearing that the prisoners brought in on drunken charges were sometimes not drunk."

"If we are going to get along, we are going to have to work together," Ball quoted the Sheriff as telling him.

On one occasion Ball said Fayette Cox and Frank White brought in a miner named Green Cornett. "I refused to jail him because he wasn't drunk," Ball said. "Then I asked him where Marshall Musick could be found and he said he didn't know. They told him they would arrest him if he did not talk. Cornett asked me to put him in jail because he was afraid the deputies would kill him. I locked him up for the night in a courthouse room."

Union miners from the R. C. Tway Coal Company testified that they, when they joined the union, were sent to Raven Rock, a place where the coal was little and the water and slate were big, where a miner could not make a living.

Miners from Clover Fork at Kitts testified that when they joined the union, they were transferred to Turnblazer's Home (named after the District president), a place similar to Raven Rock.

Martha Howard, a good-looking girl from Harlan, said she had been offered $50.00 for each organizer she could lure to a place where the thugs could work them over.

On June 10, a murder away from the trial scene shocked the court. Lester Smithers, a government witness and president of the local union at Yancy, was shot and killed while he distributed commodities to the unemployed miners of this local union. His murderers were two brothers, Verlin and Clyde Fee, non-union miners.

I had sent Smithers, a fine, outstanding union man, who was

donating his services to the union, on his mission. Eyewitnesses told me that the Fee brothers had apparently been paid by somebody to kill Smithers. They planned for one to start a fight with Smithers and then the other was to shoot him. It worked out as planned. Sheriff Cawood's chief deputy investigated the killing and testified that Fee shot in self-defense. This was cold-blooded murder.

According to the report of the deputy sheriff, these two men had been drunk and quarreling all day, but the facts are that Smithers left the warehouse one-and-a-half hours before he was killed with a truckload of groceries and was as sober as a judge when he left me. In fact, I never knew of his drinking. Eyewitnesses said that when the Fee boys started the argument with Smithers they called him a snitcher because he had been subpoenaed before the court in London. The operators were obviously not happy because the union was feeding the men who were fired because of their union activities. Smithers was a fly in their ointment. The man who committed this murder went scot-free.

The defense then began its parade of witnesses. But Charlie Dawson's legal pyrotechnics were soon over-shadowed by more sensational happenings. One of these took place on July 6 when the notorious Frank White, one of the toughest of the toughs, was shot to death at the Miles Tourist Camp, two miles from Corbin, Kentucky, where most of the defendants and defense witnesses in the conspiracy trial were staying. Chris Patterson, a former deputy sheriff who had only the day before been subpoenaed as a government witness, was at first charged with White's murder. The charge was based on a statement by gun thug Bob Eldridge who said he saw Patterson shoot White.

Patterson stoutly denied the killing, but refused to say any more. This shooting was thoroughly investigated by agents of the FBI. Their findings showed that Patterson had been released from jail in Pineville in order to testify as a government witness at the London trial. Sheriff Middleton persuaded him (with a bottle of whiskey) to stay at the Miles Tourist Camp where he was to be the "fall guy" in the murder of Frank White. White's removal had become necessary, not because he was disloyal to the thugs, but because he had proved to be such a stupid witness at the La Follette Committee hearings that the operators feared he would accidentally blurt out the truth on the witness stand during the conspiracy trial. To set the stage, White was told that he should pick a fight with Patterson, and that another thug, whom the FBI called "Mr. X," would kill Patterson. When the fracas started, "Mr. X," instead of shooting Patterson, shot over his shoulder and killed White. The story would have a happy ending for the thugs if and when Patterson was convicted of White's murder.

But the crew of hoodlums decided they could not chance a trial. Chris Patterson spent a couple of weeks in the London jail under $3,000 bond, but was released when Theodore Middleton put up that amount of money for his release. Chris was at liberty for a couple of weeks, when two gunmen picked him up in a car in Harlan one dark and stormy night. He was found the next morning lying along the road, his body riddled with bullets, obviously murdered by the same men who killed Frank White. The lips of another eyewitness were sealed forever.

A couple of days earlier another murder had swiped the headlines from Dawson's antics. The victim was Lee Fleenor, perhaps the most coldblooded thug of them all. His victim was Charlie Reno, a Harlan County miner, who was driving from Harlan County to London to appear as a government witness. Fleenor also had another reason to shoot the miner. Reno had killed Fleenor's father and served time for it. The murder occurred on the highway when Fleenor spotted Reno lying under his car, making emergency road repair. He shot him to death. But Reno's twelve-year-old son managed to surprise Fleenor, using a gun in his father's car to fire several shots, one of which creased the back of Fleenor's skull. Fleenor was never tried for this murder. As previously stated in this book, Fleenor was later sent back to the penitentiary by Governor Chandler at my request. After serving his stretch, he was paroled with the understanding that he would never return to the state. He went to Southwest Virginia where he now lives and works.

On July 22, further evidence of existence of a "perjury mill" being run by counsel for the operators was brought out in the London courtroom. Involved were Lee Fleenor's uncle, Everett Fleenor, and a Harlan attorney, E. B. Spicer, who had paid witnesses to testify falsely about the murder of Bennett Musick. Key witness was Albert Hoskins, who had previously testified for the defense that he had been in Bryan Middleton's saloon the night of the murder and had seen Belton Youngblood, one of the UMWA's organizers, and Granville, Sargent, a government witness, buy two pints of whiskey and leave on a mysterious errand with other unidentified men in two cars. Hoskins had also sworn that Youngblood and Sargent later returned and bought more liquor. It was alleged that the Musick boy was slain during their absence.

On July 22, Hoskins completely retracted his previous testimony. He said Everett Fleenor who offered him $50 in "easy money" had approached him at Evarts. All he had to do to earn the money was "to accuse Belton Youngblood and Granville Sargent of murder." Then, Hoskins stated, Fleenor took him, Vernon Kelly and John Barnes to attorney Spicer's office in Harlan. Hoskins said the three youths waited in an anteroom while Fleenor conferred with Spicer. Fleenor then came out and told them exactly what they were to say. They were then taken into Spicer's office where the attorney told them that things were not "quite ready." The next day, Hoskins testified, they returned and signed statements that had been typed by Spicer's secretary, after which Fleenor took them to the washroom and paid them the first $25 of the $50 they had been promised. Hoskins got $20 more from Fleenor the day he took the witness stand at the conspiracy trial and the last $5 a few days later.

Despite a grueling cross-examination by Chief Defense Counsel Dawson, Hoskins stuck by his guns. He said that he had decided to confess publicly to his false testimony because "I got to studying about it and knowed I done wrong."

Hoskins testimony was supported by John Barnes who also described the Fleenor-Spicer offer, but said that he later decided not to testify in court, so received only $25. The Hoskins-Barnes story received more credence when the FBI presented evidence proving that Bryan Middleton's saloon had not been in business the night of the Musick murder, February 9. Abner Turner, a silent partner in the saloon, said that the place had not opened until February 25, after being closed by the previous owner, Slemp Middleton, on January 23. Liquor, beer, and cigarette license receipts confirmed the February 25 date.

The sensational perjury testimony continued with the stories of Mrs. Lelia Bartlett and Mrs. Ester Parley, sisters, who for the first time laid the subornation of perjury activity squarely on Spicer. Their testimony was that Ben Cawood, an officer, came to their homes and told them Spicer wanted to talk to them. They went to Harlan with Cawood, both testified, and were told by Spicer that the defense "needed witnesses" in the conspiracy trial.

"We talked about the trial here," Mrs. Bartlett testified, "and I asked him what they were doing in London. He said 'they're lawing like hell.' Then he said he wanted us to come down here and be defense witnesses. "I asked him what he wanted me to say and he said I was to say that me and Ester was walking down the street in Evarts one day a few days after the Musick boy was killed and that we overheard Tick Arnett say to another man, 'It's too bad the Musick boy got killed, but we thought they were all away from home. But maybe it will all be for the best because this will build up a lot of sympathy for us. Sometimes accidents are the very best things that can happen.'"

Mrs. Bartlett said she told Spicer that she didn't even know Arnett and would not recognize him. Despite this protest, she said, Spicer dictated a statement to the stenographer and she and Mrs. Parley signed it. They took a copy of the statement back home where their father read it. Later they decided to refuse to come to London, she said, and never went back to Spicer's office. Both women said they had known the attorney for about five years.

Mrs. Parley's testimony was similar to that of her sister. She added that Spicer told them he was "making arrangements to take a carload of witnesses down to London and pay them $25.00 apiece and expenses for one day." She said Spicer asked them if $25.00 each was sufficient. Both said they did not reply. Both said they never got any money because it was promised to them only if they testified.

James Lankford was the last witness of the day on that story of perjury. He said he was asked by Spicer on two occasions to be a witness for the defense concerning the Musick killing, but that he refused to do so. He did not say that he was offered any money for being a witness.

Before the perjury testimony had started the Government concluded its proof that Youngblood was in Pineville on the night young Musick was killed and could not have been at Evarts. Several Pineville residents and members of the union-organizing group testified previously that Youngblood was at the Continental Hotel in Pineville. This story was corroborated by L. T. Arnett, James Golden, the Pineville attorney who represented the UMWA, and Youngblood himself.

After the sensation in the newspapers about perjury, the trial continued to drone along. But no one was bored. At one point, Judge Ford nearly declared a mistrial and warned the operators and thugs—particularly Merle Middleton—that any "monkey business" with the jury would land them in jail. Middleton had attempted to frighten and influence jurors by having his uncle parade in public with their relatives. Dewey and Anna Hensley who testified that Mose Middleton had asked them to provide a false alibi for himself and Merle Middleton for July 7, 1935, when a union rally at Evarts was broken up by a group of deputies, gave further perjury testimony. Hensley said that Mose suggested, "$100 was a good amount," but that he turned the offer down flat.

Just before the lawyers began their summing up, a last sensation sent the news hounds scurrying for telephones. A union miner, Boyd Isom, told the court that the Harlan Central Coal Company withheld medical care from his baby son that resulted in his death. He said that Harry Bennett, son of the mine owner, told him "if I hadn't joined the union I could have got doctor treatment for my baby before it died."

A newspaper account stated: "The effect of the statement was electrical. A woman in the audience gasped audibly and a deputy marshal rapped sharply for order." The newspaper report continued: "In the dead stillness that followed, Dawson turned savagely on the witness (Isom) in cross-examination. 'As a matter of fact, don't you know your baby got treated by the company doctor every time you called for him?' Dawson asked. I know he didn't, the witness replied." This action was inhuman but typical of the Harlan operators' method.

The government began its summing up of the case with a seven-hour presentation by Welly Hopkins. The eloquent young Texan ripped the case of the defense to bits, describing it as mere "explanations and evasions" and according to a contemporary newspaper account "declared in a ringing voice to the jury that 'if you want to see more blood spilled in Harlan County—if you want to see perjury run rampant—you can say so by a verdict of acquittal.'"

Hopkins took up each company, individual coal operator and deputy sheriff in turn and summed up all the evidence against them. He said that evidence in individual cases might seem relatively insignificant, but when considered collectively "it pyramided to a point where the conclusion that a planned conspiracy existed was inescapable."

The summing up continued, featuring a duel of wits between Dawson and the government's Schweinhaut. The concluding argument was presented by McMahon, chief counsel for the U. S., who ably reviewed the case against the Harlan County Coal operators.

The case finally was turned over to the jury on July 30, after fifty-seven days of testimony. Judge Ford asked the jurors, shirt-sleeved and gallused farmers and small tradesmen from the surrounding hills, to consider carefully the credibility of the witnesses accused by the attorneys as perjurers. He instructed that the National Labor Relations Board testimony given by George Ward and

Ben Unthank, assigned to the Association, was to be considered by them.

After three days of deliberation, the jury reported to Judge Ford on August 2 that it was hopelessly deadlocked. The foreman, L. F. Johnson of Clay County, said its members were divided seven-to-five for conviction.

The hung jury was no surprise to observers on the scene. It was made up of farmers and small businessmen whose ideology resembled that of the defendants in many ways. Some of them, although not related by blood to the defendants, had married into their families. Some of the jury members, like the Harlan County thugs and their employers, did not believe in collective bargaining and hated all labor unions and their members. The jury, like the defendants, did not believe that the war in Harlan County should be settled in court. The code of the hills, which they faithfully followed, provided that differences between man should be settled by gun and that the man who is "right" in an argument is the man who is able to walk away from a duel.

Government attorneys went through the motions of seeking a new trial, but this was merely for the records. The Harlan conspiracy trial, for all practical purposes, ended on August 2. No one was convicted legally or sent to jail. But the Harlan County operators and their thugs were convicted of being their ugly, bestial selves before the greatest court of them all—the opinion of the American public.

21

STRIKE

Soldiers and guns and troops will not mine coal in America. The time has gone by when men can be shot back into the mines.

We were all weary of litigation after the Harlan conspiracy trial. The Department of Justice and the defendants were particularly anxious not to go through the ordeal again, so a movement was initiated to settle the labor management situation in Harlan County in another way. The operators agreed to meet with representatives of the NLRB and the UMWA to negotiate a contract. For twenty-six days bargaining continued under the careful scrutiny of John R. Steelman of the U. S. Labor Department's Conciliation Service and Phillip G. Phillips of the NLRB. On August 27, 1938, an agreement was signed at Knoxville, Tennessee, that placed 12,000 miners in Harlan County under union protection. U. S. Steel's operation at Lynch, Kentucky, with 3,000 employees, was already signed up by the UMWA. The contract was signed by R. C. Tway, W. Arthur Ellison and W. H. Sinkecht for the Harlan Association, and by William Turnblazer, myself, and John Sexton for the United Mine Workers of America. O. E. Gassoway, International Board

Member from Indiana, assisted the UMWA in the negotiations.

After the contract was signed, Turnblazer and I left Knoxville to drive to Jellico, then headquarters town for District 19. On our trip home, an incident occurred that has absolutely nothing to do with this story but which still gives me a chuckle whenever I think of it.

When we reached Jacksboro, county seat of Campbell County, Bill espied an old friend sitting on his front porch close to the courthouse. Bill stopped and introduced him to me as Squire Clem Perkins. I learned later that besides being Justice of the Peace, Clem was also the county's most successful bootlegger. He was bewhiskered and had a large Bible on his lap when I met him.

Said Turnblazer, "Clem, I didn't know that you were a Bible-reading man."

"I ain't," said Clem, "but three weeks ago I bought a case of Scotch whiskey from a fellow in Cincinnati by the name of Lazarus and I want to order some more. So I have read this book from kiver to kiver trying to learn how to spell Lazarus."

When Turnblazer and I got back to Jellico the miners greeted all of our negotiators as conquering heroes. Five thousand happy coal miners and members of their families paraded through the streets, celebrating our victory. It was a beautiful feeling. "Something attempted, something done, had earned us a night's repose."

There was peace in Harlan for the next six months. During that brief period when the 1938 contract was in effect, all officials of the union, beginning with John L. Lewis, attempted to cement the bargaining machinery and create an atmosphere of good will between the contracting parties to the contract. Field workers spent on an average of sixteen hours a day, every day of the week, conferring with different groups of mine workers and teaching them the rudiments of collective bargaining. The Harlan County Coal Operators also knew nothing about collective bargaining and for years had been used to obtaining their objectives by force. Changing to collective bargaining and reason was something that was foreign to their mode of thinking and was hard for them to swallow. We tried to educate them for six months, but this ended on April 1, 1939, when all of the coal miners in the nation went on strike.

The national strike lasted until May 15. You don't need more than one guess as to which was the only operators' group in the United States that refused to sign an agreement with the UMWA. Of course, it was the Harlan Association. They had not been acting in good faith when they signed the 1938 agreement, but were only trying to get out from under their indictment by the Federal government. How well their strategy had succeeded soon became apparent.

When the national strike started our members stood fast in Harlan County. When the operators refused to sign on May 15, they continued to stick by their guns. As many labor union veterans know, the biggest problem faced in a strike situation is maintaining solidarity. This is another way of saying that the strikers' morale must be kept high and this is nearly impossible unless you are able to provide them with minimum food and shelter.

Our first problem in Harlan County in 1939 began immediately when we realized that the union would have to provide food for some of the strikers who immediately become destitute when their employment ceased on April 1. We established a large warehouse and began to buy food products to feed the families of nine thousand strikers. At first, for a couple of weeks, the job was small, but thereafter the need increased constantly. Huge amounts of food were bought and distributed at virtually all of the coal camps in Harlan County.

Some of my greatest help during this time came from a boy in his twenties, who was acting as my secretary, Matt Bunch's son, J. Carl Bunch. He bought and distributed to the miners groceries worth more than $300,000 and may have saved the UMWA, by wise purchasing, up to $60,000. During the organizing drives in Harlan County, from May 1, 1937 to September, 1939, his shrewdness in buying was talked about by all of the organizers and people who knew him. It was not unusual for our volunteer labor crew to unload four boxcar loads of flour, beans, bacon, etc., in one day

WILLIAM TURNBLAZER (left) *with the author. Turnblazer led a distinguished career as a UMWA organizer and administrator. A long-time president of District 19, he directed the organizing drives in Harlan County. In this photo, Turnblazer and Titler pose in front of bags of coal to be used in Admiral Byrd's 1938 Antarctic Expedition. Byrd chose high grade coal from Peabody Coal Company's Great Heart mine, in Kenvir, Harlan County.*

Turnblazer, Sr., should not be confused with his son, William Turnblazer, who also became president of District 19. His career was cut short when he found himself embroiled in the Yablonski assasination conspiracy in 1969. Eventually he testififed for the prosecution and his boss, "Tony" Boyle, UMWA President, was sent to prison. Yablonski had challenged Boyle for the UMWA presidency in 1969, and though he lost, Boyle though him a threat and arranged for his murder.

and to spend $10,000 per week for groceries. This was a sizeable, expensive operation that required careful, watchful management. Over one half of a million dollars worth of food was consumed by the miners in this strike.

Food for the strikers was not only supplied by the District, but also by the The International Union and the Federal government. The latter help became necessary when we were providing virtually all food eaten by nine thousand men and their families.

Carl Bunch soon discovered that he could not merely buy available food, distribute it and keep the people happy. Harlan County miners ate plain food, but they were particular about it. Carl once made the mistake of buying a carload of yellow corn meal and a carload of navy beans. The men would not touch the yellow corn meal. They insisted that corn bread had to be made from white corn meal and that yellow corn bread was "too strong for their blood." They were also persistent in their belief that white navy beans weren't fit to eat; that they must have pinto beans. So we bought white corn meal and pinto beans. One miner told me that he had tried to feed yellow corn bread to his hog, but that the hog had refused to touch it.

Our other basic problem, that of housing was a knotty legal one, involving company ownership of the houses in which the men lived. Its solution was in the long run as expensive to the union as providing food.

The dispute over housing began long before we signed the 1938 agreement with the Harlan operators. In 1937, the operators persecuted known UMWA sympathizers by securing court orders for their eviction from company houses under illegal detainers. This made it necessary for the union to put up bond in escrow to cover twice the amount of rent due on the houses during the period it was under bond. There were hundreds of these cases on the court records when the 1938 contract was signed.

After the contract was signed, it was necessary for both sides to go to court and ask that the cases be dropped. In many cases, the union paid rent for the people who had lived in these hundreds of houses for over a year.

The fact that the operators signed the 1938 agreement did not mean any drop in the UMWA's legal expenses in Harlan County. As a matter of fact, they seemed to increase steadily. As stated previously, most of the Harlan operators had signed the contract as a temporizing gesture, aimed at removing the threat of Federal prosecution for conspiracy. After they signed the contract, they spent their nights trying to figure ways to get rid of those men who were active in the union, using false allegations of unsatisfactory work, drunkenness and others too numerous to mention. Union men were jailed on trumped-up charges, making it necessary for us to hire local lawyers to see that these men were not held in jail more than two days. If absent for three days they would forfeit their rights of employment at the mine where they worked. The UMWA hired John Grady O'Hara, a young attorney just out of college, and Mr. and Mrs. John Doyle, two other attorneys in the city of Harlan, to make the rounds of the courthouse and jail each morning to see how many members of the UMWA were in jail on trumped-up charges. For those they found, our attorneys posted bond, paid their fines and got them back to work in time to save their jobs. This was quite a chore.

The UMWA also retained the firm of Golden and Lay, in Pineville, outstanding attorneys, who were on a virtual fulltime basis for us in Harlan and Bell Counties. This meant that it was necessary for us to employ five local attorneys in addition to those employed by the International Union. Much time and effort was given toward the success of our organizing drive in Harlan County by the UMWA's Senior Counsel, Henry Warrum, widely and affectionately known as "Judge," and by Earl E. Houck, director of the UMWA's Legal Department. The International Union also retained on a regular basis the firm of Townsend & Townsend, Charleston, West Virginia, whose members spent much time in Harlan County affairs.

Our short-lived era of peace was drawing rapidly to a close, although we weren't yet aware of it. In New York City, the Nation's bituminous coal operators (except those in Harlan County) were ready to sign a new contract. But in Harlan County, Judge C. E. Ball warned that he had been "requested" to ask Governor Chandler for state troops to preserve peace. He made this remark while warning twenty-eight union men and two of their wives that they would have to stop "baptizing" non-union members. It was alleged, according to contemporary newspaper accounts, that the union men and women had thrown some non-union miners into the Cumberland river near Evarts with the statement: "We baptize you in the name of the Father, the Son and John L. Lewis."

Judge Ball declared "you can't take the law into your own hands," with the additional admonishment that if the "baptizing" continued "I will place you under a peace bond you can't make." He then warned that troops might be called in.

UMWA International Representative Paul K. Reed and Attorney James Golden also warned that violence might mean that strikebreaking Kentucky National Guardsmen would come into Harlan. "We want you and all others to refrain from these baptizings, because they will cause trouble, sooner or later," Reed declared. Golden said that success in Harlan County depended upon orderly behavior by union members. Reed also warned that "someone has asked for troops."

He was right. The "someone" was Judge Ball. And the Governor, by now a lame duck captive of the Harlan operators and an avowed enemy of the UMWA, was more than willing to call out the troops and to take whatever other measures he deemed necessary to "bust the union" in Harlan County.

The last period of prolonged violence in Harlan County began on the morning of May 15, 1939, when 850 Kentucky National Guardsmen, under the command of General Ellerbe Carter, rode in to take charge. They were there at the orders of Governor A. B. Chandler, who can be almost solely charged with responsibility for bloodshed during those turbulent weeks, along with a few recalcitrant Harlan operators, whose faithful servant he was.

The national strike had centered on the UMWA's insistence that a "union shop" clause be included in the National Bituminous Wage Agreement. This clause was legal at that time under the Wagner Act and a modified version of it still exists in our wage agreement and is legal under the much more restrictive Taft-Hartley and Landrum-Griffin laws. All of the nation's operators, including those outside of Harlan in Eastern Kentucky, agreed to the union shop clause. Not the Harlan operators, though. They chose to use this as an excuse for another shot at breaking the union with the volunteered help of "Happy" Chandler and the Kentucky National Guard.

Before the troops marched, Chandler had issued a statement attempting to justify his proclamation of martial law. First of all, Chandler quoted from a letter written by Harlan County Judge, C. E. Ball, that said: "Conditions in Harlan County in connection with the labor situation have gradually grown worse during the past few weeks and have become so serious as to warrant a request for protection from the State." He, Ball, says: "It is the consensus of opinion of the people of the County, that 75 percent of the miners want to work if given protection." Later events proved Ball's estimate completely false. Only a small minority of Harlan County miners were willing to go back to work without the protection of a UMWA contract, in spite of the fact that the National Guard did prohibit picketing. Chandler then said: "During the last few weeks many miners who have desired to work have been intimidated and some of them seriously beaten." This was a deliberate falsehood.

In his press statement Chandler then wrote: I am today in receipt of a petition from 123 non-union miners who work for the Clover Fork Coal Company, and whose representatives were Tess Walter, Franklin Martin and Willie Anderson, who have represented to me that the great majority of the miners desire to go back to work immediately and will go to work if given protection by the State." There is no doubt in my mind that "Happy" received a petition from 123 non-union miners. I would like to point out, however, that 123 is a hell of a lot shy of adding up to 75% of 12,000 miners, the number of men who were on strike.

Chandler then proclaimed: "The people of Kentucky and the Nation have become weary of this controversy. I have decided, in the event this controversy is not settled by the end of this week, that the National Guard will assemble at Harlan County on Monday morning, May 15th, with instructions to give protection to every citizen of Harlan County who desires to work in the mines upon terms and conditions acceptable to him and his employer." This was a pure and simple affirmation of his faith in the righteousness of strikebreaking.

One of the statements by Chandler was to the effect that our dispute in Harlan was not between the UMWA and management, but was in reality a jurisdictional spat between two unions, one chartered by the CIO, the other by The American Federation of Labor. The Progressive Mine Workers of America (AFL) was a splinter organization with a few local unions in Illinois and scarcely a paper organization in Kentucky. Concurrently with the march of troops, the president of this so-called union, one Joe Ozanic, announced at Mount Olive, that he was conferring with Harlan County operators. The announcement, which you will note was made in Illinois, not Kentucky, included the quote from Ozanic: "I cannot discuss the nature or progress of the negotiations." There was never any progress to report in that direction.

Two weeks after the troops bivouaced in Harlan County, the Knoxville News Sentinel, not noted as a pro-union newspaper, commented on Chandler's action. I quote the full editorial, first because it is truthful, and second, because it shows that the UMWA was not alone in judging Chandler as unfit for office. Under the

National Guardsmen dismounting in Harlan.

headline: "Democracy is Born in Harlan," the News-Sentinel said:

> Not since the Civil War have people of Kentucky experienced a more alarming event than the invasion of Harlan two weeks ago by National Guardsmen who seized possession of the County to rule it in a state of undeclared martial law.
>
> Certainly there was nothing inherent in the situation itself to justify Governor Chandler's action. The Governors of at least six other states also were confronted with a mine holiday, but, although in some of these states the situation became serious, not one of them saw fit to project armed force into the troublous picture. Negotiations between miners and operators in New York had resulted in an agreement before Chandler gave the command to march. Collective bargaining, as established by law, was functioning. In Harlan, picketing during the month's holiday had been conspicuously peaceful. Law enforcement officers of the County and the regular State police were keeping vigilance. Never before during a labor dispute had the Harlan scene been so peaceful.
>
> The Governor said that responsible citizens of Harlan County reliably informed him that if he would send in troops, 75 percent of the miners would return to work. Where did he secure this "reliable" information, the public is asking, since events have proved his figures

Picket line in Harlan County.

fantastically in error. Did Governor Chandler ask the opinion of the Federal Department of Labor, specialists in that field? Did he consult the Kentucky Department of Industrial Relations, which was headed by competent Commissioner Burrows? Did he inquire of the miners themselves who, after all, were the principal parties? The governor passed them all up. Instead, he acted upon the unsupported request of County Judge Ball, a stockholder in a Harlan mine, and a petition presented by three non-union miners who had been sent to the Governor by the Whitfields of Clover Fork Coal Company.

Clover Fork Coal Company and two of the Whitfields are now under indictment in Federal Court for conspiracy to deprive miners of their civil rights. It was at their behest that the Governor ordered troops into Harlan, for, he said, the protection of civil liberties.

The real reason why "Happy" Chandler rushed to the aid of the Harlan County Coal Operators' Association have not been unsuspected. Facing political oblivion after his defeat last year, he may have remembered how Cal Coolidge broke a policeman's strike in Boston and then boomed into the Presidency. He may have considered the stinging, overwhelming beating he took at the hands of New Dealers and organized labor in the Senate race. So he hitched his wagon to a star, crashed the front page of every newspaper in the country and marched forth on a white horse to save 75 per cent of the people of Harlan County from themselves.

The result could be thought funny if the occasion were not so fraught with danger. Goaded by bayonets and cocked rifles in the hands of inexperienced and frequently unwilling youngsters, 10 per cent of Harlan's miners went back into the earth.

Like Hitler seizing Czechoslovakia, the Governor thrust into Harlan County hundreds of mystified guardsmen, bristling with automatic rifles and machine guns, ordered to shoot to kill. Civil rights were suspended or made dependent upon the uncertain decision of an officer. Peaceful picketing, guaranteed the working people by the supreme law of the land, was refused and pickets chased at the point of bayonets. Boys were ordered off the picket line, put in uniform and because they were National guardsmen, compelled to turn their guns against their fathers, brothers and fellow unionists and when an officer, appalled by such an atrocity, tried to be as human as possible, he was removed for lack of aggressiveness. Public roads and bridges were blocked unlawfully. Citizens not members of the union were detained in their normal movements without due process of law. While under escort of a guard, a scab shot a union picket.

No effort has been spared to smash the miners' organization and to herd them like slaves back into the mines. No Kentuckian who loves his state respects the Governor who vents his political spleen on hungry women and children by using the iron heel and the mailed fist of the National guard in Harlan County. Chandler will never be able to justify his childish action because it was proven unnecessary elsewhere throughout the nation.

John L. Lewis added his eloquent voice to the denunciation of Chandler. Speaking at a convention of the CIO's United Textile Workers, Lewis said that he had known Chandler a long time. Lewis said: "When he decided to run for Governor, he came to Washington to see me. He said he believed in collective bargaining. We believed Chandler because we didn't know he was talking with his tongue in his cheek.

As a result of that meeting, Lewis agreed to address a rally of coal miners at Pikeville, Kentucky, on Labor Day, 1934, to open Chandler's gubernatorial campaign. Chandler came to his hotel room after the successful rally, Lewis declared, promising "never to forget what the United Mine Workers did for him." But, said Lewis, "he left my room immediately after the conference, drove over the mountain to Harlan to keep a secret rendezvous with the Harlan operators with whom he concluded a dishonorable deal."

Lewis said that Chandler was trying to break the UMWA because coal miners had voted for Alben Barkley instead of Chandler in the 1938 campaign for a seat in the U.S. Senate. The CIO and the miners had helped thump "Happy" out of politics temporarily, so, he added: "Happy Chandler is angry—and he has a lust for vengeance. He is using his power to appease that lust. If this madman in Kentucky does not restrain that lust for vengeance, then I think there should be some authority in this country that will restrain him."

Lewis then threw down the gauntlet. "Soldiers and guns and troops will not mine coal in America. The time has gone by when men can be shot back into the mines. It will take more than a Chandler to stop the onward march of the mine workers or organized labor in this country."

The battle was joined. The voice of Lewis had been heard. But the onward marching of Union men in Harlan was to be rough and hazardous for weeks to come.

The day before the National Guard arrived, the union held a rally at Lenarue, six miles south of Harlan that drew a crowd of six thousand. Bill Turnblazer, Jim Golden, and I were the main speakers. Turnblazer tore into Chandler for having ordered troops in to break the strike. He urged the men to "stay away" from the mines, "because troops can't mine coal with bayonets." He also told the crowd "the Union will have a big war chest rolled up to feed the miners" and that if they were evicted from their houses "the United States Government will give you tents and we will feed you.

I said: "Harlan County is peaceful and has been peaceful ever since the passing of the gun thugs...there has been less murder in Harlan County, and Harlan County will be better off under the banner of the United Mine Workers."

One newspaper quoted me as saying that the coal operators were "coupon clippers and royalty collectors, including Judge Ball," and also said that I referred to the National guardsmen as "tin-horn soldiers." I do not remember exactly what I said that day, but the quotes sound like me.

In spite of everything we could do, however, on the morning of May 15, 1939, the National Guard came to Harlan County. The 850 inexperienced guardsmen were under the leadership of General Ellerbe Carter who rode into Harlan County displaying the pomp of a Roman Emperor. The general was well groomed with a well-waxed mustache, cherry red cheeks that gave the impression of being rouged, and the posterior of a chorus girl. He brought with him a personal press agent. Virtually every morning at nine o'clock, while the guard remained in the County, there was a press conference to publicize General Carter. Never in my life did I come in contact with a man who liked better to see his name and picture in the newspaper than the general from Louisville. He soon acquired the nickname of "grandma."

When the National Guard came into Harlan, the first group to arrive was their telephone crew who went to work at 2:30 a.m. tapping the telephones at the union office and in the homes of union officials. They tapped the office phone and ran a wire to a listening station at the City Hall half a block away. They tapped my home phone in the Martin Apartments next to the Post Office. They ran two wires down the pole in my back yard and assigned a guardsman to listen in after dark. We watched him with amusement for an hour while we confused him with crazy telephone messages. Then we called the Sheriff and reported a prowler in the back yard. He departed without bothering to remove the taps from the wire. Maybe he didn't know how.

On May 15th, I wrote Governor Chandler that I was resigning my positions as a member of the State Unemployment Compensation Advisory Board and also the State Wage and Hour Board. I told him that I did not want to contaminate a good thirty-year union record by association with his administration. When questioned by reporters, "Happy" said that if I had not resigned it would have been necessary for him to fire me. According to the Louisville Courier Journal the ex post facto record made by "Happy" in Frankfort shows I was fired.

The deadline for reopening of Harlan County mines with National guard protection was at 2:00 p.m. on May 15th. The union had picket lines at thirty-seven mines. All entrances and roads to these mines were to be kept open to non-union miners by National guardsmen armed with machine guns, rifles and bayonets. Union pickets were not armed. The stage was being set for more tragedy in Harlan County. The troops were armed with the most modern weapons available but were without experience in their use. A trigger-happy soldier is dangerous. But a raw rookie soldier is even worse. He never knows who or when he is going to shoot.

The first week began a series of tragic and near-tragic incidents that turned the miners' hatred toward the guardsmen themselves. These occurred because of the inexperience and stupidity of the soldiers themselves and the maniacal determination of their superiors to protect Harlan County scabs.

The first took place on May 18th at the High Splint mine near Clover Fork where the National Guard alleged that unknown union men had fired two fusillades of shots at non-union miners.

I halfway believe that this was a demonstration staged by General Carter for the benefit of out-of-town newspapermen. But he did stop a truck and arrest its thirty-six occupants, all of whom were union men. Three guns were found in the bed of the truck but ownership could not be established. The men were released after being charged with violation of the Kentucky Motor Vehicles Act, namely, too many people riding in one truck.

The events at Totz, a little camp owned by the Harlan Central Coal Company, on May 19th were more serious. General Carter had promised us that 150 pickets would be permitted at Totz if they were peaceful and if they were under the discipline of a representative of the Union. Our representative, James D. Scott, was not permitted to pass a National guard road blockage, and two hundred Union sympathizers at Totz, including some women and children, were herded at gun point in the hot sun on a forced one-mile march away from the mine. Our people were peaceful limped and walked the mile as well as they could and were rewarded for their good behavior by being called "a bunch of bums" by General Carter.

Food line for striking miners in Harlan County.

National Guardsmen and striking miners in Harlan County.

A few days later the first shooting of the new war took place. A non-union miner, John Padgett, shot a union man, Elmer McLaughlin, who was not a picket but an onlooker while Padgett was arguing with some women who had rightfully called him a scab. With him all during the affair was a National guard private named Obie Littrell who not only failed to disarm Padgett when he threatened to shoot into the group of women, but actually protected him and enabled him to escape after he shot McLaughlin, an innocent bystander, in a fit of wild temper. General Carter was asked by newspaper reporters why he had not disciplined Private Littrell. He excused the soldier's action by saying he was "young and inexperienced." Littrell was twenty-six years of age and had served in the guard for two years.

It soon was apparent to all of us except a few hard-nosed Harlan operators and "Happy" Chandler that public sentiment was on the side of the strikers. The Knoxville News-Sentinel late in May carried the editorial lambasting Chandler, printed earlier in this chapter. A reporter for the same newspaper, Carleton Waldos wrote a by-lined story, "Rule by Bayonets," that ridiculed the presence of the National Guard in Harlan County. He said that many of the troops openly sympathized with "the Jones Boys," as the strikers had become widely known, and fraternized with them in public. Representative Andrew Jackson May, (D-Ky.) chairman of the House Military Affairs Committee, said in Washington that it was "inconceivable" to him that "military force was necessary in the Harlan field." May's constituents were mostly coal miners and operators. On May 23rd, Kentucky's Commissioner of Industrial Relations, W. C. Burrows, issued a statement protesting against use of troops in Harlan County. He also wrote Chandler a letter of resignation, which said: "The main reason I am taking this action is because I am unalterably opposed to the presence of troops in Harlan County. I believe that I have demonstrated during the past three years of my association with the state administration, that I believe in mediation rather than force in settling of all labor disputes."

"During this administration, we have been faced with more labor difficulties than during all the other administrations combined. However, at no time has it been necessary to ask for troops until you decided to send them to Harlan County last Monday."

After the letter of resignation had been made public, Chandler called Burrows in for a conference. The Governor, a soft-soap expert from way back, persuaded Burrows to withdraw his resignation, thus saving a little face.

Another hopeful trend toward a break in the operators' solid front was the fact that some of the mines were signing individual contracts with the Union. Although at first no member of the operators' association signed up, we were meeting with Secretary George Ward from time to time. Although these negotiations were temporarily fruitless, at least the lines of communication were open.

June, 1939 was a relatively quiet month, filled with tension, but relatively empty of sensation. The newspapers got excited when the High Splint mine was shot up again. No one was hurt and a "full scale investigation" discovered nothing but some empty rifle shells nearby. On June 20th, Bill Turnblazer announced that the Creech Coal Company had signed a Union-Shop contract with the UMWA, the first member of the Harlan County Coal Operators' Association to do so. George W. Creech, vice-president, signed for the Company, Turnblazer, as District 19 President, myself as Secretary-Treasurer, organizer Robert Hodge, and members of the local union scale committee, signed for the UMWA.

At the beginning of July it had become obvious to us that the situation had again become stalled on dead center. The National Guard was still chauffeuring scabs to work in government-owned vehicles. Creech had signed up, but other members of the operators' association had no intention of doing so. Early in the month, the silence was shattered by a dynamite blast that destroyed a $4,000 cutting machine at the Stanfill mine of the Mahan-Ellison Coal Company. The mine was empty at the time of the explosion and the damage was not discovered until later. The company said that the damage amounted to $20,000, and "Happy" Chandler dramatically announced that the state would give a $250 reward to anyone who turned in the perpetrators of the outrage. The company, the operators' association and the County also said they would each pay an additional $250 to the finder, or a total of $1,000. (No one was ever found.) It seemed paradoxical to me that Chandler would offer a $250 reward for the person or persons destroying a mining machine, yet offered not one red cent for the arrest of the bushwhackers who shot up Bill Clontz's house, shot Tom Ferguson in the back or murdered Bennett Musick.

At the same time the operators had tried again to use the courts to cripple the strike. Cleon Calvert, representing four non-union stooges, had asked for a temporary injunction to prevent forty-three Harlan and Bell County operators from working their mines under the "Union Shop" clause in their contract with the UMWA. Special Judge J. B. Hannah, of Ashland, Kentucky, sitting in Harlan Circuit Court, denied Calvert's request. Thomas E. Townsend, James

Golden and W. R. Lay represented the UMWA in this case. This was a legal victory for us but the real struggle was again to be the pitheads in the county. On July 9th, I called a meeting of Harlan County union miners at Lenarue. Bill Turnblazer spoke and called for reforming of picket lines to "curtain production" and to "get some men out of the mines while the Great Lakes trade is going on. Turnblazer said: "You have the right to peaceful picketing and to peacefully persuade non-union men not to work."

John L. Lewis was personally represented at this meeting by District 6 President, John Owens of Columbus, Ohio, who in 1947 became International Secretary-Treasurer of the Union. He told the crowd of several thousand miners "the death of labor unions is the first step in crushing democracy."

After the meeting a member of the National Guard stationed near Lenarue kicked one of our men who had just been released from the hospital. Although this was reported to Major Fred Staples, nothing was done.

The next day I ordered reformation of the picket lines. The stage had been set for one of the last big battles in Harlan County. If I had known what was to happen to me personally in the next few days, I might have been tempted to take a vacation—but I didn't.

22

The Battle of Stanfill

The soldiers, it was learned later, had been given a "fix" of cocaine or morphine before they were sent into the jail to murder me.

The last big battle of 1939 in Harlan County was named for the little mining camp where it took place—Stanfill, nine miles southwest of the City of Harlan. The mine there was owned by the Mahan-Ellison Coal Company and was the same one where a mining machine had been dynamited a week before.

This so-called Battle of Stanfill was initially described as an attempt by National guardsmen to defend themselves against an attack by UMWA pickets. The press agent for the Kentucky National Guard quickly and widely disseminated this version, but later eyewitness accounts differed from this considerably, to say the least.

Two men died at Stanfill on July 12th. Both were Union pickets, killed with National guard weapons. The only weapons used in this one-sided battle belonged to the guardsmen. Those who died were Dock Caldwell, of Wilson-Berger, who was killed outright and Daniel Noe, of Elcomb, who was shot through the abdomen and died three days later. Three other UMWA members were wounded, Noble Bowman, of Chevrolet, John Kennedy, of Gulston, and Frank Laws, of Crummies. Two National guardsmen were also wounded, Captain John Hanberry, who started the fracas, and Private W. T. Mason.

The truth about what happened is based on interviews with twenty or more eyewitnesses and my own personal participation in some of the events.

On July 12th, I had arranged for setting up picket lines at five mines that were working non-union. The Stanfill mine was one of these. This was a case where there was no trouble in getting sufficient pickets to picket the mines. Our big trouble was having too many. Everybody who was out of work in Harlan County wanted to go on the picket line and do his duty to preserve the freedom which had been brought him by the Union. All pickets were requested to leave their firearms and weapons at home. It was later learned that this request was carried out to the letter. Later, when the pickets were searched on the morning of July 12th at Stanfill after the riot, there was not one gun found on a mine worker picket.

The riot started after a group of pickets moved toward the mine entrance where a non-union motorman was running an electric mine locomotive back and forth, hooking up a trip of cars to go into the mine. One of the pickets, Dock Caldwell, pulled the motor trolley pole off the wire. Captain Hansberry was standing close by, was nervous, became panicked, pulled his gun and started shooting Dock Caldwell in the chest as fast as he could pull the trigger of his automatic pistol. Caldwell was mortally wounded and the other pickets became incensed at the cold-blooded murder. A picket grabbed a rifle from a National guardsman, Private Mason, and hit him over the head with it and then shot Hansberry. This was the only shot fired by a picket and it was fired with a National guard rifle. A dozen or more shots were fired into the pickets by the Guardsmen, wounding Dan Noe and several others. Others were cut around the hands and head with bayonets.

The account given by the National Guard said that somebody had first shot Captain Hansberry and that after he was shot, he started firing. This, of course, was false. The next day General Carter and Colonel Roy Easley held a press conference at which they displayed a bunch of firearms, which they alleged had been taken from the pickets. Seven of the ten guns purported to have been taken from the pickets were army issue, .38 and .45 Colts, carried by the soldiers, which had been laid out on the table and photographed for the purpose of fooling the public and creating sentiment for the National guardsmen. The public was not taken in by this. Dozens of people who saw the picture of the display of firearms in the Knoxville News-Sentinel laughed at the boldness of the National Guard's attempt to fool the public with false propaganda.

Although I was not present at the riot itself, July 12th was a pretty busy day for me, too. At 6 a.m., two miners knocked at my front door, and told me that a gun battle had taken place at Stanfill. Both of these men were bleeding profusely and I immediately took them to the Harlan Hospital, which was only a block away. Then my wife and I left for Stanfill to see what could be done to help our people. I had no more than landed at Stanfill when I saw the National Guard troops lining up the pickets into a military formation to march them nine miles to Harlan and put them in jail.

When I got out of my car at Stanfill, it was immediately ordered by Major Fred Staple that I be taken back to Harlan and put in jail with the rest of the "damn murderers." A burly sergeant with a nervous trigger finger put me in an army truck along with several others, and sat beside me with a .45 pistol pointed at my head the entire way into Harlan, talking real tough. I advised him that with his nervous finger that pistol might go off and he said he didn't care a damn. After I was put in the army truck, my wife got in our automobile and went back to Harlan. She picked up Mrs. John Doyle and the camera and went back toward Stanfill to take some pictures of the pickets being marched into Harlan. On her way into Harlan, she picked up two pickets who had been in the fracas at Stanfill and gave them a ride. As she crossed the railroad tracks below the mine, a pig belonging to Jack Angel ran across the road and was hit by her automobile and killed. Angel was a mine foreman and was in charge of the non-union miners at Stanfill on the morning of July 12th. Afterward, he threatened to sue me if I did not pay for the pig, so I gave him ten dollars to settle the case.

When Mrs. Titler returned to our home in Harlan, she was advised that Dan Noe was calling for his wife, who lived at Stanfill. She immediately started back to get Mrs. Noe to bring her in to the hospital so she could be with her wounded, soon-to-die husband. When she got more than halfway toward Stanfill, she met the National guard which had several hundred pickets lined up along the road. She stopped and got out of the car to take some pictures. A line sergeant saw her and attempted to take the camera away from her. She smacked him in the nose with it and bloodied his nose. The sergeant then took the camera away from her and smashed it. Apparently General Carter and his staff were not too well pleased with the way they were handling the police duty in Harlan County, because they issued orders to smash every camera that took a picture of anything that was going on. Mrs. Titler was arrested and roughly shoved into her car when she told a Guardsman that she was not physically able to walk into Harlan with the pickets.

When the National guardsmen got to the outskirts of Harlan, they immediately encountered a gallery of spectators along the street who were watching the "parade." The inexperienced guardsmen became confused and did not know how to handle the crowd. They knew little or nothing about their weapons so in trying to keep the crowd back, some of their rifles were accidentally discharged and many onlookers were wounded. UMWA organizer Martin Hurd was marching in the picket line when a disturbance took place at the corner of Main and Clover Streets. During the confusion he broke ranks and ran through several back yards and escaped. He stayed out of the County for a week, after which he returned and was not bothered. Neither was he charged with banding or confederating; neither was he forced to make bond.

Mrs. Titler and I were put in jail along with 221 others involved in the Stanfill affair. No bond was set for any of the defendants for three days, so the Harlan jail became the Titler family home for that period. Ben Middleton, the jailor, was a cousin of Theodore, but was friendly to the Union and a good friend of mine. He allowed Mrs. Titler and me to share a cell by ourselves. He also allowed us to put sheets on the bed, bring in a radio and make the place look homey. Four hours after we were placed in jail, two National guard enlisted men and two commissioned officers were slipped into the jail by gun thug Charlie Rose while Ben Middleton was out to lunch. Somebody had sent them in there for the express purpose of assassinating me in cold blood. They expected to find me alone in a cell where they could kill me without witnesses and claim self-defense. Instead, they found my wife with me, which undoubtedly saved my life. The two commissioned officers stayed outside the cell door and Rose let the other two men into the cell where they started pushing me around with the muzzles of their guns in the hope that I would resist and they could shoot me. Mrs. Titler took a hand in the fight and the soldiers were confused about how to proceed. One soldier pulled his gun and was going to shoot me, but six women in an adjacent cell, seeing the drawn guns, began screaming, which confused him further, so that again no shot was fired. By this time, five or ten minutes—which seemed like a century to me—had passed and Ben Middleton returned from lunch. He ran all four of the soldiers out of the jailhouse and fired Charles Rose, deputy jailor, for letting them in.

The soldiers, it was learned later, had been given a "fix" of cocaine or morphine before they were sent into the jail to murder me. One was a known drug addict from Barboursville.

Finally, on July 15th, County Judge Cam E. Ball called an examining trial on charges placed against 23 UMWA defendants after the Stanfill riot. All defendants except Mrs. Titler and me were placed under $1,000 bond. I was charged with sedition, forcible rebellion and armed attack on a National guardsman. A peace warrant against me was sought. My total bond was $21,000. Mrs. Titler, who was under the care of a physician, was the only defendant released after arraignment. UMWA Attorneys Golden and Lay signed her bond. However, immediately after her release she was rearrested on the courthouse steps by County Attorney Bert O. Howard, and a Deputy Sheriff and charged with aiding prisoners to escape, because she had driven two of the Stanfill pickets to Harlan on the day of the riot. Golden and Lay arranged bond for her on this second charge. Golden, Paul Reed and others arranged for Union men to escort her from the courthouse to a waiting car, which whisked her to Middlesboro, in Bell County. On the same day this hearing was held, a Union miner, Bill Roberts, was killed by a scab at the Stanfill mine, Willie Fee. It was ironic that Judge Ball set Fee's bond for a vicious murder at $5,000, while my bond was $21,000.

I stayed in the Harlan jail until bonds had been signed for all of the defendants. I signed the last bond —my own—on July 18th, got into a car and drove with my wife to Knoxville to sit in on negotiations for a new contract with the Harlan operators. When we arrived at the Farragut Hotel, Mrs. Titler and I were met by Bill Turnblazer and escorted to a banquet at which we were the honored guests.

The operators were succumbing to pressure from the outside and the realization that "Happy" Chandler and the National guard were not enough to defeat the UMWA and the Federal Government. I participated in the Knoxville negotiations for three days at which all the terms and conditions of the contract were worked out that put the remaining five thousand UMWA members working for members of the Harlan County Coal Operators' Association under contract for two years. This agreement was strictly a compromise. We did not get the "union shop" and the operators did not get the "penalty clause."

SADIE TITLER AND GEORGE J. TITLER *and their dog, Johnny, 1938. This picture was taken the day following their six-day stint in jail after the Battle of Stanfill.*

23

The Final Days of Bloody Harlan

> *Every Union man who contributed anything to the task in Harlan County carries a proud feeling close to his heart that he is leaving to posterity a better world in which to live.*

The signing of the 1939 contract did not necessarily mean that Harlan County was peaceful. From an outward viewpoint, everything seemed to be going along fairly well but the inside story was different. The Harlan County coal operators had a contract shoved down their neck, which they did not like, by the power of the United States Government's Conciliation Service, plus the sword of Damocles hanging over their heads, the threat of a retrial of the conspiracy charges against them. They had signed the contract reluctantly and immediately began to drag their heels in living up to it.

Of course, Mrs. Titler and I were still under bond on charges arising out of the July 12th riot at Stanfill. On July 26, a special grand jury in the Harlan Circuit Court returned 102 indictments with recommendations for bonds totaling more than a half million dollars. Among those indicted, together with recommended bonds, were the following: William Turnblazer, conspiracy to hinder military organization, $10,000, and banding and confederating,

$5,000; George J. Titler, aiding and abetting malicious shooting and wounding, $5,000, conspiracy to hinder military organization, $10,000, and banding and confederating, $5,000; Mrs. George J. Titler, banding and confederating, $5,000. The Titler family was still "wanted." I kept looking for our pictures on the post office bulletin board. The Judge, who had met Mrs. Titler in church on several occasions, reduced her bond to $1,000 and said he didn't believe she would leave Harlan while her husband was there.

Now that all the members of the Harlan County Coal Operators' Association were under contract and also federal indictment, 225 miners also indicted in state court, the attorneys for both sides started legal manipulations to clean the slate and start anew. All cases against both sides were dropped. This action conserved the best interests of all parties concerned and brought Harlan County back into the Commonwealth of Kentucky. (For fifteen years, it had flourished as a separate state.)

This did not mean that Harlan County suddenly became a paradise for union coal miners. The operators had lost a battle and had been forced into signing a contract. But the job of getting them to negotiate and bargain collectively in good faith was no easy task. Litigation and small acts of violence still lay ahead. After disposition of charges against UMWA defendants in the Stanfill riot, the next order of business was clearing the board of several hundred eviction cases. This was placed in the hands of the attorneys, James Golden and W. R. Lay, who did a remarkable job of clearing up this phase of the feud.

One device used by the operators to stall on contract compliance involved company doctors. Even after the contract was signed, when men took medical examinations to see if they were physically fit to work in the mines, the operators connived with their doctors to turn union men down. It was then necessary for the union to take them to other doctors for an impartial physical examination, after which we had to use the fairly slow grievance machinery in the contract to force the operators to put these men to work.

The company doctor problem, and the hospital problem to which it was closely related, had always plagued Harlan County coal miners. Medical care was a major headache during strike periods because the operators would not permit company doctors to treat anyone living in their camps that was on strike. No outside doctor would go into the camps because it would have been a breach of medical ethics to do so. Therefore, it was necessary for us to fetch the sick from camps on strike before they could receive medical care or hospitalization.

Because of this situation, Mrs. Titler became the guardian angel of all pregnant women in the coal camps or any women or children ailing from other causes. One young lady by the name of Davis, living in the Clover Fork camp of Kitts, was expecting. She had a kidney ailment and it was necessary for Mrs. Titler to go into the camp with an ambulance to bring her out and take her to a hospital. The father of the aforementioned lady, Harrison Reedy, was a deputy sheriff, about six feet three inches tall, weighing two hundred thirty pounds. It fell to his lot to serve a warrant on Mrs. Titler the second time she was arrested and taken to jail. This was only ten days after Mrs. Titler had favored his daughter. He was a mean-looking man with the heart of a lamb, so when it became necessary for him to serve the warrant, he brought his wife along to the house to serve the warrant and he cried the whole way to the jail while Mrs. Titler and his wife walked down the street ahead of him. Mrs. Titler has had many a laugh in telling the story of the crying deputy sheriff taking her to jail. She always contends that he was the kindest man in Harlan and was out of place as a deputy sheriff.

Throughout the several months' shutdown in 1939, it became the duty of Mrs. Titler to look after the layettes of the expectant mothers in the coal camps. This became quite a chore and it was not unusual for her to buy twenty-five layettes a week. Every time I went home for lunch, the front room would be full of women sipping tea and talking "shop" while Mrs. Titler took their applications for layettes and listened to their troubles. Because of the crowded condition of the living room, on several occasions it was necessary for me to go through the kitchen door in order to get into the house. One day I eavesdropped at the kitchen door to see what women talked about when they assembled in groups of four or five. It seems that two of the women who were requesting layettes were from the same family, a mother and daughter. In the conversation, it was brought out that one of the women was having her first baby and the other her ninth. The mother, who was having the ninth child, said she lived according to the Bible. She said: "The Bible says 'Go ye forth and multiply.'" Whereupon the daughter spoke up and said: "Mrs. Titler, don't let mother pull your leg. She wasn't thinking of the Bible when she got that way. I know from experience."

The conversation then changed to the subject of large families. A woman from Liggett said that the largest families in Harlan County came from her hometown. She said it was not uncommon for a woman in Liggett to have twelve or thirteen children. She said: "Why, Ioe Glancy has eleven and he is only thirty-eight years old and is a grandpap."

Some one asked why the families in Liggett were bigger than anywhere else in the county. One woman volunteered the information that the coal train came up Caterns Creek in the morning about four o'clock and woke everybody up. She said it was too late to go back to sleep and it was too early to get up and this was what accounted for the big families. Everybody laughed. I didn't think it was funny for a poor, tired coal loader to be awakened at four in the morning by a coal drag.

To the striking miners of Harlan County and their wives, Mrs. Titler became a living legend. She was their Mother Jones (a fiery old-time labor organizer who worked with coal miners all over the nation) and Florence Nightingale rolled into one. Her complete lack of physical fear was amazing to all who knew her. She always said that the gun thugs, ruthless and cold-blooded as they were, would not kill a woman. In retrospect, I am sure she was right. Even the gun thugs were bound by the "code of the hills" or Harlan County custom, whichever title you prefer. That code included deep respect for women and also demands that the male protect the female with his life if need be. Many outsiders believed that Harlan County males were rude when they saw a man walking down the street with his wife trailing two or three steps behind him. This custom is left over from pioneer days when the man of the family walked down the forest trails ahead of his family to look for wild animals and Indians and to protect his wife and children from them.

If she had any characteristic that exceeded her fearlessness, it was her generosity. In the four years we lived in Harlan, she gave away most of her own clothes, made payments on cars, washing machines and radios that were in danger of being lost to the finance company and also paid hospital and doctor bills. When we arrived in Charleston, West Virginia, in 1941, we had three thousand dollars worth of IOU's, (which we burned), sixty dollars in cash and a million dollars worth of beautiful memories.

Violence was not quite ended in Southeastern Kentucky. It slowed down considerably, but four gunfights of note took place while I was still a part of the District 19 family. The first occurred on September 30, 1939, when UMWA organizer George Gilbert was ambushed on Forester's Creek. Gilbert appeared on crutches before County Judge Ball to swear out warrants against John Osborne and Walter Blanton, of Layman, in connection with the shooting, after which he was treated at a hospital in Pineville. Paul Reed told reporters that doctors removed eighteen buckshot from Gilbert's knee.

About four and a half months later, a much more serious occurrence—the murder of a fine young man—took place at Crockett, near the Leslie County line in Bell County.

The owners of the Clover Fork Coal Company in Harlan County, the Whitfield family, owned a mine at Crockett where UMWA Local Union 7644 had jurisdiction. The local union president was Lewis Hatmaker, a young, outstanding man about thirty years of age. On February 15, 1940, a neighbor who worked with him at the Crockett mine, known as Kentucky Ridge Coal Company, and a close friend of Superintendent Ed. Whitfield, Bob Helton, came to Hatmaker's house with a shotgun on the pretense of going hunting. He left his gun on the porch and came into the Hatmaker house and talked a while and was treated to a couple of drinks of moonshine, according to Ruth Hatmaker, Lewis Hatmaker's wife. The men used pickled corn as a chaser, she said.

After spending about two hours in the Hatmaker house, Helton asked Hatmaker to take a walk. They walked over to the Kentucky Ridge Company commissary where Helton shot Hatmaker in the back in cold blood without provocation, then turned his gun in to the company commissary, who apparently owned it.

At the trial, the prosecution checked for evidence to show that an officer of the company had hired Helton to shoot Hatmaker, but Helton would not talk. He was indicted on February 17, tried and sentenced on March 9, 1940 to life in state prison. There was no reason given at the trial for shooting Hatmaker. It was thought by people close to the situation that Hatmaker was exercising his duties as a local union president too well to suit the union-hating Whitfields, and was ordered executed.

On April 1, 1941, the nation's mines were shut down when operators, including those in Harlan, refused to sign a contract with the UMWA. During this short strike, one of the most vicious mass murders in Harlan County history took place at Crummies Creek. The murderer was gun thug Bill Lewis, who was killed four months later, and his victims, all union men, were Virgil Hampton, Oscar Goodlin, Charles Ruth and Ed Tye. Details of the Crummies Creek massacre were told earlier in this book. Soon after this, the Harlan operators signed a contract with UMWA that included the union shop clause.

The last "battle" in District 19 took place more than a year later. By January 1, 1941, Harlan and Bell Counties were 95 per cent organized. The only nasty non-union outpost was the Fork Ridge mine just across the Kentucky line in Tennessee, a short distance from Middlesboro. The mine was operated by C. W. (Dusty)

Rhodes, president and general manager. Searchlights were placed on the tipple and plug-uglies guarded the mine property with tommy guns. Every time a union organizer attempted to talk with a Ford Ridge employee, he took his life in his hands.

Rhodes was a large, reckless young man who arrogantly told union men that if miners attempted to picket his mine, he would slaughter them. For months, he and Bob Robinson, a former Tennessee highway patrolman, had been parading around with their Tommy guns and challenging the miners to a fight. More than half of the employees had been signed up by the UMWA, but Rhodes ignored their demands and hired more thugs.

On April 15, 1941, the union decided to post a picket line in the safest place they could find. The pickets chose stations where they could take cover in case they were attacked by company guards, and then moved to a strategic place near the mine. When the caravan of cars came to a stop at the state line and started to unload, the fifty pickets were greeted with a broadside from fifteen or eighteen armed guards who had word they were coming and had preceded the pickets to the state line. On the first volley, one picket was killed and more than a dozen were wounded, nine seriously enough to be hospitalized.

When James Ridings, A. T. Pace and George Gilbert, union representatives, were getting out of their car, Gilbert was shot in the leg, and Ridings, in addition to having his necktie shot off, also had his clothes perforated by bullets. The pickets took cover behind trees, rocks and cars and returned the fire, killing Rhodes, the company president, E. W. Silvers, company vice president, and Robinson, the company guard.

Sam Evans, a union member, was killed. The nine men in the hospital who were jointly charged, along with Turnblazer, Ridings and Pace in the Tennessee murder warrant were: R. W. Lawson, Bell County deputy sheriff Alford Smith, Walter Pilly, Earl Alley, John Holland, Clayton Webb, Millard Forester, and A. J. Napier. Some of these men were from Kentucky and some from Tennessee.

The battle raged across the state line and more than a thousand shots were fired. When the smoke had cleared away, a question arose as to which state had jurisdiction in the courts. When engineers from the two states tried to determine where the state line really was, they found some one had moved the line stake 400 feet over into Tennessee and that Kentucky had paid for paving four hundred feet to road in Tennessee to bring the hard-top road four hundred feet closer to the mine. Finally the engineers decided that Rhodes, Silver and Robinson had been killed in Tennessee. Where the union men were killed or wounded was immaterial, because no one would be tried for their killing.

While the two states were trying to determine who had jurisdiction, Ridings and Pace were advised by counsel to disappear in order to keep from rotting in jail while the states argued over jurisdiction. They went to Huntington and Charleston, West Virginia and registered in a Charleston hotel under aliases of Smith and Jones. When the phone rang in their room, it was a long distance operator asking for Mr. Smith or Mr. Jones. Pace had forgotten his assumed name and told the operator that she had the wrong number. The call was from their attorney, who finally contacted them and advised them to come to Middlesboro and make bond. They did so, posting five thousand dollars bond each. Their bond was signed by Floyd Ball of Middlesboro and William Russell.

On April 24, Governor Prentice Cooper of Tennessee asked extradition on Turnblazer, Ridings, Pace and the nine wounded union men in the Middlesboro Hospital. Ridings and Pace were placed in jail in Tazewell, Tennessee, without bond, charged with first-degree murder. While Pace and Ridings were in the Claiborne County jail, Mrs. Pace and Mrs. Ridings went to Tazewell to visit their husbands. After they left the jail and started back to Middlesboro, Mrs. Ridings suggested to Mrs. Pace that the best way to help the men was to pray for them. Mrs. Pace was not a praying woman, so she suggested to Mrs. Ridings: "You pray and I will cuss and then we will see what happens." This system seemed to have worked fine. Ridings and Pace were soon free on bond after habeas corpus proceedings were instituted by union counsel.

Ridings and Pace went to trial December 8, 1941, for murder and a jury of Claiborne County citizens promptly found them "not guilty." The trial for murder did not mar the fine reputation enjoyed over the years by these two men. As a matter of fact, many people felt they were entitled to medals for service rendered to the community beyond the call of duty.

Rhodes and Robinson had attempted to rule by force rather than reason. The gun rule they had established was the Frankenstein monster that destroyed them. They lived by the gun and died by the gun. Fork Ridge later produced coal under a union contract, a contract paid for with blood and sorrow.

This was the last gun battle in southeastern Kentucky or Tennessee over the UMWA's right to organize. The feudal coal barons learned a valuable lesson from this encounter, namely that times were changing. They could no longer murder miners like dogs with impunity and with the protection of state governments. They had been taught that workingmen, for the first time in American history, were thought of as first-class citizens.

Thinking back, I realize that the Harlan County gun thugs in reality got nothing for their efforts to drive out the union. Most of them died violent deaths. The ones who survived or died natural deaths had their consciences to live with. How they did it, I do not know. Below is a partial list of those gun thugs who died as they had lived—violently.

> Bill Randolph, who quit a miner's job to become a trigger-happy thug at Three Point, after killing five men and becoming Chief of Police of Harlan Town, shot behind the ear when he was not looking by Clarence Middleton.
>
> Lonnie Ball, committed suicide.
>
> Wash Irwin, assassinated by his "buddies."
>
> Frank White, murdered by a paid killer.

Carl Scott and Joe Allen, both killed by a single shotgun blast of a confederate.

John Middleton, killed by Bill Dean.

Perry G. Noe, killed by John Lee.

Bryan Middleton (the Sheriff's brother) who was never a thug and the best man in his family, shot by Shorty Baumgardner.

Chris Patterson, assassinated by his confederates.

Charles Rose, shot by one of his pals while driving a car through Brookside.

Bill Lewis, killed in 1941 supposedly by Bill Dean, in the Harlan County Courthouse while guarding ballot boxes.

One-eyed Earl Jones, died in a gunfight.

Among those who died natural deaths was the kingpin thug, Theodore Middleton, who died of a heart attack in 1942 before he had a chance to enjoy fully the loot he had acquired during his heyday as High Sheriff of Harlan County. Another thug, Allen Bollen, died of cancer. Several of the operators died of insanity or lingering ailments. One of them, Sherman Howard, was shot to death while trying to highjack a ballot box.

Three of the meanest of the deputies are still living. The chief thug, Ben Unthank, is living quietly in Harlan, trying to atone for his sins as a Deacon in the Baptist Church. Lee Hubbard has moved to Tennessee and is reported to be preaching the gospel as a minister of the Church of God. Lee Fleenor lives in Southwest Virginia, where he works as a small coal miner-operator. Let it be said in behalf of Lee Fleenor, that since he went to Virginia he has turned out to be a good citizen in every respect.

Reading the history of Harlan County can only bring one to these conclusions: First, might does not make right. Second, right will always prevail over wrong in the long run if the "right" people have the courage and tenacity to hang on to their principles and properly present their case in the courts of public opinion.

The United States Supreme Court is the highest court in our land when it comes to interpreting the written law. The court of public opinion is supreme in interpreting the unwritten law. Only men's individual consciences can determine the difference between right and wrong.

These hired guns that sold their souls for $125 a month died before their time and no doubt faced their Creator with a guilty conscience and a worried mind. What does a man gain if he acquires worldly things and loses his soul? I am of the opinion that every one of these late deputies in the light of their fates would live different lives if they had the opportunity to live again.

With the union men who took part in the organizing of Harlan County, it is a different story. I am convinced that as these men look back over their lives, they all conclude that the course they charted was good and right and if the opportunity presented itself again, they would not change their course in any way. Every Union man who contributed anything to the task in Harlan County carries a proud feeling close to his heart that he is leaving to posterity a better world in which to live.

Organizing Harlan County was not just a job to me. It was the most vivid four years of my life, an experience I will never forget. The men who worked with me were—those who live still are—the best and truest friends I have ever had. It was in Harlan County that I had my real baptism in fire and blood and learned all over again how much the United Mine Workers of America meant to thousands of men who were willing to die that it might live. To me, the UMWA's organizing drive in Harlan County will ever be a symbol to those who carry on in the labor movement. Harlan County was organized—but labor's agony will never end.

Epilogue

> *Most male residents of Harlan County today still carry pistols but these are used to commit murders in the traditional American way—when liquored up, in disputes over property or women, or just for the hell of it.*

The rugged topography of Harlan County in 1962 is the same as it was twenty-two years ago. But conditions are different. A war has been fought. Literally thousands of small mines have been opened and closed.

Immediately after World War II the Union's strength was at its highest peak ever. The trying days of 1946 to 1950 brought forth the UMWA Welfare and Retirement Fund, which has done more for the coal miners in Harlan County than we dreamed of in the bloody days of the 1930s.

The Fund's Harlan Memorial Hospital stands as a symbol of the fact that union coal miners no longer are cast aside when they are injured, broken down, or too old to work. It is the biggest employer in the City of Harlan today.

This hospital and nine other like it have opened careers in medicine to sons of coal miners who have the ability to aid and comfort the ailing and sick in the remote mountain areas near Harlan. Its

School of Professional Nursing has meant that hundreds of miners' daughters, whose only hope of a career previously had been for a drab married life and a "passel of hungry young 'uns," will now have a profession they can work at for the rest of their lives.

Other changes in Harlan have not been for the best, perhaps. In the late 1940s, Harlan County, with its miners fully employed at union wages, had the highest per capita income in the State of Kentucky. Today, due to mechanization and a long-time depression in the coal industry, Harlan has become a pocket of unemployment and tragic poverty. Able-bodied, strong men unable to find jobs, whose unemployment compensation benefits have expired, are subsisting on meager handouts of government surplus food and what little money State Welfare will provide. In the early days, Harlan County children wore clothing made of flour sacks because their fathers were union men. Today, other helpless little children wear flour sacks and go barefooted because of a failure in our economic system.

Harlan is no longer "Bloody Harlan," at least so far as the union and the operators are concerned. The last coal strikes during World War II and in the period 1946-1950 were without bloodshed. The men merely laid down their tools and went home. Even in 1959, when the operators tried to break the union contract, a strike resulted in only one death which was under circumstances so obscure that one is led to believe that it was not a labor dispute death at all, but merely a crime of passion or the result of a private feud.

Most male residents of Harlan County today still carry pistols but these are used to commit murders in the traditional American way—when liquored up, in disputes over property or women, or just for the hell of it. A new attitude toward labor disputes has made violence and gunplay unprofitable and unnecessary. The operators today use the Taft-Hartley law instead of hiring gun thugs.

The UMWA is not as strong in Harlan as it was in its heyday. Unemployment and hunger breed scabs. There are far too many men working in little dog holes in Harlan and elsewhere in our southern coalfields. They are underpaid and work long hours in unsafe surroundings. They will be there as long as the coal market is depressed and as long as men merely need a pick, a shovel and a five-dollar license fee to become coal operators. This is a new challenge to our union. The challenge has been recognized but the problem is not solved. But I am sure that our leaders and members will win out again in Harlan, just as we did in the bloody days recounted in this book.

www.ingramcontent.com/pod-product-compliance
Lightning Source LLC
Chambersburg PA
CBHW070420010526
44118CB00014B/1834